Frontispiece to Herrick's *Hesperides: or, The Works Both Humane & Divine of Robert Herrick, Esq.*, 1648. By permission of the Houghton Library, Harvard University.

Robert HERRICK

a reference guide

A
Reference
Guide
to
Literature

Everett Emerson
Editor

Robert HERRICK

a reference guide

ELIZABETH H. HAGEMAN

G.K. HALL & CO.

70 LINCOLN STREET, BOSTON, MASS.

012
H 566h

Library of Congress Cataloging in Publication Data

Hageman, Elizabeth.
  Robert Herrick : a reference guide.

  (Reference publication in literature)
  Includes indexes.
    1. Herrick, Robert, 1591-1674—Bibliography. I. Title.
II. Series.
Z8400.H33 1983 [PR3513] 016.821′4   82-11763
ISBN 0-8161-8012-1

This publication is printed on permanent/durable acid-free paper
MANUFACTURED IN THE UNITED STATES OF AMERICA

Had it not been their candor scornes to give
Fames Funeralls to Princes whilst they live
Or that their Synode did desire to see
The final Act of his Mortalitie
Some Johnson, Drayton, or some Herick would
Before this time have charactred the Mould
Of his perfections; and in living Lines,
Have made them knowne before these mourning times.

> Richard James, The Muses Dirge,
> 1625

Ships lately from the Islands came,
With Wines, though never heard'st their name.
Montefiasco, Frontiniac,
Viatico, and that old Sack
Yong Herric took to entertaine
The Muses in a sprightly vein.

> Anon. "To Parson Weeks. An
> Invitation to London," Musarum
> Deliciae: or, The Muses Recrea-
> tion, 1655

And then Flaccus Horace,
    He was but a sowr-ass,
And good for nothing but Lyricks,
    There's but One to be found
    In all English ground
Writes as well; who is hight Robert Herick.

> Anon. "Upon the Infernal Shades
> of the Authors Poems: or, The
> hooded Hawk," Naps Upon Parnassus,
> 1658

vii

Contents

The Author

Elizabeth H. Hageman, who received her doctorate from the University of North Carolina, is now an associate professor of English at the University of New Hampshire. Since 1973 she has edited "Recent Studies in Renaissance Literature," a series of bibliographical essays appearing in each issue of English Literary Renaissance. In addition to "Recent Studies in Herrick" in that series, she has published articles and reviews in journals such as Studies in Philology, The Sixteenth Century Journal, Renaissance Quarterly, and Shakespeare Quarterly.

Preface

This bibliography is intended to provide students of the seventeenth-
century poet Robert Herrick with an annotated, chronological survey
of criticism written in English from 1648, the date of publication of
Hesperides: or, The Works Both Humane & Divine of Robert Herrick
Esq., through mid-1981. It differs, then, in extent and function
from earlier bibliographies of Herrick. Samuel A. and Dorothy R.
Tannenbaum's work (1949.1 in this bibliography) offers a series of
lists, each in alphabetical order, of a wide variety of primary and
secondary material; its terminal date is 1948. Twenty years later,
George Robert Guffey updated that bibliography with a chronological
list of sixty-one items published between 1949 and 1965 (1968.4).
More recently, Ted-Larry Pebworth and others have compiled a forty-
page "Selected and Annotated Bibliography" (1978.28) which focuses on
criticism written between 1910, the date of F.W. Moorman's Robert
Herrick: A Biographical and Critical Study (1910.11), and 1976.
The present study includes more materials than does Pebworth's, and
its chronological arrangement will allow readers to trace the development of various trends in Herrick criticism as later critics
repeated, modified, and/or dissented from earlier discussions of
Herrick's poetry.

My first aim has been to list and annotate all chapters, articles,
and books devoted exclusively to criticism of Herrick's work; to that
list, I have added more general works such as Virginia Tufte's The
Poetry of Marriage (1970.13) and William A. McClung's The Country
House in English Renaissance Poetry (1977.5) which offer substantial
treatments of Herrick. Although I have omitted manuscript theses
listed by the Tannenbaums (1949.1), I have included dissertations on
Herrick noted in Dissertation Abstracts and Dissertation Abstracts
International, as well as dissertations from Harvard, Yale, Cambridge,
and Oxford Universities not abstracted in those volumes. In addition,
I have listed, insofar as I have been able to discover them, dissertations that include chapters or parts of chapters on Herrick. In
all cases, dissertations are listed under the years they were sub-
mitted, rather than the years their abstracts were published. Because the G.K. Hall series in which this bibliography appears focuses
on criticism, I have excluded editions of Herrick's poetry that

xi

contain no critical apparatus (the World's Classics Editions, for instance) and the many selected editions that include only brief introductory statements reiterating commonplaces about Herrick and his work. Bibliographies of Herrick criticism are listed, as are reviews—but not brief notices—of book-length studies of Herrick and of editions of his poetry.

Encyclopedias and biographical dictionaries like The Dictionary of National Biography (1891.2), anthologies like George Ellis's Specimens of the English Poets (1790.1), and literary histories like W.J. Courthope's A History of English Poetry (1903.3) are included when their comments bear on the development of criticism of Herrick and on his literary reputation. Similarly, I have cited essays making brief comments on Herrick when they have been quoted so often that they have become part of the "canon" of Herrick criticism (1851.2 and 1870.1, for instance), when, because they are written by literary figures such as Ralph Waldo Emerson (1835.1) or Gerard Manley Hopkins (1935.1 and 1935.2), they provide especially illuminating visions of Herrick and/or their authors; or when, though brief, they offer unique critical arguments (1936.5 and 1939.5, for example). Several items which might otherwise have been omitted on grounds of insignificance have been included simply because of their being, on the basis of Tannenbaum entries, difficult to locate; it is my hope that the bibliographic details and annotations I have provided in those entries will aid students to find them and/or to determine whether their contents are in fact necessary to their own research. Although I have concentrated on criticism written in English, I have, whenever I have been able to locate it, listed criticism written in other languages.

Publications for each year are listed alphabetically by their authors' or editors' names, except that editions of Herrick's poetry appear first in each year's entry, with front matter and text pages listed separately in order to give the user an indication of the amount of scholarly apparatus accompanying each. I have provided information on reprints of books and articles under the original publication dates; additional, later entries appear only for those items that have been extensively revised. Except for titles in direct quotations, I have given titles of Herrick poems in the form used by J. Max Patrick, who edited the most recent complete edition (1963.1). In the interest of simplicity, however, I have omitted italics in poem titles.

The title page of Herrick's 1648 volume designates his poems as Hesperides; or The Works Both Humane & Divine of Robert Herrick Esq.; a separate title page calls the last 272 poems in the volume His Pious Pieces (1648.1). It is, therefore, sometimes difficult by title alone to determine whether critics writing about Hesperides poems refer to the entire volume or only to the 1130 secular poems. To avoid confusion, I have used the phrase "the 1648 volume" when critics certainly refer to the collected poems and the title

Hesperides when they write only about the secular poetry. Readers are advised to consult both entries in the Subject Index.

Finally, each item I have listed but not seen is designated by an asterisk.

ACKNOWLEDGMENTS

My first and deepest thanks for help with this volume go to Jill Freeman, an undergraduate English major at the University of New Hampshire, without whose diligent and good-humored help in finding Herrick items and in compiling, indexing, and proofreading this bibliography the work could not have been completed. I am grateful, too, to a number of colleagues and friends for help and advice at various stages in this project: Carl Dawson, Jerome Dees, A. Leigh DeNeef, Everett Emerson, James Harner, Terence Logan, Jean Miller, J. Max Patrick, Ted-Larry Pebworth, and Dale Randall; and to librarians (especially Reina Hart, Barry Hennessey, Diane Tibbetts, Jane Russell, and Deborah Watson) at the University of New Hampshire, at Harvard, Cambridge, and Oxford Universities, at the Library of Congress, and at the British Library. I owe thanks for financial assistance with various parts of the project to the Department of English and the Graduate School of the University of New Hampshire and, for permission to print the frontispiece from Herrick's 1648 volume, to the Houghton Library, Harvard University. Nan Collins and Carol Demeritt typed the manuscript with patient and cheerful sympathy for my concern for accuracy. Responsibility for errors in detail or in judgment is, of course, mine.

This work is dedicated to the memory of two Renaissance scholars and loyal friends, Margaret B. Bryan and Dennis G. Donovan.

Introduction

The extent to which Herrick's poetry was admired--or even known--
within his own century is difficult to determine, but J. Max Patrick
has argued convincingly that "'neglected' is too strong a term for
the reception of Herrick's poetry by his contemporaries" (1978.27;
see also items listed under "Reputation" in the Subject Index of this
bibliography). Indeed, in the sixteen years between the publication
of Herrick's 1648 volume and his death in 1674, "almost a hundred of
[his poems] were reprinted, usually without credit to him, in 28 different collections" (Patrick, 1963.1). It seems best, however, to
qualify Patrick's statement that Herrick's "greatness was inadequately
recognized while he lived and for more than two hundred years after
his death" (1978.27). For while it is true that Herrick's name was
all but unknown during the eighteenth century (see 1933.1, 1933.2,
and 1947.9), by 1874 Herrick had been denigrated by Robert Southey
(1831.1 and 1851.2) and praised by Ralph Waldo Emerson (1835.1),
Elizabeth Barrett Browning (1842.1), Mary Russell Mitford (1852.1),
Leigh Hunt (1854.3), Robert W. Buchanan (1861.1), A. Bronson Alcott
(1872.1), and by anonymous writers in the Retrospective Review and
Blackwood's Edinburgh Magazine (1822.1 and 1839.2). His poems were
available in a number of editions, including a selected edition by
John Nott (1810.1) and complete editions by Thomas Maitland (1823.1)
and W. Carew Hazlitt (1869.1). He had been published in America
(1856.1) and mentioned four times in the first volume of Notes and
Queries (1850.1, 1850.2, 1850.3, and 1850.4)--a periodical in which
observations on Herrick's poetry and his life have appeared regularly
up to the present day.

Although few of those who wrote about Herrick before 1875 offered
detailed analyses of his work, the years between 1797 and 1874 do
provide some true landmarks in Herrick scholarship. In this context,
one must note John Nichols's work on Herrick's family and his life
(1797.1 and 1798.1); Nathan Drake's discussion of the poetry, which
includes a number of topoi that recur in later Herrick criticism--the
ideas that Devonshire life was a significant cause of Herrick's best
poems, that the 1648 volume is a mixture of excellent and tasteless
poetry, that Herrick is a descendant of Catullus, and that his best
verse is characterized by "grace and polish" (1804.1); Barron Field's

account of Herrick anecdotes he heard while on a visit to Dean Prior
(1810.2); and W. Carew Hazlitt's printing in his edition (1869.1)
poems not in the 1648 volume and the Herrick letters first recorded
by Nichols (1798.1).

In 1875, Edmund Gosse published the first of several appreciative
essays on Herrick (1875.2; see also 1876.4, 1880.1, and 1903.6), and
the following year the indefatigable Alexander Grosart published his
three-volume edition of The Complete Poems (1876.1). Although Gosse
and Grosart disagreed over such matters as whether Herrick was influenced more by Catullus or Martial, whether Herrick was interested
in political matters, and whether he was a "carefree lyrist" (Gosse)
or a careful craftsman (Grosart), they agreed that the poems in the
1648 volume are "a vast confused collection . . . tossed together"
(Gosse, 1903.6), that Herrick's versification is superior to Waller's,
and that the epigrams are best forgotten.

In their squeamishness about the epigrams, Gosse and Grosart were
typical of nineteenth-century and even early twentieth-century critics. In 1823, Thomas Maitland had justified including all the poems
in his edition by supposing that it was "more likely to be deposited
in the libraries of the curious, than to become familiar to the ordinary readers of drawing-room poetry" (1823.1); in 1884, Henry Morley
omitted eighteen pages of poems unfit for "reading . . . in our
English homes" (1884.1); and in 1891, Alfred Pollard relegated the
epigrams to a detachable appendix (1891.1). In 1899, Laurie Magnus
edited a Temple Classics Edition in which some poems and parts of
poems are replaced by asterisks--a practice repeated in the Everyman's
Library edition of 1908 (see 1897.1). Not until F.W. Moorman's
Biographical and Critical Study of 1910 can one find praise like the
following: "we must regard [Herrick] as one of the greatest masters
of the epigrammatic art, and as the only English poet who can bear
comparison with the epigrammist of the Greek Anthology" (1910.11).
Even Moorman, however, dismissed the satiric epigrams on the ground
that "The most that can be said for them is that they are neither
more witless nor more foul than those written by many other epigram-
mists of the Renaissance." Herrick's next biographer, Floris
Delattre, was willing to acknowledge a strain of "brutalité" in
Herrick's work (1911.2), and in 1933, M.L.S. Lossing argued that the
very absence of "refinement" in the epigrams is a significant aspect
of a poet whose hallmark is "an immediate presentation of sensation"
(1933.7). From that time forward, an increasing number of readers
have accepted, even admired, Herrick's occasional "brutalité" (see
especially, 1976.7 and 1978.9).

If nineteenth-century readers failed to admire the epigrams,
however, they appreciated the lyrics enough to call Herrick "the
Burns of his time" (1874.5), second only to Shelley in the list of
England's greatest lyrists (1880.1), a poet of great "naturalness of
feeling" (1892.6). Indeed, in his preface to Pollard's edition of
the poems, A.C. Swinburne asserted that Herrick "is and will probably

always be the first in rank and station of English song-writers"
(1891.1). Toward the end of the century, critics began to emphasize
more somber moods in the 1648 volume. Henry Morley, for example,
introduced his edition with the theory that "In the texture of his
book he evidently meant to show the warp and woof of life. He aimed
at effects of contrast that belong to the true nature of man"
(1884.1). Both Ernest Rhys (1887.1) and Edward Everett Hale (1892.8)
observed in Herrick's later verse a "note of a profound apprehension
of the dangers in which the country was being involved" after 1640
(1887.1). Alfred Pollard suggested that the "Temple" or "Book" of
heroes within the 1648 volume was written "in his sedater middle age"
(1892.9); and Frederic Ives Carpenter saw Herrick and his fellow
Cavaliers writing verses tinged by "the quiddities of the metaphysics, the self-reproaches of the mystics and the devotees, and the
darkness of Puritanism" (1897.5).

Just before the turn of the century, Alfred Pollard published a
revised edition of The Hesperides and Noble Numbers (1898.1); the
notes in that edition include references to a number of sources of
Herrick's poems--sources identified by the Reverend Charles P. Phinn,
whose copiously annotated copy of Grosart's edition (1876.1) is now
in the British Library. In the same year Pollard published an article providing 112 additional passages from classical and English
writers that may be sources for Herrick's poems (1898.4). In the
decades that followed, a number of writers noted Herrick's exploitation of motifs from classical, English, and Continental writers.
F.W. Moorman placed Herrick squarely in the English tradition
(1910.11 and 1917.5); Floris Delattre treated his poems in terms
of the Renaissance concept of imitatio and of the Renaissance
admiration of Greek and Latin literature (1911.2); and Herbert
Grierson placed both Herrick and Milton in traditions established
by the Pléiade, "Herrick catching all the pagan grace and fancy
of their lighter Anacreontic strains to which he gave certainly
no less of classical perfection and style" (1906.2). In an edition of The Poetical Works that was to remain the standard text
until L.C. Martin's edition of 1956 (1956.1) and J. Max Patrick's
of 1963 (1963.1), Moorman examined Herrick's "thorough, and at times
relentless, revision of his verses" and noted work by Phinn and
Pollard (1903.7 and 1903.8) and W.F. Prideaux (1905.4) which argues
for Herrick's revising pages of the 1648 volume while it was in the
printing office (1915.1). Two years later, in The Cambridge History
of English Literature, Moorman once again articulated his sense of
Herrick as a songster in a "day when England was a nest of singing
birds"--and as "a careful and deliberate artist who practiced with
unfailing assiduity the labor of the file" (1917.5). The seeming
contradiction between Herrick the singer of songs and Herrick the
deliberate craftsman continued to inform essays on Herrick published
in the 1910s and 1920s; in 1933, Oliver Elton reconciled the two
ideas about Herrick by saying he "is one of the calculating poets--
and hence his air of spontaneity" (1933.4).

Introduction

Both William Empson (1930.2) and F.W. Bateson (1934.2) saw Herrick as a poet whose language is richly ambiguous, and in their preface to The Oxford Book of Seventeenth Century Verse Herbert Grierson and Geoffrey Bullough presented him in the mainstream of seventeenth-century poets whose work is "troubled . . . by the intrusion of the intellect, a spirit of inquiry impatient of traditional, conventional sentiment" (1934.4). Cleanth Brooks included two examples from Herrick in his argument that seventeenth-century poetry "is basically and generally a poetry of wit" (1939.1; see also Bateson, 1950.2), and Leah Jones treated Herrick as an important predecessor of the eighteenth century (1940.1). Two influential voices, however, minimized Herrick's place in English poetry. In his review of Grierson's and Bullough's Oxford anthology, F.R. Leavis excluded Herrick from the "line of wit" he admired in poetry from Donne to Dryden (1935.3). T.S. Eliot, in a lecture printed first in the Welsh Review and then in the Sewanee Review, uttered the judgments that Herrick is a "purely natural and unself-conscious man, writing his poems as the fancy seizes him" and that his volume, unlike George Herbert's Temple, lacks a "continuous conscious purpose" (1944.1).

Nine months before Eliot's lecture appeared in print, however, Allan H. Gilbert published an essay noting how many of Herrick's verses deal with death and arguing that the voices in Herrick's poems are those of dramatic personae rather than of Herrick himself (1944.2). Gilbert's understanding of the variety of personae whose muses inform the 1648 volume and of the serious reverberations of much of the verse has been echoed in Sydney Musgrove's The Universe of Robert Herrick (1950.4), in Thomas R. Whitaker's essay on the "Christian-Dionysian" ambiguity in Herrick's verse (1955.10), Cleanth Brooks's analysis of "Corinna's going a Maying" (1947.1), in G.R. Hibbard's examination of the ethical views expressed in Herrick's country-house poems (1956.6), in Harold Swardson's treatment of Herrick's poetry as an assertion of "an alternative to narrowly pious Christian attitudes" (1956.10), and in Roger B. Rollin's Ph.D. dissertation on Herrick's development of pastoralism (1959.12). Revised and published (1966.6), Rollin's work argues that Herrick's 1648 volume meets Eliot's criterion that a major book of short poems will be informed by "a unity of underlying pattern" (1944.1), for Herrick's pastoral persona is concerned with "the affirmation of life, the confrontation of death, and the transcendence of both through art" (1959.12).

Rollin agrees with Musgrove that Herrick is "a poet of stature less only than the greatest . . . of his age" (1950.4). That evaluation is probably one with which most critics of seventeenth-century literature would now agree. In treating Herrick as a representative figure within a complex and multifaceted century, recent scholars have simultaneously affirmed the view of Herrick as a conscious artist and have enlarged our perceptions of the period as a whole. Essays written in the mid- and late 1970s investigated topics such as Herrick's political and religious stance (1978.17 and 1978.33, for example), his sense of history (1974.3 and 1979.7), and his place (with Marvell, the poet whom Leavis claimed was more serious than Herrick) as a mannerist poet (1978.19). In the 1970s, the most active writers on Herrick were probably the generic critics, who placed him squarely in his seventeenth-century milieu and argued for his conscious exploitation and development of genres familiar to Renaissance readers. Among important pieces of generic criticism, one should note Rosalie L. Colie's brief but influential analysis of "The Argument of his Book" (1973.3); other examples include Heather Asals's treatment of the epigrams (1976.1), William A. McClung's and Heather Dubrow's of the country-house poems (1977.6 and 1979.3), and A. Leigh DeNeef's of ceremonial poetry (1969.2; revised and published as 1974.4).

In seeing Herrick as a conscious craftsman whose volume represents a complex world view, these readers return, albeit with the language of more sophisticated critical methodologies, to topoi found in earlier Herrick criticism by scholars like Alfred Pollard (1891.1), Edward Everett Hale (1892.8), F.W. Moorman (1910.11), and Floris Delattre (1911.2). Unwilling to repeat Swinburne's lavish praise of Herrick the English songster (1891.1), recent critics accord him what is in our age a higher compliment: the compliment of studying his language, his poetic structures, and his two-part volume of poems with rigorous care. Only three articles--all brief notes--were published on Herrick in 1980. At this writing, in mid-1981, three more articles treating Herrick have been published. Those statistics might be indicative of a decline in Herrick's reputation. More likely, I think, they suggest that after the flurry of activity surrounding the 1974 tercentenary of his death, Herrick is now accepted as a significant poet for whom we need not find labels like "great" or "good" or "charming" and whose work we will continue to study both in his seventeenth-century context (as a royalist, an Anglican, a critic of life and art) and in an ahistorical context of poets whose "Verses out-live the bravest deeds of men" (H-791).

Writings about Robert Herrick

1648

1 Hesperides: or, The Works Both Humane & Divine of Robert
     Herrick Esq. London: John Williams & Francis Eglesfield,
     398 + 79 pp. Facsimile reprint. Menston, England: Scolar
     Press, 1969.
          Single volume containing 1,130 poems, followed by 272
     poems that are introduced by a separate title page (dated
     1647) designating them His Noble Numbers: or, His Pious
     Pieces. A variant title page for the entire 1648 volume
     adds "and are to be sold by Tho: Hunt, Book-seller in
     Exon."

1675

1 PHILLIPS, EDWARD. Theatrum Poetarum; Or a Compleat Collection
     of the Poets, Especially the most Eminent, of all Ages.
     Pt. 2, "The Modern Poets." London: for Charles Smith,
     p. 162. Facsimile reprint. Hildesheim and New York:
     Georg Olms Verlag, 1970.
          After Robert Heath, treats "Robert Herric [sic], a
     writer of Poems of much about the same standing and the
     same Rank in fame with the last mention'd, though not par-
     ticularly influenced by any Nymph or Goddess, except his
     Maid Pru." Says Herrick offers pleasant pastoral images,
     "which but for the interruption of other trivial passages
     might have made up none of the worst Poetic Landskips."

1687

1 WINSTANLEY, WILLIAM. "Robert Herric" [sic]. In The Lives of
     the most Famous English Poets; or, the Honour of Parnassus
     . . . To the Reign of His Present Majesty King James II.
     London: H. Clark, for Samuel Manship, pp. 166-67. Facsim-
     ile reprint. Gainesville, Fla.: Scholars' Facsimiles and
     Reprints, 1963.

1687

After an independent judgment of Herrick as "one of the
Scholars of <u>Apollo</u> of the middle Form, yet something above
George Withers" (the poet treated just before Herrick),
quotes (without attribution) Phillips's comments describing
Herrick's "Poetick Landskips" and comparing him to Robert
Heath (1675.1).
Excerpted: 1901.1.

1701

1   PRINCE, JOHN. <u>Danmonii Orientales Illustres: or, The Worthies</u>
<u>of Devon</u>. Exeter: Sam. Farley, p. 334.
Closes the entry on Sir Edward Giles by printing his
epitaph with the information that "The Author of this Epitaph was Mr. <u>Herrick</u>, at that time Vicar of the Parish of
<u>Dean-Prior</u>, and very Aged; but in his Youth he had been an
eminent Poet, as his printed Works declare."

1714

1   WALKER, JOHN. <u>An Attempt Towards Recovering an Account of the</u>
<u>Numbers and Sufferings of the Clergy of the Church of</u>
<u>England,   . . . who were Sequester'd, Harrass'd, &c. in the</u>
<u>late Times of the Grand Rebellion</u>. Pt. 2. London: W.S.
for J. Nicholson, R. Knaplock, R. Wilken, B. Tooke,
D. Midwinter, and B. Cowse, p. 263.
Quotes the incumbent at Dean Prior who writes that
Herrick "was a Sober and Learned Man; and was Presented to
this Living by his Majesty King <u>Charles</u> I. on the Promotion
of Dr. <u>Potter</u> to the See of <u>Carlisle</u>. After his Ejectment
he retired to <u>London</u>; and having no Fifths paid him, was
subsisted by Charity, until the Restoration; at which time
he returned to this Vicaridge."
Revised by A.G. Matthews: 1948.10.

1721

1   WOOD, ANTHONY à. "Robert Heyrick [sic]." In <u>Athenae</u>
<u>Oxonienses: An Exact History of all the Writers and</u>
<u>Bishops Who have had their Education in the most Antient</u>
<u>and Famous University of Oxford</u>. 2d ed. Vol. 2. London:
for R. Knaplock, D. Midwinter, and J. Tonson, pp. 122-23.
Title page of second edition indicates it is "very much
Corrected and Enlarged: with the Addition of above 500 new
Lives from the Author's Original Manuscript"; the biography

of Herrick is one of the new lives added in this edition.
Mistakenly places Herrick at Oxford and asserts he "was
elected Fellow of Alls. Coll. from that of S. John's as it
seems, in the year 1628, but took no Degree, as I can yet
find." Notes Herrick "lived near the River Dean-Bourne"
and was "forced to leave that place," but mentions nothing
about his having been vicar of Dean Prior. Notes the publication of Hesperides and Noble Numbers, which "made him
much admired in the time when they were published, especially among the generous and boon Loyalists, among whom
he was numbred as a sufferer." Believes that "afterwards
he had a Benefice conferr'd on him (in Devonsh. I think)"
by the Earl of Exeter and records that he lived in
Westminster after the Restoration. Names Richard Heyrick
(treated in vol. 2) as a kinsman. (Richard Heyrick is also
listed as having been elected a fellow of All Souls after
having taken a degree at St. John's.)
    Corrected edition: 1817.1. Excerpted: 1901.1.

1769

1   GRANGER, Rev. J. "Robert Herrick." In A Biographical History
    of England from Egbert the Great to the Revolution. Vol. 1,
    Pt. 2. London: for T. Davies, p. 496.
       Includes Herrick in "Class IX. Men of Genius and of
Learning" during the reign of Charles I. Describes the
frontispiece of the 1648 volume and presents Herrick as a
prolific poet; cites Phillips's statement that Herrick was
inspired by his maid Prue only (1675.1) and notes that the
poems' qualities suggest she was an inadequate muse. Refers the reader to Wood (1721.1) for commendation of the
divine poems.
      Excerpted: 1901.1.

1790

1   [ELLIS, GEORGE.] "Robert Herrick." In Specimens of the Early
    English Poets. London: for Edwards, pp. 205-7.
       Headnote to three Herrick poems ("A Meditation for his
Mistresse," "Sonnet" ["To a Gentlewoman, objecting to him
his gray haires"], and "The mad Maids song") indicates that
he is the author of the 1648 Hesperides, which "contains
two little pieces, 'the Primrose' and 'the Inquiry,' which
are printed in Carew's poems." (In Hesperides, "the
Inquiry" is entitled "Mistresse Elizabeth Wheeler, under
the name of the lost Shepardesse.")

1796

1 D., O. Comments on Herrick. <u>Gentleman's Magazine</u> 66
      (September):736.
          Adds details to Eugenio's comments in 1796.3: Dr.
      Barnaby Potter preceded Herrick as vicar of Dean Prior;
      John Syms succeeded him. Says that "Farewell to Dean-
      Bourn" ("To Dean-bourn, a rude River in Devon") has been
      passed down orally in the parish and that the parishioners
      believe Herrick to have authored <u>Poor Robin's Almanack</u>.
      Asks whether the latter could be accurate.

2 ERUDITUS, LEVITER [pseud.]. Comments on Herrick and other
      matters. <u>Gentleman's Magazine</u> 66 (August):645-46.
          Response to W.F.I. (1796.4): Herrick is mentioned by
      Phillips (1675.1) and Winstanley (1687.1). Adds biographi-
      cal details to Eugenio (1796.3) and agrees with Phillips's
      judgment of the poems (1675.1). Notes allusions to Herrick
      in <u>Naps upon Parnassus</u> (1658) and <u>Musarum Deliciae</u> (1655).

3 EUGENIO [pseud.]. Comments on Robert Herrick. <u>Gentleman's
      Magazine</u> 66 (June):461-62.
          Gives details on Herrick's life and works from Wood
      (1721.1), Thomas Rymer (<u>Foedera</u>, <u>Tom</u>. xix, p. 138), Granger
      (1769.1), and Walker (1714.1); refers the reader to Wood
      (1721.1) for commendation of the religious poems. Prints
      poems by Herrick on pp. 509-10.

4 I., W.F. Query about several English poets. <u>Gentleman's
      Magazine</u> 66 (May):384-85.
          Asks for information about six "old poets," including
      Robert Herrick, the author of <u>Hesperides</u>.
          Response: 1796.2.

1797

1 N[ICHOLS], J. Letters of Robert Herrick the poet. <u>Gentleman's
      Magazine</u> 67 (February):102-3.
          Corrects Wood's assumption that Herrick was at St. John's
      or All Souls, Oxford (1721.1) by printing two letters from
      Herrick to his uncle and a note of hand showing he was at
      St. John's College and Trinity Hall, Cambridge.

1798

1 NICHOLS, JOHN. "Houghton." In The History and Antiquities of
   the County of Leicester. Vol. 2, Pt. 2. London: by and
   for the author, pp. 611-36.
       In the section on Houghton, treats the Herrick family
   (pp. 615-36)--leading up to Robert Herrick the poet. Provides a genealogy of the Eyrick or Heyrick family from
   1450 to 1797; traces family members' lives; prints letters
   from various Herricks and seven poems by Robert Herrick
   addressed to Nicholas Herrick and his family. Treats the
   poet Robert Herrick on pp. 631-34: provides biographical
   details; prints five letters and one note of hand from
   Herrick to his uncle Sir William Herrick to show that he
   was a student at Cambridge rather than Oxford; prints a
   number of the poems, closing with the final lines of
   Hesperides ("To his Book's end this last line he'd have
   plac't, / Jocund his Muse was; but his Life was chaste") as
   descriptive of "His general character."
       See 1797.1 for an earlier printing of two of Herrick's
   letters and the note of hand.

1804

1 DRAKE, NATHAN. "On the Life, Writings and Genius of Robert
   Herrick." In Literary Hours; or, Sketches, Critical, Nar-
   rative, and Poetical. 3d ed. Vol. 3. London: for
   T. Cadell and W. Davies, Nos. 42, 43, and 44; pp. 25-88.
       Brief biography in no. 42 includes the speculation that
   Herrick's happiest years were those he spent at Dean Prior;
   accounts for his present lack of fame by his failure to
   weed inferior poetry out of his collection. Stresses
   Herrick's similarity to Catullus and praises "the grace
   and polish of his versification." No. 43 prints some of
   Herrick's amatory, Anacreontic, and Horatian poems, and
   no. 44, moral and descriptive poems--all with brief ex-
   planatory and evaluative comments. Concludes, "Out of
   better than fourteen hundred poems, included in his
   Hesperides and Noble Numbers, not more than one hundred
   could be chosen by the hand of Taste. These, however,
   would form an elegant little volume, and would perpetuate
   the memory and genius of HERRICK."
       Excerpted: 1901.1.

1 Select Poems from the Hesperides, or Works Both Human and
     Divine of Robert Herrick, Esq. Edited by J[ohn] N[ott].
     Bristol: J.M. Gutch; London: Longman & I. Miller,
     iv + 253 pp.
        Advertisement directs the reader to Drake's Literary
     Hours and to Nichols's History of Leicester for details
     of Herrick's biography (1804.1 and 1798.1) and explains
     that Nott has included some 300 poems from the 1648 volume
     in spite of Drake's assertion that of the 1400 lyrics "one
     hundred only could be selected by the hand of taste. In
     selecting with such limitation, too many beauties, I am
     persuaded, would be left behind: I have presented the pub-
     lic with nearly three times that number, and I trust the
     offering will not be thought intrusive; yet I will not say,
     but that I have been too profuse in my display of these
     choice flowers, and have woven too luxuriant a wreath, in-
     cited by my partiality for their original cultivator."
        Brief annotations provide sources, analogues, and bio-
     graphical details. Index of titles.

2 [FIELD, BARRON.] Review of Nott's edition of Select Poems
     from the Hesperides, of John Fry's 1810 edition of poems by
     Carew, and Headley's Select Beauties of Ancient English
     Poetry, revised by Henry Kett in 1810. Quarterly Review
     4 (August):165-76.
        Applauds Nott's action in providing poems from a "de-
     parted genius" (1810.1), but wishes he had followed Drake's
     idea that one hundred poems would be sufficient for a se-
     lection (1804.1). Suggests seven excellent poems from
     Hesperides which might be added to a second edition, quot-
     ing "Upon a Child. An Epitaph" and "His Letanie, to the
     Holy Spirit" in full. Reports a recent visit to Dean
     Prior, where he found many villagers able to recite lines
     from Herrick and no one who did not know "Farewell to Dean
     Bourn" ("To Dean-bourn, a rude River in Devon"). Tells of
     a ninety-nine-year-old woman, Dorothy King, who recited
     five poems from Noble Numbers and who recounted a number of
     Herrick anecdotes: he had a pet pig that drank out of a
     tankard; one day he threw his sermon at the congregation,
     cursing them for not listening. Prefers Herrick to Carew,
     even though their styles are so similar that internal evi-
     dence will not determine which of them wrote "The Inquiry"
     ("Mistresse Elizabeth Wheeler, under the name of the lost
     Sheapardesse") and "The Primrose." After commenting on
     Fry's and Kett's editions, concludes with a discussion of
     whether modern spelling ought to be adopted for Renaissance

texts; believes that the original orthography is important only when, as in Chaucer and Shakespeare, it influences the rhyme. (For authorship of this review, see 1854.1.)
Excerpted: 1901.1.

1817

1   BLISS, PHILIP. "Robert Heyrick" [sic]. In Athenae Oxonienses: An Exact History of all the Writers and Bishops Who have had their Education in the University of Oxford by Anthony Wood. Corrected and enlarged by Bliss. Vol. 3. London: for F.C. and J. Rivington and others, cols. 250-52.
Prints 1721.1, with corrections and additions in brackets. Notes that Herrick was in fact a Cambridge graduate, adds Dean Prior as the name of his parish, and so on. Praises Hesperides, noting Nichols's, Drake's, and Nott's publications of selections (1798.1; 1804.1; and 1810.1); wishes Nott had included twice as many poems.

1819

1   CAMPBELL, THOMAS, ed. Specimens of the British Poets with Biographical and Critical Notices, and An Essay on English Poetry. 7 vols. London: John Murray. 1:235-36; 4:67-74.
Sees a few of Herrick's poems as evidence of his being "a writer of delightful Anacreontic spirit," but opines that less than 10 percent of his poems are free of "coarseness and extravagance" (1:235-36). Prints five Herrick poems, prefaced by a paragraph characterizing his "vein of poetry [as] very irregular, but where the ore is pure, it is of high value." Refers to Nichols (1798.1) for biographical details and poems showing family connections. Closes by noting the Noble Numbers poems, "where his volatile genius was not in her element" (4:67-74).
Several reprints and later editions. Excerpted: 1901.1.

1820

1   HAZLITT, WILLIAM. Lectures Chiefly on the Dramatic Literature of the Age of Elizabeth. London: Stodart & Steuart; Edinburgh: Bell & Bradfute, pp. 251-55.
Sees Herrick as "an amorist, with perhaps more fancy than feeling, though he has been called by some the English Anacreon." Quotes several of the poems.
Later editions. Excerpted: 1901.1.

1822

1 ANON. Essay on Robert Herrick. <u>Retrospective Review</u> 5
(August):156-80.
Intends to provide lyrics omitted by Drake (1804.1) and
to "[embellish] our pages with the rare and singular
things" Herrick's volume offers. Claims that Herrick ex-
cels Waller and Carew, even in spite of the occasional "in-
delicacy" and "coarseness" of some of his poems; indeed,
Herrick is "the very best of English Lyric Poets." Praises
characteristics like charm, pathos, and hearty joyfulness
in Herrick's verse and then prints some twenty pages of his
poems--including "The Dirge of Jephthahs Daughter" from
<u>Noble Numbers</u>, even though the writer sees that volume as
generally insignificant.

1823

1 <u>The Works of Robert Herrick</u>. Edited with a Biographical
Notice by Thomas Maitland [Lord Dundrennan]. 2 vols.
Edinburgh: for W. and C. Tait, xxx + 288 pp.; 296 +
xxxviii pp. Reissued as <u>The Poetical Works of Robert</u>
<u>Herrick</u>. London: William Pickering, 1825.
"Biographical Notice" (pp. v-xxx) provides a life (foot-
noting Wood, Nichols, Nott, and others) and includes a survey of Herrick's reputation to 1823. Justifies Herrick's
lapses in taste by claiming he "was not an <u>immoral</u> poet,
writing in <u>moral</u> times. . . . He rather sacrificed his own
taste to that of his age, and yielded to what he could
neither alter nor improve." Admires Herrick's treatment
of country life and sees him as "at all times, and in every
sense, an <u>English</u> poet." Contrasts Waller's versification,
which is correct and majestic, to Herrick's "melody, sweet-
ness, and variety of rhythm." Declares he has printed the
whole of the 1648 volume without hesitation, for "the present reprint is more likely to be deposited in the libraries
of the curious, than to become familiar to the ordinary
readers of drawing-room poetry."
Table of contents at the end of vol. 2.

1824

1 [PROCTER, BRYAN WALLACE.] <u>Effigies Poeticae: On the Por-</u>
<u>traits of British Poets Illustrated by Notes Biographical,</u>
<u>Critical, and Poetical</u>. Vol. 1. London: James Carpenter,
pp. 102-3.

No. 49: An engraving by E. Smith after Marshall's
frontispiece. Notes Herrick looks like Southey. Says
Herrick is a frivolous, elegant poet, and quotes "Upon a
Lady that dyed in child-bed."

1826

1   RYAN, RICHARD. Poetry and Poets: Being a Collection of the
     Choicest Anecdotes Relative to the Poets of Every Age and
     Nation. Together with Specimens of Their Works and
     Sketches of Their Biography. Vol. 2. London: Sherwood,
     Gilbert, & Piper, pp. 148-54.
     Prints a number of extracts to show that even though a
     few of Herrick's poems are a "disgrace" to Hesperides,
     "the dross bears no proportion to the ore, and the latter
     is of the purest description." Quotes a number of his
     predecessors' comments on Herrick, notes his place as
     "Laureat of the Faeries," and lists thirty-nine mono-
     syllabic fairy-like names from the epigrams.

1831

1   SOUTHEY, ROBERT. Lives of Uneducated Poets, to Which are
     Added Attempts in Verse by John Jones. London: John
     Murray, pp. 85-86.
     After praising John Taylor, the Water Poet, writes that
     "we have lately seen the whole of Herrick's poems repub-
     lished, a coarse-minded and beastly writer, whose dunghill,
     when the few flowers that grew therein had been trans-
     planted, ought never to have been disturbed. Those flowers
     indeed are beautiful and perennial; but they should have
     been removed from the filth and ordure in which they are
     embedded."
     Several reprints. Excerpted: 1901.1.

1834

1   WILLMOTT, ROBERT ARIS. Lives of the Sacred Poets. London:
     John W. Parker, pp. 192-95.
     Brief account of Herrick's life followed by appreciative
     comments on Noble Numbers, the source of Herrick's "most
     lasting fame." Quotes all or part of the following: "His
     Letanie, to the Holy Spirit," "A Thanksgiving to God, for
     his House," "The Dirge of Jephthahs Daughter," and "His
     Prayer for Absolution."

1835

1   EMERSON, RALPH WALDO. "Ben Jonson, Herrick, Herbert, Wotton."
Eighth lecture in a series on English literature delivered
at the Masonic Temple in Boston, 31 December.
        Includes four pages on Herrick. After evaluating him as
a poet who understood the poetic significance of homely details but "pushed that privilege too far" and included some
truly "base and even disgusting themes" in his poems,
quotes several poems to show Herrick's ability to work with
language. Observes that "He has and knows he has a noble
idiomatic use of English, a perfect plain style from which
he can at any time soar to a fine lyric delicacy or descend
to the coarsest sarcasms without losing his firm footing."
        Printed in The Early Lectures of Ralph Waldo Emerson,
vol. 1, ed. Stephen E. Whicher and Robert E. Spiller
(Cambridge, Mass.: Harvard University Press, 1959),
pp. 337-55. Emerson makes similar comments on Herrick's
language in "Art and Criticism," a lecture published in The
Complete Works of Ralph Waldo Emerson, vol. 12, Natural
History of Intellect and Other Papers, ed. Edward M.
Emerson (New York: Wm. H. Wise & Co., 1893), p. 296.
Several reprints. See also The Journals and Miscellaneous
Notebooks of Ralph Waldo Emerson, vol. 5, ed. Merton M.
Sealts, Jr. (Cambridge, Mass.: Harvard University Press,
Belknap Press, 1965), pp. 42-43.

1837

1   CUNNINGHAM, GEORGE GODFREY. "Robert Herrick." In Lives of
Eminent and Illustrious Englishmen . . . To the Latest
Times. Vol. 3. Glasgow: A. Fullarton & Co., pp. 300-301.
        Brief comment on life and works, quoting "To Daffadills"
as evidence of Herrick's being "a minor poet of consider-
able merit" and lamenting Herrick's lapses of taste.
        Reprinted in George Godfrey Cunningham, The English
Nation: or a History of England in The Lives of English-
men, pt. 11 (Edinburgh and London: Fullarton, Macnab &
Co., n.d.), pp. 488-89.

1839

1   Selections from the Hesperides and Works of the Rev. Robert
Herrick. Edited by Charles Short. London: John Murray,
xiv + 216 pp.

Memoir sketches the life; assumes most of Herrick's
poems were written in Devonshire "and appear to flow, not
from a discontented but a placid and happy mind." Conclusion treats the question of Herrick's reputation: even
allowing some "blemishes" in the poems, claims Herrick is
"one of the greatest of the English lyric poets." Quotes
earlier commentators on Herrick throughout the memoir.
Ends with a list of significant men from Devon. Prints
poems under the following headings: "Invocations,"
"Selections," "Amatory Odes," "Fairy-Land," "Pastorals,"
"Anacreontic and Bacchanalian," and "Moral and Pathetic."

2 ANON. "Dii Minorum Gentium. No. I. Carew and Herrick."
   Blackwood's Edinburgh Magazine 45 (June):782-94.
   Compares Carew and Herrick, two "representatives of
kindred as well as contemporary genius, and the objects of
similar and nearly equal commendation," finding Carew to be
"greatly superior to his competitor." Quotes a number of
the poems to illustrate Herrick's "strange sensuality and
want of refinement," the "affectionate tenderness and
. . . easy and natural expression" (but lack of real
passion) in the love poetry, and the easy liveliness in
"Corinna's going a Maying." Concludes that whereas Carew
is to be praised for "the soundness of his thoughts, the
rectitude of his feelings, and the selection of his language," Herrick deserves commendation for "the liveliness
of his images, the facility of his style, and the variety
of his numbers."

3 HALLAM, HENRY. Introduction to the Literature of Europe, in
   the Fifteenth, Sixteenth, and Seventeenth Centuries.
   Vol. 3. London: John Murray, pp. 510-11.
   Brief notice of Herrick, who is "sportive, fanciful,
and generally of polished language."
   Excerpted: 1901.1. Various later editions.

1842

1 [BROWNING, ELIZABETH BARRETT.] Review of The Book of the
   Poets published by Scott, Webster, and Geary (second part).
   Athenaeum, 11 June, p. 522.
   Calls Herrick "the Ariel of poets, sucking 'where the
bee sucks' from the rose-heart of nature, and reproducing
the fragrance idealized"; by contrast, Carew uses "all such
fragrance as a courtly essence, with less of self-
abandonment and more of artificial application."
   Reprinted in Elizabeth Barrett Browning, The Greek
Christian Poets and the English Poets (London: Chapman &

1842

Hall, 1863), p. 145; Essays on the Greek Christian Poets
and the English Poets (New York: J. Miller, 1963), p. 164.
The latter volume has been reprinted several times. Excerpted: 1901.1.

1843

1   DYCE, Rev. ALEXANDER. The Poetical Works of John Skelton.
     Vol. 1. London: Thomas Rodd, p. cxxix. Reprint. New
     York: AMS Press, 1965.
         Lists poems on pp. 10, 97, and 268 of the 1648 volume as
     examples of poems in Skeltonics written after Skelton.
     (The poems to which Dyce refers are "No Spouse but a
     Sister," "To the Lark," and "An Hymne to the Muses.")
     Response: 1948.6.

1844

1   Hesperides: or Works Both Human and Divine of Robert Hearick
     [sic]. Edited by Henry G. Clarke. 2 vols. Clarke's
     Cabinet Series. London: H.G. Clarke & Co., 224 pp.;
     254 pp.
         Memoir by G.T.F. presents the life and works of a
     "jocund and joyous" poet whose "blemishes" can be attrib-
     uted to the age in which he lived. Poems printed in eleven
     categories: "Invocations," "Amatory Odes," "Anacreontic
     and Bacchanalian," and "Epithalamium" (vol. 1); "Pastoral
     and Descriptive," "Fairy Land," "Charms and Ceremonies,"
     "Epitaphs," "Aphorisms," "Encomiastic Verses," and "Moral
     and Pathetic" (vol. 2). Index at end of each volume.

1846

1   Hesperides: or the Works Both Humane and Divine of Robert
     Herrick Esq. With a Biographical Notice by S[amuel]
     W[eller] S[inger]. 2 vols. London: William Pickering,
     xxvii + 288 pp.; 325 pp.
         "Biographical Notice" relies heavily on Maitland's
     (1823.1); adds direct quotations from Maitland, Campbell
     (1819.1), and the Retrospective Review (1822.1). Prints
     the five letters Nichols includes in the History of
     Leicester (1798.1). Table of contents at the end of
     vol. 2.
         Several reprints; for American reprint, see 1856.1.
     Preface excerpted: 1901.1.

12

2 HERRICK, JEDEDIAH. <u>A Genealogical Register of the Name and
   Family of Herrick, from the Settlement of Henerie Hericke
   in Salem, Massachusetts 1629, to 1846, with a Concise
   Notice of their English Ancestry</u>. Bangor, Maine: Samuel
   S. Smith, 69 pp.
       Lists Robert Herrick as an English ancestor of the
   American family.

1848

1 <u>Selections from Herrick for Translation into Latin Verse</u>.
   Preface by the Rev. A.J. Macleane. London: George Bell,
   xii + 76 pp.
       Preface objects to recent censorship of Herrick's poetry
   and notes that the poems in this volume are those most re-
   sembling classical verses.

1849

1 ANON. Essay occasioned by recent editions of works by
   Tennyson, Shelley, and Keats. <u>Edinburgh Review</u> 90
   (October):388-433.
       Brief mention of Herrick as an example of "the southern
   spirit" whose "thoughts were instinct with the true classical spirit" (p. 414).

1850

1 BARRY, J. MILNER. "A Note on Robert Herrick, Author of
   'Hesperides.'" <u>Notes and Queries</u> 1 (9 March):291-92.
       Describes a visit to Dean Prior in search of information
   about the date of Herrick's death: he was unable to find a
   tombstone, but reports that the register records that
   "Robert Herrick Vicker was buried ye 15th day October,"
   "1674." Inquires after a selection of Herrick's poems by
   Singer.
       Response: 1850.4.

2 B[ARRY], J. M[ILNER]. "Poor Robin's Almanack." <u>Notes and
   Queries</u> 1 (18 May):470.
       Inquires who was the actual author of the almanac at-
   tributed, by nineteenth-century parishioners of Dean Prior,
   to Herrick. (See index, <u>Poor Robin's Almanack</u>, for comments on its authorship.)

1850

3   GUTCH, J.M. "Herrick's Hesperides." <u>Notes and Queries</u> 1
    (30 March):350.
        Prints an answer to "Gather Your Rose-Buds" ("To the
    Virgins, to make much of Time") from John Forbes's <u>Cantos,
    Songs, and Stanzas, &c.</u>, 3d ed. (Aberdeen, 1682).

4   S[INGER], S[AMUEL] W[ELLER]. "My Love and I for kisses
    played, &c." <u>Notes and Queries</u> 1 (11 May):458.
        Ends note with response to 1850.1: it was Dr. Nott who
    published a selected edition of Herrick (1810.1); Singer's
    contribution to Herrick studies is his preface to the
    Pickering edition of <u>Hesperides</u> (1846.1).

                          1851

1   MILLS, ABRAHAM. "Robert Herrick." In <u>The Literature and the
    Literary Men of Great Britain and Ireland</u>. Vol. 1. New
    York: Harper & Brothers, pp. 212-18.
        Introduces seven poems by Herrick with appreciative com-
    ments on the life and work of "one of the most exquisite of
    the early English lyrical poets."
        Several reprints.

2   SOUTHEY, ROBERT. "Herrick." In <u>Southey's Common-Place Book</u>.
    Edited by John Wood Warter. Fourth Series. London:
    Longman, Brown, Green, & Longmans, pp. 303-5.
        Quotes Phillips's judgment of Herrick (1675.1) and then
    objects further that "Without being intentionally obscene,
    he is thoroughly filthy, and has not the slightest sense of
    decency." Admits that Herrick's verses have some value in
    that he "has noticed more old customs and vulgar supersti-
    tions than any other of our poets."
        In a note, Warter (Southey's son-in-law) suggests that
    Southey's judgment is "somewhat severe" and calls attention
    to "His Prayer for Absolution" and other examples of Her-
    rick's piety from <u>Noble Numbers</u>.

                          1852

1   MITFORD, MARY RUSSELL. "Old Poets: Robert Herrick--George
    Wither." In <u>Recollection of A Literary Life; or, Books,
    Places, and People</u>. New York: Harper & Brothers,
    pp. 142-51.
        Presents Herrick as one of many Jacobean poets whose
    works belie the misapprehension that Waller is the first

true writer of harmonious English verse. Quotes some thirteen poems to show the subtle grace of Herrick's lines.
Various reprints. Excerpted: 1901.1.

1853

1 [KING, RICHARD JOHN.] "Robert Herrick and his Vicarage."
   Fraser's Magazine 47 (January):103-9.
        Letter purporting to be "From the Rev. M. Howlett, in
   Devonshire, to H. Townley, Esq., in London," praising
   Herrick's verse, presenting some of his poems, and recount-
   ing information from the parish register at Dean Prior and
   other sources of Herrick's biography. Describes the arrangement of Hesperides as like "some quaint old Roman-
   catholic procession, in which shaven friars and morris-
   dancers, saintly relics and frisking dragons, follow each
   other in the happiest confusion"; Herrick combines "worthless" imitations of classical poets, "coarsest" epigrams,
   and excellent lyrics in his book. Believes that Herrick
   found folk customs in Devonshire that he would otherwise
   not have encountered and that he "enjoyed all the advan-
   tages of Sir Edward Giles's close neighborhood" there.
   Prints Sir Edward's epitaph, "supplied by Herrick" for Dean
   Church and poems illustrating Herrick's interest in the
   country landscape; goes on to suggest that Herrick became
   increasingly dissatisfied in Devon as the year 1648 ap-
   proached. Notes his years in London, about which we know
   little, his return to Devon, and his death in 1674.
        Reprinted in Richard John King, Sketches and Studies:
   Descriptive and Historical (London: John Murray, 1874),
   pp. 363-77.

1854

1 CUNNINGHAM, PETER. "Herrick and Southey." Notes and Queries
   10 (8 July):27.
        Reveals that his friend Barron Field told him that he,
   not Southey, wrote 1810.2.

2 HAZLITT, WILLIAM. "Robert Herrick." In Johnson's Lives of
   British Poets Completed by William Hazlitt. Vol. 1.
   London: Nathaniel Cooke, pp. 281-84.
        Outlines the life, including stories from Field
   (1810.2): Herrick was popular at Dean Prior, his pet pig
   drank from a tankard, and so on. Cites Pickering's preface
   (actually written by Maitland [1823.1]) as a source of his

1854

information about Herrick's friends; assumes he visited the
Triple Tun with Jonson in the years following his ejection
from Dean Prior (Jonson died before that date). Includes
italicized phrases from Wood (1721.1), but does not note
the source of comments like Herrick was "equally popular
with the generous and boon loyalists, who looked upon
Herrick as a fellow-sufferer with themselves in the cause
of monarchy." Does not know when Herrick died. Assumes
that Herrick's only poetic work not included in Hesperides
is "The New Charon, Upon the death of Henry Lord Hastings."

3 HUNT, LEIGH. "On Poems of Joyous Impulse." Musical Times,
   and Singing Class Circular 6 (1 May):37-39.
       Traces dithyrambic poetry from Catullus through the
   nineteenth century, including Herrick, who "is remarkable
   for his spirit of enjoyment." Quotes from "An Ode to Sir
   Clipsebie Crew," which he calls a "burst of geniality."
       Reprinted: Lawrence Huston Houtchens and Carolyn
   Washburn Houtchens, eds., Leigh Hunt's Literary Criticism
   (New York: Columbia University Press, 1956), pp. 540-51.

4 WHITFELD, Rev. H.J. "Dean Prior." In Rambles in Devonshire,
   with Tales and Poetry. London: Simpkin, Marshall, & Co.,
   pp. 75-83.
       Recounts a journey on horseback from Totnes to Dean
   Prior, where he finds a place quite unlike "what we should
   expect from the Author of the Hesperides." Sees the valley
   of the Dean Bourn as too lovely to deserve Herrick's "quer-
   ulous reproaches."

1855

1 ANON. "Herrick and Milton." Notes and Queries 12 (1 September):164.
       Observes similarities between lines 1-16 of "Epithalamium
   on Sir Clipseley Carew and his Lady" ("A Nuptiall Song") and
   lines 710-21 of Milton's "Samson Agonistes."
       Reprinted: Panorama of Life and Literature 2 (March,
   1856):323.

1856

1 Hesperides: or the Works both Humane and Divine of Robert
   Herrick, Esq. 2 vols. The British Poets. Boston: Little,
   Brown & Co.; New York: James S. Dickerson, xxii + 340 pp.;
   325 pp.

Reprint--with minor corrections and emendations--of
1846.1.
Revised edition: 1857; later reprints.

2   ANON. "Robert Herrick." Oxford and Cambridge Magazine 1
(September):517-30.
An appreciative account of Herrick's life and works, in
which the writer imagines Herrick enjoying evenings with
the Mermaid Club and speculates that he spent some time in
court before moving to Dean Prior. Laments the loss of the
merry England of Herrick's May Day and Christmas poems;
notes Herrick's royalism. Contrasts Noble Numbers with
Herbert's religious verse: "Herbert had more fancy,
Herrick the more vivid imagination." Cites some of the
fairy poems. Closes with regret that Herrick "allowed
himself to pander to the corrupt taste of his age," for his
best verses are those about nature: "no sooner does he as-
sume the character of a gay cavalier than the fire of genius
seems quenched by the torrent of coarseness and sensuality
which disfigures so much of his writings."

1857

1   ANON. "Herrick's Julia." Household Words 16 (3 October):
322-36.
Expresses appreciation for Herrick at his best--the
Herrick who "moves with a seemly gait and talks to us co-
herently." Sketches Herrick's biography, assuming that
Herrick's "melodious poems" were written at Dean Prior and
that, in an attempt to please current tastes, "he delib-
erately, and with malice of aforethought" wrote a number
of truly unpleasant poems after being ejected from his post
there. Imagines Herrick during his happy years in Dean
Prior and uses details from the poems to conjure up images
of Herrick's mistresses, especially of Julia, who was "An
exquisite name--and nothing more--in the History of Poetic
Literature," yet a real person in Herrick's life.

2   [HUBBARD, F.M.] Review of the 1856 American edition of
Hesperides. North American Review 84 (April):484-501.
Sees Herrick as one of the lesser poets who are "of a
brilliancy that is all their own, and shining with a steady,
pure, untroubled splendor." Gives an account of Herrick's
life and work, dispraising some of the poems as "rubbish"
and praising the "rich simplicity" of the language of the
best poems. (William Frederick Poole, comp., Poole's Index

17

1857

to Periodical Literature, rev. ed., vol. 1, pt. 1
[Gloucester, Mass.: Peter Smith, 1958], p. 588, attributes
this review to Hubbard.)

1859

1   The Poetical Works of Robert Herrick, Containing his
    "Hesperides" and "Noble Numbers." With a Biographical
    Memoir by E. Walford. London: Reeves & Turner, xi +
    608 pp.
        After quickly tracing Herrick's reputation to 1859 and
    presenting an outline of his life, urges the reader to for-
    give Herrick any shortcomings in the morality of his verse
    and to remember that if Herrick had been a "voluptuary," he
    would not have been so well remembered by his parishioners
    at Dean Prior. Table of contents.

2   MASSON, DAVID. "Survey of British Literature. 1632." In The
    Life of John Milton Narrated in Connection with the Politi-
    cal, Ecclesiastical, and Literary History of his Time.
    Vol. 1, 1608-1639. Boston: Gould & Lincoln; Cambridge:
    Macmillan & Co., pp. 387-514.
        Includes Herrick (pp. 467-69) as an "incipient" poet in
    1632; sees the 1648 volume as a collection of "little bits
    of song or epigram" written by "an Anacreon or Catullus in
    holy orders." Points to Herrick's "epicurean" melancholy.
        Revised edition: 1881. Several reprints. Excerpted:
    1901.1.

1860

1   HAGGARD, W.D. "Robert Heyrick." Notes and Queries, 2d ser.
    10 (1 September):174.
        Asks whether the Heyrick mentioned in 1860.2 is the
    author of Hesperides, and queries why the poet was ex-
    pelled from his living at Dean Prior.
        Response: 1860.3.

2   NICHOLS, JOHN GOUGH. "An Elizabethan Marriage." Notes and
    Queries, 2d ser. 10 (11 August):101-3.
        Prints a fragment of a verse epistle from the Heyrick
    papers at Beaumanor. Suggests it was written by Gwilliam
    Robinson for the marriage of the eldest son of Robert
    Heyrick of Leicester.
        Responses: 1860.1, 3.

1864

3   . "Robert Herrick, The Poet." <u>Notes and Queries</u>, 2d
ser. 10 (3 November):356.
    Responding to the query in 1860.1, observes that the
poet Herrick was the nephew and godson of Robert Heyrick
of Leicester.

1861

1 [BUCHANAN, ROBERT W.] "Robert Herrick, Poet and Divine."
<u>Temple Bar</u> 1 (January), 166-74.
    Compares <u>Hesperides</u> by "that Bacchus of versifying
clergymen" and <u>The Complete Angler</u> by "that highly respect-
able old gossip Izaak Walton" as two books that make ex-
ceedingly pleasant reading. Quotes a number of Herrick's
poems to show how delightfully fanciful they are. Prefers
the poems about country life and dislikes the epigrams.
(Buchanan claims authorship of this essay in the opening
sentence of "Holy Mr. Herbert," <u>Temple Bar</u> 2 [July]:
475-89.)
    Reprinted as "Herrick's Hesperides: A Note on an Old
Book," in Robert W. Buchanan, <u>David Gray, and Other Essays,
Chiefly on Poetry</u> (London: Sampson Low, Son, & Marston),
pp. 221-36.

1862

1 COLLIER, WILLIAM FRANCIS. "Robert Herrick." In <u>A History of
English Literature in a Series of Biographical Sketches</u>.
London: T. Nelson & Sons, pp. 170-71.
    Paragraph praising Herrick as "perhaps the sweetest of
the lyrists who sang in the seventeenth century."

1864

1 ANON. "Lyrists: Herrick--Ben Jonson--Carew." <u>Dublin
University Magazine</u> 63 (April):380-84.
    Sees Herrick as "more natural than either Carew or
Jonson, and though devoid frequently of the fine taste of
the latter, his verses exhibit in their diction the presence of an imagination sensitive and picturesque, which is
not to be found among song-writers since the age of
Elizabeth until the present, and in the present in scarcely
the lyrics of any other poet except Tennyson." Maintains
that Herrick is a "modern Anacreon," and quotes a number of

1864

"the pretty songs and verses" from Hesperides, occasionally
noting the influence of other classical poets.

1868

1 MACDONALD, GEORGE. "Wither, Herrick, and Quarles." In
England's Antiphon. [London]: Macmillan & Co.,
pp. 159-73.
   Presents Herrick (pp. 163-71) as "the jolly, careless
Anacreon of the church [who] threw down at length his wine-
cup, tore the roses from his head, and knelt in the dust."
Quotes Herrick's assurance that "Jocund his muse was, but
his life was chaste" as a partial apology for Hesperides
and criticizes him for being "guilty of great offences, and
the result of the same passion for lawless figures and sim-
ilitudes which Dr. Donne so freely indulged." Praises Noble
Numbers, from which he quotes eight poems. The book as a
whole traces English religious poetry from thirteenth-
century lyrics through Tennyson.
   Excerpted: 1901.1.

1869

1 Hesperides: The Poems and other Remains of Robert Herrick Now
First Collected. Edited by W. Carew Hazlitt. 2 vols.
Library of Old Authors. London: John Russell Smith,
xxx + 526 pp.
   Preface indicates that Hazlitt has "prevailed upon the
publisher" to allow him to rework an edition that would
otherwise have been primarily a reissue of 1846.1. (A note
to the preface indicates that Singer's essay is a "lame
paraphrase" of the "Biographical Notice" in 1823.1.)
Judges Hesperides to include both "beauties and excellen-
cies" and "passages of outrageous grossness." "Biographical Notice" includes, in brackets, Hazlitt's corrections
and additions to Singer's work in 1846.1. Appendix prints
poems from manuscript sources, manuscript versions of
printed poems, and poems attributed to Herrick by Hazlitt
(including "King Oberon's Clothing"); fourteen letters from
Herrick to his uncle Sir William Herrick; and the pedigree
of Herrick's family from Nichols, 1798.1 (with corrections). Index at end of vol. 2.
   Revised edition: 1890.1. Preface excerpted: 1901.1.

2   ANON. Review of Hazlitt's edition of Hesperides. Every
     Saturday 8 (18 September):378-80.
         An appreciative account of Herrick's poetry counters
     Hazlitt's characterization of him as a "noble savage"
     (1869.1). Calls for an edition of selected poems to intro-
     duce Herrick to a wider audience.

3   ANON. Review of Hazlitt's edition of Hesperides. Notes and
     Queries, 4th ser. 3 (29 May):520.
         Notice of "the most complete edition of Herrick which
     has yet been given to the world" (1869.1).

4   MILLER, JOSIAH. "Robert Herrick." In Singers and Songs of
     the Church: Being Biographical Sketches of the Hymn-
     Writers in All the Principal Collections. 2d ed. London:
     Longmans, Green, & Co., pp. 60-61.
         Two paragraphs on life and work of an "eccentric and
     talented poet."

1870

1   LOWELL, JAMES RUSSELL. "Lessing." In Among My Books.
     Boston: Fields, Osgood, & Co., pp. 291-348.
         Praises Ben Jonson who "could soar and sing with the
     best of them; and there are strains in his lyrics which
     Herrick, the most Catullian of poets since Catullus, could
     imitate, but never match" (p. 341). (The italics, which
     are mine, indicate the part of Lowell's sentence which is
     quoted in many subsequent studies of Herrick and Catullus.)

2   SAUNDERS, FREDERICK. Evenings with the Sacred Poets: A
     Series of Quiet Talks about the Singers and Their Songs.
     New York: Anson D.F. Randolph & Co., pp. 236-37.
         Brief praise of Herrick's religious poetry accompanied
     by excerpts from Noble Numbers.
         Several reprints.

1872

1   ALCOTT, A. BRONSON. "Books." In Concord Days. Boston:
     Roberts Brothers, pp. 133-42.
         Includes brief praise of Herrick who "wrote sweet and
     virtuous verse, with lines here and there that should not
     have been written."
         Various reprints. Excerpted: 1901.1.

1873

1   CHANTER, J.R. "The Early Poetry of Devonshire: With a
    Calendar of Devonshire Poets." Transactions of the
    Devonshire Association for the Advancement of Science,
    Literature, and Art 6:501-46.
        Includes a paragraph (p. 529) on Herrick who resided in
    Devonshire for twenty years; observes that at times he "is
    not very complimentary either to the country or its people."

1874

1   ANON. "English Vers de Société." Quarterly Review 137
    (July):105-31.
        Review article treating Lyra Elegantiarum; a Collection
    of some of the best Specimens of Vers de Société, &c.,
    edited by Frederick Locker (1867) and five other anthologies
    of verse. Treats Herrick on pp. 108-10, where he is de-
    scribed as a poet whose various moods lead him to "[exem-
    plify] a party whose aspect of moral and intellectual
    paradox is its distinguishing note in history." Thinks
    Herrick's "lewdness" led him into trouble with the Puritans
    and made him popular during the Restoration. Also sees his
    verse as having a "special charm" that makes it interesting
    quite apart from the historical circumstances in which it
    was written.

2   D., C. Query about Herrick's "To Anthea." Notes and Queries,
    5th ser. 2 (24 October):328.
        Asks the meaning of Protestant in the lines "Bid me to
    live / Thy Protestant to be" in "To Anthea, who may command
    him any thing."
        Response: 1874.4.

3   D[ENNIS], J[OHN]. "English Lyrical Poetry." Cornhill Maga-
    zine 29 (June):698-719.
        Includes comments on Herrick (pp. 706-8), whose verse is
    "often graceful, but it is never elevating"--in contrast to
    Spenser, whose "Epithalamion" and "Prothalamion" are far
    more admirable. Disagrees with Palgrave's judgment (The
    Golden Treasury of Songs and Lyrics, 1861) that Herrick's
    and Waller's poems are "more finished art" than Eliza-
    bethan lyrics.
        Reprinted in John Dennis, Studies in English Literature
    (London: Edward Stanford, 1876), pp. 288-355 (Herrick is
    treated on pp. 311-15).

4   R., R.; BUCKLEY, W.E.; and WARREN, CHARLES F.S.   Replies to
     C.D.'s Query about Herrick's "To Anthea." Notes and
     Queries, 5th ser. 2 (26 December):521-22.
          In response to 1874.2, R.R. notes the Latin root of
     Protestant means "to speak as a witness": "the poet here
     means, that if Anthea bid him to live, he will do so, and
     protest or make known her many adorable qualities, and how
     worthy she is to be loved."
          W.E. Buckley suggests that to protest means "to give
     repeated assurances of his love and devotion, even if his
     love should not be returned."
          Charles F.S. Warren believes Herrick "simply means he
     will be [Anthea's] devotee, will 'protest' in her defence
     if necessary, and 'protest' his love for her to herself and
     everybody else too."

5   [SMITH, GEORGE BARNETT.] "English Fugitive Songs and Lyrics."
     Edinburgh Review 140 (October):355-82.
          Includes Herrick as one of a number of examples of the
     "naturalness" of "early" poetry of England; suggests he was
     "the Burns of his time, and was imbued with something of
     the reckless soul of the great north-countryman"
     (pp. 361-63).
          Reprinted as "English Fugitive Poets," in George
     Barnett Smith, Poets and Novelists: A Series of Literary
     Studies (London: Smith, Elder, & Co., 1875; New York:
     D. Appleton & Co., 1876), pp. 365-422. Excerpted: 1901.1.

                              1875

1   BOUCHIER, JONATHAN. "Herrick and Ausonius." Notes and
     Queries, 5th ser. 4 (11 December):471.
          In response to 1875.3, adds two intermediate steps
     between Ausonius' Idylls, 14, and Herrick's "Gather ye
     Rosebuds" ("To the Virgins, to make much of Time"):
     Tasso's Gerusalemme Liberata, canto xvi, stanza 15, is
     translated in Spenser's Faerie Queene, II, xii, 75.
          Discussion continued: 1876.5.

2   G[OSSE], E[DMUND] W. "Robert Herrick." Cornhill Magazine 32
     (August):176-91.
          Presents Herrick as "a genuine specimen of an artist,
     pure and simple," for he is the only Caroline poet utterly
     unaffected by the political turmoil surrounding him. Notes
     the influence of Jonson's masques upon Herrick's fairy
     poems, suggesting that the latter are "a kind of final
     compendium of all the poets of the XVIIth century imagined

1875

about faeries." Outlines Herrick's early life and then uses poems from Hesperides to describe his pleasant years in Devonshire. Sees him as a carefree lyrist, a Renaissance neopagan whose only serious topic is his desire for fame. Conflates images from the poems to describe Julia, who "bore him one daughter" and who inspired him to write a book of poems marred only by the epigrams, which are "generally very gross, very ugly, and very pointless." Praises Herrick's capturing details of "homey country life," yet contrasts him with William Browne, whose work includes "a real notion of Devonshire rock and moor, which Herrick never so much as suggests." Treats the epithalamia, fairy poetry, and Noble Numbers briefly. Indicates his preference for Herrick's versification over Waller's and speculates on Herrick's interest in the classics--disputing any real resemblance to Catullus and observing some similarities with Martial. Imagines the end of Herrick's life as happy and observes that by the time he died in 1674, the "bewigged and bepowdered" eighteenth century was about to begin.

Reprinted: Littell's Living Age 127 (30 October 1875): 285-94, and in Edmund Gosse, Seventeenth-Century Studies: A Contribution to the History of English Poetry (London: Kegan Paul, 1883), pp. 113-39. Several reprints. Excerpted: 1901.1.

3   STORR, F. "Herrick and Ausonius." Notes and Queries, 5th ser. 4 (18 September):226.
Observes that Herrick borrows from Ausonius' Idylls, 14, in "Gather ye Rosebuds" ("To the Virgins, to make much of Time").
Responses: 1875.1; 1876.5.

4   WINTERS, W. "MS lines in Fuller's 'Historie of the Holy Warre,' 1640." Notes and Queries, 5th ser. 3 (20 March): 227.
Asks for confirmation that fourteen lines "On the title and Author" written in a seventeenth-century hand in a copy of Fuller's Holy Warre are, as he suspects, by Herrick.

1876

1   The Complete Poems of Robert Herrick. Edited with Memorial-Introduction and Notes by the Rev. Alexander B. Grosart. 3 vols. Early English Poets. London: Chatto & Windus, cclxxxv + 182 pp.; xxvii + 304 pp.; xxiv + 316 pp.

"Dedicatory Letter" to Swinburne expresses hope he will
approve Grosart's decision to present a complete edition.
Preface traces Herrick's reputation and the publishing
history of poems from the 1648 volume and outlines contents
of this edition. Presents all of the poems because "it
is . . . a thing of truth as against falsehood that the
Works shall be made accessible in integrity of text--all
save students of our Literature being warned off to
'Selections' specially provided" by others.

Part 1, "Biographical," of the "Memorial-Introduction"
contains new data on Herrick's family and his life (as
Phinn's annotations--see below--indicate, Grosart makes
occasional errors).

Part 2, "Critical," presents Herrick as a "genius of a
unique and masterful sort--no mere dainty weaver of words
into rhyme." Explains discrepancy between contents an-
nounced in "The Argument of his Book" and actual contents
of the 1648 volume by proposing that (1) Herrick intended
to publish a separate volume of verse-celebrations of
friends and eminent contemporaries and (2) the epigrams
"were evidently written off after a laugh over Martial, or
at some odd or offending parishoners," but that Herrick's
overenthusiastic publisher convinced him "to entrust him
with his 'Book of the Just' and his miscellaneous Manuscripts of Epigrams and the like, and his marked copy of
'Wit's Recreations.' Whereupon he or some unskilled sub-
ordinate proceeded to intermix these additions with the
others. That the Poet himself had nothing to do with the
arrangement or disarrangement lies on the surface." Disputes Hazlitt's attributions of additional poems to
Herrick (1869.1). Compares MS copies of poems with versions published in the 1648 volume to show that "Herrick
worked with a fine artistic patience and genuine concen-
tration and consecration on his Verse." (Also compares
sixty-two Hesperides poems with versions in a copy of
Witt's Recreations that he mistakenly believes predates
the 1648 volume. See 1891.1 for a correction of this
error.) Quotes a number of the poems to show Herrick's
attitudes toward love, nature, and the king and his court;
sees Herrick as an Epicurean and disputes Gosse's dispraise
of him (1875.2). Dislikes the epigrams, but enjoys the
lyrics, whose versification he praises over Waller's.
Maintains that Herrick is indebted more to Catullus than
to Martial: "'Allusive reading,' rather than assimilative
is what I discover in Herrick's Poems."

Acknowledges that poems in Noble Numbers are generally
inferior to those in Hesperides and notes Herrick's quiet
confidence in the fame he will receive eventually. Proposes

1876

that the replica of the Marshall portrait in this edition,
unlike earlier, inferior copies, "interprets to us his Book
and unmistakenly gives us assurance of a Man, every inch of
him."

The remainder of vol. 1, all of vol. 2, and pp. 1-88 of
vol. 3 contain Hesperides; pp. 90-113 of vol. 3 present
"Golden Apples," nine poems not in the 1648 volume; and
pp. 117-224 of vol. 3 print Noble Numbers. The poems appear with their original punctuation, capitalization, and
italics. Each volume has a separate table of contents. At
the end of vol. 3 are an alphabetical index of first lines,
a glossarial index, and an index of names.

(The Rev. Charles Percy Phinn's annotated copy of
Grosart, which Pollard used in the preparation of his notes
for the revised edition of his text [1898.1], is now in the
British Library.)

2   ANON. Review of Complete Poems of Robert Herrick, by Grosart.
     Saturday Review of Politics, Literature, Science, and Art
     42 (4 November):576-77.
         On the whole, praises Grosart's commentary and indexes
     and is glad to have a complete edition of the poems: "if
     it includes much which we might wish Herrick had not writ-
     ten, Mr. Grosart has done well in doing everything, for the
     use of scholars and students, and duly warns others 'off to
     selections especially provided.'"

3   DENNIS, JOHN. "English Rural Poetry." In Studies in English
     Literature. London: Edward Stanford, pp. 356-91.
         Gives William Browne and Herrick "a rather prominent
     place as rural poets." Quotes from Herrick's poems of
     country life and maintains that they are derived from his
     knowledge of Devonshire, rather than from literary sources
     (pp. 364-69).

4   GOSSE, EDMUND W. Review of Complete Poems of Robert Herrick,
     by Grosart. Academy 10 (25 November):513-15.
         Mixed praise of Grosart's work (1876.1); principal ob-
     jections are to the "Memorial-Introduction," which is too
     extensive for the general reader, contains too many typo-
     graphical errors, and includes an inaccurate "correction"
     of Gosse's suggestion that Herrick is indebted to Jonson's
     "Oberon" (1875.2)--Grosart is under the misapprehension
     that "Oberon" is not about fairies. Praises collation of
     poems printed in Witt's Recreations with Hesperides, but
     wishes for collations of poems printed in Wit a Sporting
     (1657). Reiterates his own opinion that the 1648 volume

was published shortly before the king's execution in the
face of Grosart's supposition that it appeared early in
1648.

5   R., R.   "Herrick and Ausonius."   Notes and Queries, 5th ser. 5
    (12 February):135-36.
        Responds to 1875.1 and 1875.3 by quoting the Book of
    Wisdom, c.ii.v.5-9, which is one of many literary passages
    whose imagery and theme resembles "Gather ye Rosebuds"
    ("To the Virgins, to make much of Time").

                            1877

1   ANON.   Review of Chrysomela, by Palgrave, and Complete Poems,
    by Grosart.   Athenaeum, 7 July, pp. 7-9.
        Briefly traces Herrick's increasing fame since 1796 and
    describes Hesperides as embodying "the singular charm of
    perfect ease, self-knowledge, and delicate literary taste."
    Notes the difficulty in analyzing Herrick's "pure litera-
    ture," yet observes there is much to be done in the study
    of Herrick's tactful use of his English predecessors:
    Drayton, Marlowe, and others.   Maintains that Herrick
    avoided the harmful influence of Donne and learned from
    Jonson--especially from the masques, which influence
    Herrick's fairy poetry, and Underwoods, which praise the
    pastoral life and which present a variety of verse forms
    which Herrick exploited.   Praises Palgrave's selection of
    poems appropriate for the general reader (1877.2) and
    Grosart's careful editing of the complete 1648 volume
    (1876.1).   Objects to Grosart's extravagant praise couched
    in an "unfortunate" prose style, but appreciates Palgrave's
    succinct preface.   Corrects a few of Palgrave's and
    Grosart's annotations.

2   PALGRAVE, F.T.   "Robert Herrick."   Macmillan's Magazine 35
    (April):475-81.
        Stresses how little we know about Herrick, even how
    little we learn about him from his poems.   Notes the
    strong influence of Continental literature upon English
    poetry of the sixteenth and seventeenth centuries, includ-
    ing upon Herrick, but sees him as "wholly free from
    Italianizing tendencies" and allegory and remarkably free
    from classicism: "we have, perhaps, no poet who writes
    more consistently and earnestly with his eye upon his
    subject."   Believes he has little in common with his im-
    mediate predecessors or his contemporaries, except for

1877

Jonson whose model provided appropriate discipline for
Herrick, "to whom the curb, in the old phrase, was more
needful than the spur." Emphasizes Herrick's craftsmanship
and judges him "the first place as lyrical poet, in the
strict and pure sense of that phrase, among all who flour-
ished during the interval between Henry V. and a hundred
years since."
    Reprinted: Littell's Living Age 133 (12 May 1877):
349-54, and, with the addition of three pages treating his
editorial practices, as the preface to Francis Turner
Palgrave, Chrysomela: A Selection from the Lyrical Poems
of Robert Herrick, Golden Treasury Series (London:
Macmillan & Co., 1877). Several reprints; revised edition
in 1898. Excerpted: 1901.1.

1879

1   DESHLER, CHARLES D. Afternoons with the Poets. New York:
        Harper & Brothers, pp. 133-37.
        Presents Herrick as "the most delightful of all the
    minor English poets [of his age], and rarely equalled in
    any other." Praises "Corinna's going a Maying" as almost
    equal to Spenser's "Epithalamion," "which it resembles as
    being an outburst of spontaneous gayety and youthful glad-
    ness, inspired by love and perfect physical enjoyment."
    Quotes four sonnets--"The Argument of his Book," "To the
    Genius of his house," "To the right Honourable Mildmay,
    Earle of Westmorland," and "The parting verse" to Mrs.
    Bridget Lowman--all of which "are very delightful . . .
    though sometimes . . . softened by an accompaniment of
    gentle seriousness."

1880

1   GOSSE, EDMUND W. "Robert Herrick." In The English Poets:
        Selections with Critical Introductions by Various Writers
        and a General Introduction by Matthew Arnold. Edited by
        Thomas Humphry Ward. Vol. 2, Ben Jonson to Dryden.
        London: Macmillan & Co., pp. 123-29.
        Presents Herrick as the greatest pastoral poet and
    (except for Shelley) the greatest lyrist of England.
    Maintains that although Herrick's work is far more like
    Martial's than like Catullus', his "imagination was
    steeped in antique literature. . . . he contrived to
    assimilate into his work more of the temper of Theocritus
    and of the lyrists of the Anthology than any English writer

of the century." Describes him as "a Pagan and a hedonist," a follower of Ben Jonson in--for example--the fairy poetry which is indebted to Oberon, the Fairy Prince. Believes Herrick to be more interested in himself than in any other topic and maintains that the religious poems are theologically weak, but successful literature when secular details "adorn" sacred themes. Closes by placing Herrick "pre-eminent among [poets] of the second class" because he lacks the passion of poets like Burns and Shelley.
    Several reprints. Excerpted: 1901.1.

1882

1   Selections from the Poetry of Robert Herrick. With Drawings by Edwin Abbey. New York: Harper & Brothers, 188 pp.
    Preface by Austin Dobson offers effusive praise of Herrick's "idyllic" and "amorous" Hesperides and "the vesper-chiming of the Noble Numbers."
    Several later reprints.

2   LINTON, W[ILLIAM] J[AMES], ed. Rare Poems of the Sixteenth and Seventeenth Centuries. New Haven, Conn.: Appledore Private Press, p. 242n. Reprints. Boston: Roberts Brothers; London: K. Paul, Trench & Co., 1883.
    Note: "The 'H' is so rich in jewelry that the most careless selection can hardly be satisfactory. Yet being so rich, there might have been more independent taste. One is led to ask how much of popular favouritism even in literature is, like fashion in clothes, due to dictation of the purveyors." Four poems are printed on pp. 91-95.
    Reprinted: 1901.1.

1883

1   ANON. Review of Dobson's Selections. Atlantic Monthly 51 (February):277-79.
    Qualifies praise of Dobson's preface and the illustrations by Abbey (1882.1) by noting "a kind of forced, though sympathetic quaintness" in both the prose and the pictures.

2   ASHE, T. "Robert Herrick." Temple Bar 68 (May):120-32.
    Essay on Herrick's life and work, emphasizing the range of his poetry. Finds Herrick "the most genuine of the minor poets of his day"; sees him as "essentially English" despite his imitations of classical writers; prefers his

1883

fairy poems and objects to his epigrams: "His indecency
may have been the fault of his age, but his coarseness was
his own."
Reprinted: Littell's Living Age 157 (26 May 1883):
485-91. Excerpted: 1901.1.

3   DENNIS, JOHN. "Robert Herrick." In Heroes of Literature:
English Poets: A Book for Young Readers. New York:
E. & J.B. Young & Co.; London: Society for Promoting
Christian Knowledge, pp. 96-106.
An appreciative account of Herrick's poetry; recommends
Palgrave's Chrysomela (1877.2) and Gosse's criticism
(1875.2).
Excerpted: 1901.1.

4   SMITH, H. ECROYD. "Poor Robin." Notes and Queries, 6th ser.
7 (28 April):321-22.
Identifies Robert Winstanley of Saffron Walden as Poor
Robin—an attribution established by Mr. Joseph Clarke of
the Roos, Saffron Walden. Prints a bibliography of
Winstanley's publications.

1884

1   Hesperides: or, Works both Human and Divine of Robert
Herrick. Edited by Henry Morley. Morley's Universal
Library. London and New York: George Routledge & Sons,
319 pp.
Introduction (pp. 1-8) presents a brief biography and
characterizes the 1648 volume as a book arranged so its
poems will "show the warp and woof of life." Believes
Herrick to be, "in range of thought and fulness of natural
music, second only to Robert Burns." Indicates he has
omitted eighteen pages of poems which "would interfere with
the free reading of Herrick in our English homes"; directs
the scholar to Grosart's complete edition (1876.1) and the
reader interested in selections to Palgrave's Chrysomela
(1877.2).
Later editions. Introduction excerpted: 1901.1.

*2 ANON. "Robert Herrick." Southern Collegian 16 (February):
163-67.
Cited in Tannenbaum (1949.1), item 338.

3   COUCH, T.Q. "Popular Antiquities of Cornwall (Fasts and
    Festivals)." <u>Western Antiquary; or, Devon and Cornwall
    Note-Book</u> 4 (June):1-2.
        Account of traditional celebrations of May Day in
    Cornwall, including mentions of children and adults in
    Polperro gathering branches of budding hawthorn and elm
    (both called May) and of young people in Padstow singing
    a morning song as they walk through the countryside.
    Quotes stanza 1 of "Corinna's going a Maying" as a literary
    expression of these festivities.

4   HARRIS, HOWARD. "Christmas in the Seventeenth Century."
    <u>Western Antiquary; or, Devon and Cornwall Note-Book</u> 4
    (December):131-33.
        Quotes poems from Herrick that treat Christmas festivi-
    ties: bringing in the Yule Log (called "Mock" in Cornwall);
    enjoying the Wassail-bowl; playing games like Blindman's
    Buff, Shoe the Mare, and Twelfth-tide Cake; hanging rose-
    mary, bays, mistletoe, holly, and ivy; feasting until St.
    Distaff's Day (the day after Twelfth Night); and concluding
    Candlemas festivities by saving a part of the Christmas
    brand to fuel next year's Yule Log.

<u>1885</u>

1   F., W.G.D. "Dean Swift's Mother." <u>Notes and Queries</u>, 6th
    ser. 11 (4 April):264-65.
        Notes two references to an Abigail Herrick in records of
    Wigston Magna, which is four miles from Leicester, and sug-
    gests she was Swift's mother. Does not know whether her
    family was connected with the Herricks of Beaumanor.

2   HUTTON, LAURENCE. <u>Literary Landmarks of London</u>. Boston:
    J.R. Osgood & Co.; London: Trübner & Co., pp. 136-37.
        Notes that Herrick was born in Wood Street, Cheapside,
    and that the church in which he was baptized (St. Vedast,
    Foster Lane) was destroyed in the London fire--as was the
    bookseller's shop in St. Paul's Church Yard where <u>Hesperides</u>
    was sold. During the years of the Commonwealth, he lived
    "for some time in St. Anne's Lane (now St. Anne's Street),
    running from Orchard Street to Great Peter Street,
    Westminster."
        Various later reprints and revisions.

1885

3   PEACOCK, EDWARD. "Heyrick or Herrick Family." <u>Notes and</u>
       <u>Queries</u>, 6th ser. 12 (26 September):258.
           Calls attention to an account of the Rev. Tobias
       Heyrick in <u>The Antiquities of Gainford</u>. (Does not mention
       Robert Herrick.)

4   PICKFORD, JOHN. "Heyrick or Herrick Family." <u>Notes and</u>
       <u>Queries</u>, 6th ser. 12 (22 August):143-44.
           Cites comments by King (1853.1) on Herrick's ancestry
       and observes that in 1857 William Perry Herrick of Beau-
       manor Park, Leicestershire, placed a tablet commemorating
       Herrick in Dean Prior Church. Calls attention to monuments
       to later Heyricks in Gainford, co. Durham, and in Repton
       Church, Derbyshire.

<u>1886</u>

1   DOUGLAS-LITHGOW, R.A. "Notes Upon the Life and Genius of the
       Poet Herrick." <u>Transactions of the Royal Society of Liter-</u>
       <u>ature</u> 14:183-232.
           Draws on laudatory opinions expressed by Gosse, Singer,
       and others to present an appreciative survey of Herrick's
       life, works, and reputation. Closes with an evaluation of
       Herrick's excellence; like Palgrave (1877.2), Douglas-
       Lithgow sees Herrick as the "most charming lyrical poet"
       in England between Chaucer and Burns. Ends with two long
       effusions quoted from 1823.1.

2   JESSOPP, AUGUSTUS. "Poor Robin." <u>Notes and Queries</u>, 7th ser.
       1 (26 June):508.
           Asks for identification of the "Poor Robin" to whom
       Roger North refers in his <u>Autobiography</u>.
           Response: 1886.4.

3   PALMER, F.S. "Herrick and His Verse." <u>Harvard Monthly</u> 3
       (October):8-13.
           Appreciative account of Herrick's work to answer those
       who find his poems "trivial and pretty" or "loose and
       coarse."

4   RUSSELL, CONSTANCE. "Poor Robin." <u>Notes and Queries</u>,
       7th ser. 2 (17 July):57.
           In response to 1886.2, identifies Herrick as the author
       of <u>Poor Robin's Almanack</u>.

1887

5 SANBORN, KATE. "The Vanity of Genius from Pindar to Dickens."
   In The Vanity and Insanity of Genius. New York: George J.
   Coombes, pp. 1-103.
      Cites "His Poetrie his Pillar" to indicate Herrick's
   awareness of his own worth (pp. 51-53).

                          1887

1 Hesperides: Poems by Robert Herrick. Edited with Notes by
   Herbert P. Horne. Introduction by Ernest Rhys. The
   Canterbury Poets. London: Walter Scott, xxxviii + 301 pp.
      Rhys's introduction presents Hesperides as a "late pre-
   sentation of the work of a poet who was known, if at all,
   because of old association with the 'sons' of Ben." A
   brief life builds to the assertion that the later verse
   includes a "note of profound apprehension of the dangers
   in which the country was being involved." Sees the volume
   as a record of Herrick's mind and characterizes his place
   in English letters: "It is the way in which Herrick adds
   to and completes this natural lyrical impulse by the
   further grace of verse taught by the Latin verse-writers
   and their English disciples, that makes him so consummate
   an artist within his range."
      Horne's "Editor's Note" explains that the 194 poems have
   been selected and arranged to show "the change from
   Herrick's early poems with their supreme daintiness and
   touch of Elizabethan conceit to his later work with its
   almost classical severity, and feel the gradual growth of
   the delicate pathos increase by bitter degrees until at
   length it breaks out into those piercing cries frequent
   enough among his latest poems." Notes--many attributed to
   Grosart (1876.1) or to Palgrave (1877.2)--at the end of the
   volume.
      Introduction excerpted: 1901.1.

2 HAMILTON, WALTER, ed. Parodies of the Works of English and
   American Authors. Vol. 4. London: Reeves & Turner,
   292 pp.
      Prints seventeen parodies of poems by Herrick.

3 MORRILL, JUSTIN S. "Robert Herrick." In Self-Consciousness
   of Noted Persons. Boston: Tickner & Co., pp. 90-91.
      Believes Herrick's "His Poetrie his Pillar" reveals "a
   rank growth of conceit."
      Excerpted: 1901.1.

1887

4   SAINTSBURY, GEORGE. "Caroline Poetry." In A History of
     Elizabethan Literature. London and New York: Macmillan &
     Co., pp. 354-93.
        Places Herrick at the "head" of the "numerous and re-
     markable" poets of the Caroline period. Finds nothing to
     praise in the epigrams, but admires the "secular vigour"
     of the other Hesperides poems and the "spiritual vigour"
     of the pious poems. Prefers the secular verses, but re-
     jects Gosse's judgment that Herrick is a pagan (1875.2).
     Ends the chapter with an "Apology for Caroline Poetry" in
     which he maintains that the Caroline writers are "sons of
     Donne," defends them against labels like "decadent," and
     asserts that never since that period have we seen "such
     blending of classical frankness, of medieval simplicity
     and chivalry, of modern reflection and thought."
        Reprinted several times. Excerpted: 1901.1.

                              1888

1   ALPHA [pseud.]. "Herrick." Notes and Queries, 7th ser. 6
     (1 December):436.
        Asks for details about Herrick's early education.
     Response: 1888.4.

2   BOUCHIER, JONATHAN. "Herrick." Notes and Queries, 7th ser. 6
     (6 October):268.
        Asks for eighteenth-century allusions to Herrick and
     queries whether Herrick's Julia was a real or imaginary
     person.
        Responses: 1888.3; 1889.3.

3   MARSHALL, EDWARD H. "Herrick." Notes and Queries, 7th ser. 6
     (1 December):436-37.
        Responds to 1888.2 by quoting Field's comments on
     Herrick's reputation in his Quarterly Review article
     (1810.1) and by quoting R.J. King (1853.1): "Who 'stately
     Julia' was I cannot guess."
        Response: 1889.3.

4   MASKELL, J. "Herrick." Notes and Queries, 7th ser. 6
     (22 December):496.
        Responds to 1888.1 with the information that Herrick did
     not attend Westminster School. Accounts for his obviously
     fond references to Westminster by noting that Ben Jonson
     was a Westminster resident and that after he was expelled
     from Dean Prior, Herrick lived in St. Anne's Lane.

5   R., R. "Primrose Path." Notes and Queries, 7th ser. 6
     (21 July):49.
          As part of a comment on Shakespeare's use of the phrases
     "primrose path" and "primrose way," prints Herrick's "The
     Primrose" and "To Primroses fill'd with morning-dew" from
     the 1648 volume.

6   SYDNEY, WILLIAM. "A Famous Devonshire Divine of the 17th
     Century." Western Antiquary; or, Notebook for Devon,
     Cornwall, and Somerset 7 (March):232-33.
          Appreciative account of Herrick's life and works.

                              1889

1   HORDER, W. GARRETT. The Hymn Lover: An Account of the Rise
     and Growth of English Hymnody. London: J. Curwen & Sons,
     pp. 74-76.
          Brief mention of Herrick, after Wither and before
     Milton, as one of several seventeenth-century poets who
     wrote a few poems suitable to be sung as hymns. Prints
     part of "His Letanie, to the Holy Spirit" because it "is
     in parts tender and beautiful."

2   LANG, ANDREW. "On Vers de Société." In Letters on Litera-
     ture. London and New York: Longmans, Green, & Co.,
     pp. 145-55.
          Paragraph on Herrick calls him "the inexhaustible in
     dainties" and claims his Julia is "no vaporous Beatrice,
     . . . but a handsome English wench."
          Several later editions. Excerpted: 1901.1.

3   R., R. "Herrick." Notes and Queries, 7th ser. 7
     (5 January):15-16.
          In response to 1888.2 and 1888.3, notes the reference
     to Herrick in Naps upon Parnassus, published in 1658, and
     quotes Phillips's judgment of Hesperides to refute the
     idea that Phillips "pass[ed] over" Herrick in Theatrum
     Poetarum (1675.1).

4   SWINBURNE, ALGERNON C. A Study of Ben Jonson. New York:
     Worthington Co.; London: Chatto & Windus, pp. 98-100.
     Reprint. Lincoln: University of Nebraska Press, 1969.
          Presents Herrick as a "humble admirer and studious
     disciple" whose work transcends that of his master, Ben
     Jonson.

<u>1890</u>

1 <u>Hesperides: The Poems and Other Remains of Robert Herrick</u>.
   Rev. ed. 2 vols. Edited by W. Carew Hazlitt. Library of
   Old Authors. London: Reeves & Turner, lxxix + 223 pp.;
   xxvi + 286 pp.
       Footnote to "Biographical Notice" indicates that it is
   "Enlarged and revised from Maitland and Singer; and in fact
   the account is almost rewritten." Now includes the speculation that after leaving Cambridge, Herrick was employed
   at Whitehall, "and we should assign to this period and
   circumstance the composition of those pieces among the
   'Noble Numbers' which bear a relation to that institution."
   Inserts comments on Herrick as "the English Catullus" and
   on the order of poems in the 1648 volume, which Hazlitt
   sees as "a repertory of pieces thrown together in an utter
   jumble, as if Herrick had handed the loose MSS. to the
   printer as they had lain by him in readiness for the
   press." Prints nine poems not included in the 1648 volume.
   Table of contents for each volume.

2 GUINEY, LOUISE IMOGEN. "English Lyrics Under the First
   Charles." <u>Harper's New Monthly Magazine</u> 80 (May):946–59.
       Surveys eleven poets from James Graham (Montrose) to
   William Drummond, all of whom she describes as writers
   "coming . . . in the breathing-space between two mighty
   eras [the Elizabethan period and the Restoration], flut-
   tering, as it were, between the pinnacles of old achieve-
   ment, their memory so vapor-like, their work so experi-
   mental and light." Finds it necessary to say little about
   Herrick because he is now loved by "Every modern lover of
   spring grass, of holiday music, of mistletoe and country
   cream." Notes Harper's recent edition of Herrick's poems
   (1882.1).

3 HENLEY, W.E. "Herrick." In <u>Views and Reviews: Essays in
   Appreciation</u>. London: David Nutt, pp. 112–15.
       An appreciation of Herrick's "freshness of spirit" and
   his "charming and innocent curiosity." Believes that the
   poems from <u>Noble Numbers</u> resemble the "homely mixture of
   the sacred and the profane" of Spanish Catholics more than
   other English religious verse—even "the erotic mysti-
   cism of Richard Crashaw." Admires "their sincerity and
   earnestness" and "their grace of line and inimitable
   daintiness of surface."
       Excerpted: 1901.1.

4   MITCHELL, DONALD G.   "Robert Herrick."   In <u>English Lands,</u>
     <u>Letters, and Kings</u>.   Vol. 2, <u>From Elizabeth to Anne</u>.
     London: Sampson Low, Marston, Searle, & Rivington,
     pp. 120-26.
          A survey of the life and work of one of nature's "own
     singers."
          Excerpted: 1901.1.

                         1891

1   <u>The Hesperides & Noble Numbers</u>.   Edited by Alfred [W.] Pollard
     with a Preface by A.C. Swinburne.   2 vols.   The Muses'
     Library.   New York: Charles Scribner's Sons; London:
     Lawrence & Bullen, xxvi + 318 pp.; 404 pp.
          Swinburne's preface (pp. ix-xiv) celebrates Herrick as
     "the crowning star" of Elizabethan poets and maintains that
     he "is and will probably always be the first in rank and
     station of English song-writers."   Admits that some of the
     poems are to be deplored for their lack of taste, but
     claims that Herrick chose to alternate poems of "the rank-
     est and intolerable odour" with his many poems "of natural
     or artificial perfume" to relieve the monotony of his
     volume.
          Pollard's "Life of Herrick" (pp. xv-xxvi) outlines
     Herrick's biography, declining to speculate on the order of
     composition of the poems.   In a note to "Comfort in Calam-
     ity" (2:291), however, proposes that "the first five
     hundred poems of <u>Hesperides</u> [represent] the intended col-
     lection of 1640, with a few additions, and the last six
     hundred [are] later, and I must add, inferior work.   This
     is borne out by the absence of any manuscript versions of
     poems in the second half of the book."
          Numbers poems in the order they appear in the 1648 vol-
     ume, using separate numbering for <u>Hesperides</u> and <u>Noble</u>
     <u>Numbers</u>, but prints the epigrams last in a detachable
     appendix (2:357-98).   Adds nine poems not included in the
     1648 volume (2:257-72).   Notes at the end of each volume
     include earlier versions of some of the poems from British
     Museum manuscripts and identifications of Herrick's friends
     and of sources for the poems.
          Appendix 1 (2:302-5) corrects Grosart (1876.1) by noting
     that the 1645 edition of <u>Witt's Recreations</u> contains one
     Herrick poem, "The Description of a Woman," not published
     in Herrick's 1648 <u>Hesperides</u>.   The 1650 edition of <u>Witt's</u>
     <u>Recreations</u> includes some sixty-two poems also printed in
     <u>Hesperides</u>:   "The differences, though mostly unimportant,
     are too great for the <u>Witt's Recreations</u>' editor to have

pilfered direct from Hesperides. . . . The Witt's Recreations' text thus represents an earlier stage in Herrick's
poetic development, though it was not printed until after
Hesperides." Appendix 2 (2:305-11) maintains that Herrick's
three Oberon poems were probably written in 1626 "and cannot be dissociated from Drayton's Nymphidia, published in
1627, and Sir Simeon Steward's 'A Description of the King
of Fayries clothes.'" Describes the copy of A Description
of the King and Queene of Fayries . . . (1635) owned by the
Bodleian Library, which contains (as do a number of contemporary manuscripts) both Steward's poem and Herrick's "A
Description of his Dyet." Appendix 3 (2:312-14) disputes
the attribution to Herrick of Poor Robin's Almanack. Indices to persons mentioned and to first lines at the end of
vol. 2.
    Reprinted: Darby, Pa.: Arden Library, 1979. Swin-
burne's preface reprinted as "Robert Herrick," in his
Studies in Prose and Poetry (London: Chatto & Windus,
1894), pp. 44-48; as the "Note on Herrick," in Flower Poems
by Robert Herrick, ill. Florence Castle (New York: E.P.
Dutton & Co.; London: George Routledge & Sons, 1905),
pp. 9-18; and in The Complete Works of Algernon Charles
Swinburne, vol. 5, ed. Sir Edmund Gosse, C.B., and Thomas
James Wise, Bonchurch Edition (New York: G. Wells; London:
W. Heinemann, 1926), pp. 260-63; reissued in New York:
Russell & Russell, 1965. Revised edition: 1898.1.

2   BULLEN, A.H. "Robert Herrick." In The Dictionary of National
    Biography. Vol. 26. Edited by Leslie Stephen and Sidney
    Lee. London: Smith, Elder, & Co., pp. 253-54.
        Account of Herrick's life, works, and reputation to
    1891. Brief appreciation concludes, "In his 'Hesperides'
    he is the most frankly pagan of English poets, but his
    'Noble Numbers' testify to the sincerity of his Chris-
    tianity."
        Several reprints. Excerpted: 1901.1.

3   PRIDEAUX, W.F. "'The Spark,' by Thomas Carew." Notes and
    Queries, 7th ser. 12 (14 November):396.
        Noting that Carew's works were published the year after
    his death but that Herrick edited his own volume, argues
    that "The Primrose" is likely Herrick's. (Believes, how-
    ever, that "The Spark" is by Carew, not John Suckling, in
    whose volume it also appears.)

4   REPPLIER, AGNES. "English Love-Songs." In <u>Points of View</u>.
      Boston and New York: Houghton, Mifflin & Co., pp. 30-63.
      Reprint. London: Gay & Bird, 1892.
          An essay on "the artless candor" with which love poets
      present their ladies; includes comments on the poetic (if
      not the historical) reality of Herrick's Julia.
          Excerpted: 1901.1.

1892

1   ANON. Review of Pollard's edition of <u>Hesperides</u>. <u>Athenaeum</u>,
      23 July, pp. 124-25.
          Finds some discrepancy between Pollard's provision of
      full and excellent notes for the scholar and the pub-
      lisher's decision to present the book "tricked out in
      daintiness and elegance" as though it were meant for the
      dilettante. Agrees with most of Swinburne's judgments of
      Herrick's excellence, rejecting only his comparison of
      Herrick to Marlowe and proposing that some of the poems in
      <u>Noble Numbers</u> do match the "sincerity and sweetness" of the
      secular poems--"although they rarely match the latter in
      felicity."

2   ANON. Review of Pollard's edition of <u>Hesperides</u>. <u>Nation</u> 54
      (17 March):217.
          Brief praise of the edition (1891.1), qualified by the
      comment that Swinburne's preface is "entertaining, though
      he has, as usual, next to nothing to set out with all his
      brave manner."

3   ANON. Review of Pollard's edition of <u>Hesperides</u>. <u>Notes and
      Queries</u>, 8th ser. 1 (16 January):59.
          Praises the edition (1891.1) as "a delight to sight and
      to touch" and proclaims Swinburne's preface "a model of
      inspired criticism and eulogy." Advises readers to ignore
      the epigrams.
          Response: 1892.10.

4   ANON. Review of Pollard's edition of <u>Hesperides</u>. <u>Spectator</u>
      68 (13 February):238-40.
          Approves the decision to print the epigrams separately
      and suggests that even more of the sensuous poems could
      have been weeded out of <u>Hesperides</u> (1891.1): Herrick "has
      a gift of song so exquisite of its kind, that one regrets
      all the more the false and debasing notes that so often
      mar its sweetness."

1892

5   B., C.C. "Herrick's Poems." <u>Notes and Queries</u>, 8th ser. 1
    (21 May):422.
        In response to 1892.10, asks for the "real history" of
    "The Primrose."
        Response: 1892.12.

6   CHOATE, ISAAC BASSETT. "Robert Herrick." In <u>Wells of English</u>.
    Boston: Roberts Brothers, pp. 211-16.
        An appreciative account of a poet who (except for occa-
    sional and lamentable coarseness) wrote lovely poems with
    great "naturalness of feeling."

7   COLSON, F.H. "Herrick in Devonshire." <u>Transactions of the</u>
    <u>Devonshire Association for the Advancement of Science,</u>
    <u>Literature, and Art</u> 24 (July):70-75.
        Argues that although Herrick probably appreciated some
    aspects of Devonshire life and was interested in its folk
    customs, his verse is not truly about nature or country
    life. Believes, then, that when Herrick (at the age of 38)
    moved to Devonshire, he was "sobered partly by isolation,
    partly by clerical responsibility" and that (except for
    some moments of lightheartedness) he turned to sacred
    poetry and wrote the poems in <u>Noble Numbers</u>. Suggests he
    printed the 1648 volume because he was in need of money.

8   HALE, EDWARD EVERETT, Jr. <u>Die Chronologische Anordnung der</u>
    <u>Dichtungen Robert Herricks</u>. Inaugural-Dissertation zur
    Erlangung der philosophischen Doctorwürde. Halle:
    Hofbuchdruckerei von C.A. Kaemmerer & Co., 56 pp.
        Argues against Grosart's theory that Herrick's printer
    determined the order of poems in the 1648 volume (1876.1).
    Seeing poems in the first part of <u>Hesperides</u> as most
    closely related to "The Argument of his Book" and noting
    the number of epigrams in the latter part of <u>Hesperides</u> and
    in <u>Noble Numbers</u>, postulates that the structure of the
    volume is generally chronological and that, as a rule,
    poems in <u>Noble Numbers</u> were written after <u>Hesperides</u> poems.
    Taking into account those poems that can be dated, divides
    the career into three broad periods: Cambridge and London
    years, 1629-40, and 1640-48. Sees Herrick becoming in-
    creasingly somber as he progresses through these three
    periods, but cautions that daily changes in mood would
    allow him to write different kinds of poems soon after one
    another. Studies such attributes of the verse as run-on
    lines in his couplets (the later couplets are closer to
    Waller's and Pope's in that their lines are end-stopped).

9   POLLARD, ALFRED W. "Herrick and his Friends." Macmillan's
    Magazine 67 (December):142-48.
        Asserts that "in his sedater middle age, when his
    poetry had lost something of its fire, [Herrick] set him-
    self to construct a poetic temple to commemorate the vir-
    tues of the men and women he most loved or honored."
    Identifies many of the people--John Seldon, Dr. Alabaster,
    and others--whom Herrick treats in his "Temple" or "Book"
    of heroes. Speculates that the decade between Herrick's
    leaving Cambridge and his moving to Dean Prior were his
    "most poetically" productive and notes how many of the
    poems show "a knowledge and love of the classics," probably
    gained during his Cambridge years. Notes Herrick's cleri-
    cal friends and those who were musicians; treats his
    patrons: Charles I, the Duke of Buckingham, the Earl of
    Westmorland, and others. Ends with Endymion Porter to whom
    Herrick addressed five poems.
        Reprinted: Littell's Living Age 196 (21 January 1893):
    220-26, and Alfred W. Pollard, Old Picture Books with other
    Essays on Bookish Subjects (London: Methuen, 1902),
    pp. 200-215. Excerpted: 1901.1.

10 PRIDEAUX, W.F. "Herrick's Poems." Notes and Queries, 8th
    ser. 1 (9 April):290.
        Praises Pollard's "beautiful edition of this artless,
    yet artful lyrist" (1891.1). Notes a "trifling omission
    or two," including the fact that "The Primrose" (as
    Prideaux noted in 1891.3) was first printed in an edition
    of Carew's poems.
        Responses: 1892.5, 12.

11 Q[UILLER] C[OUCH], A.T. "A Literary Causerie." Speaker 5
    (16 January):82-84.
        Praises Pollard's edition of Hesperides (1891.1), but
    wishes Swinburne's preface had included comments on
    Herrick's particular qualities rather than only a eulogy
    of his excellence. Agrees with Henley (1890.2) that
    Herrick is "definite" (detailed); quotes several poems to
    show that he combines "definiteness with grace." Adds that
    Englishmen love Herrick's poetry because they love the
    countryside he describes; closes with agreement with
    Swinburne's assertion that Herrick's craftsmanship is the
    source of his immortality.

12 R., R. "Herrick's Poems." Notes and Queries, 8th ser. 1
    (11 June):481.
        Responding to 1892.5, calls attention to his earlier
    printing of "The Primrose" exactly as it appears in
    Herrick's 1648 volume (1888.5).

1893

1   The Poetical Works of Robert Herrick. Edited by George
      Saintsbury. 2 vols. Aldine Edition of the British Poets.
      London and New York: George Bell & Sons, liii + 293 pp.;
      xxiv + 308 pp.
          Introduction (pp. xv-liii) expresses lukewarm praise of
      Herrick's poetry, outlines his life (stressing how little
      is known about it), and maintains that variants available
      in seventeenth-century books (including Witt's Recreations)
      and manuscripts "are after all somewhat apocryphal, and
      possess very little interest for those who do not care for
      the mint and anise and cummin of literature." (Does pro-
      vide variants "of real interest" in an appendix.) Indi-
      cates distaste for the epigrams, some appreciation of poems
      in Noble Numbers ("I take Herrick to have been not in the
      least a 'Pagan,' but very much of a 'natural man'"), and
      admiration for Hesperides poems. Closes, "A little of
      Herrick calls for the broom and the dust-pan, but taking
      him altogether, he is one of the English poets who deserve
      most love from lovers of English poetry, who have most
      idiosyncrasy, and with it most charm." Uses a single num-
      bering system for Hesperides and Noble Numbers. Includes
      nine poems attributed to Herrick but not in the 1648 vol-
      ume. Index of first lines at end of vol. 2.
          Several reprints. Introduction reprinted, with the
      first ten pages excised and last sentence rewritten, as
      "The Poetry of Herrick," in George Saintsbury: The Memo-
      rial Volume (London: Methuen & Co., 1945), pp. 112-23; and
      in A Saintsbury Miscellany: Selections from his Essays and
      Scrap Books (New York: Oxford University Press, 1947),
      pp. 112-23; excerpted as "Appreciation of Herrick," Liter-
      ary Era 1 (1894):25.

2   ALLINGHAM, WILLIAM. "Ramble the Sixth: Dean Prior." In
      Varieties in Prose. Vol. 1. London and New York:
      Longmans, Green & Co., pp. 123-37.
          An essay on Herrick's works occasioned by a visit to
      Dean Prior: mixed praise and dispraise of a poet Allingham
      obviously considers to be a writer of generally pleasant
      but inconsequential verse. Notes Herrick's imitations of
      "coarse and even filthy" classical poets, especially
      Martial; believes that his best poetry will be long
      remembered.

3 PANCOAST, HENRY S. "The Seventeenth Century Lyrists." In
   Representative English Literature: From Chaucer to
   Tennyson. New York: Henry Holt & Co., pp. 210-16.
       Describes Herrick as the greatest lyrist of a group made
   up of Donne, Lovelace, Carew, Suckling, Herbert, Crashaw,
   Vaughan, and Quarles. Juxtaposes Herrick's and Carew's
   blithe epicureanism with Milton's more rigorous "high
   seriousness and religious faith of Puritanism" as it is
   expressed in "Lycidas." Prints two of Herrick's lyrics.
   Later reprints. Excerpted: 1901.1.

4 WEATHERLY, CECIL. "Robert Herrick." Spirit Lamp 3
   (10 March):67-71.
       Celebrates Herrick's mirth and his ("more prominent")
   melancholy: "Herrick's charm and grace are so obvious that
   they must appeal to every one; he is too delicate to ana-
   lyse, for the effect is somewhat fleeting, and apt, if too
   keenly, too subtly pressed, to fade away."

                            1894

1 ANON. "The Aldine Herrick." Saturday Review of Politics,
   Literature, Science, and Art 77 (13 January):50-51.
       Review of Saintsbury's 1893 edition. Agrees with
   Saintsbury that the poems appearing in Witt's Recreations
   are apocrypha, rather than Herrick's own revisions. Finds
   "the personal element in his poetry [to be] one of the
   chief sources of its charms."

2 PICKFORD, JOHN. "Portrait of Robert Herrick." Notes and
   Queries, 8th ser. 6 (20 October):306.
       Speculates that the engraved portrait of Herrick on the
   title page of his 1648 Hesperides is by William Marshall.
   Responses: 1894.3-4.

3 TERRY, F.C. BIRKBECK, and JEWELL, ALFRED. "Portrait of Robert
   Herrick." Notes and Queries, 8th ser. 6 (22 December):
   493-94.
       Responding to 1894.2 and 1894.4, Terry quotes Grosart's
   remarks on the engraving of Herrick's portrait by W.J.
   Alais that appears in his edition of The Complete Poems
   (1876.1). Jewell notes the same engraving.

1894

4   WALFORD, E., and COLEMAN, EVERARD HOME. "Portrait of Robert
      Herrick." Notes and Queries, 8th ser. 6 (3 November):359.
        In response to 1894.2, Walford notes the portrait of
      Herrick in his edition of the poems (1859.1); Coleman notes
      the one in Pollard's edition (1891.1).

                              1895

1   Selections from the Poetry of Robert Herrick. Edited by
      Edward Everett Hale, Jr. Athenaeum Press Series. Boston:
      Ginn & Co., 1xx + 200 pp.
        Introduction provides a brief life and presents
      Hesperides as a book of poems about country life, about
      Herrick's "dainty mistresses," and about his many friends.
      In a note to p. xxvi, explains that Herrick's temper is
      akin to Horace's, but that their verses are formally dis-
      similar. Finds hints as to Herrick's interests and pre-
      occupations in the poetry. Stresses the difficulty in
      determining the chronology of the poems, for they are pre-
      sented "in one grand confusion," but summarizes argument of
      1892.8 to suggest a probable order for the poems and sug-
      gests that Herrick's moods were variable enough to allow
      him to write contradictory poems soon after one another.
      Demonstrates the variety of verse forms and vocabulary to
      be found in the poems; examines run-on lines and couplets
      in longer poems; and postulates that Herrick's development
      led him to write more "correct" couplets later in his
      career. Agrees with Gosse that the sacred poems are gen-
      erally inferior (1875.2) and speculates that they were
      written last: "the poet was trying a new vein and, as it
      turned out, no very successful one." Notes, glossary, and
      index to first lines. Introduction excerpted: 1901.1.

2   ANON. Review of Hale's Selections. Bookman (New York) 2
      (December):336.
        Praise of Hale's choice (1895.1) of representative poems
      (including some lesser examples of Herrick's art). Finds
      the notes inappropriate: some say too little, some too
      much.

3   FLETCHER, ROBERT. Medical Lore in the Older English Drama-
      tists and Poets (Exclusive of Shakespeare). Baltimore:
      Friedenwald Co., 35 pp.
        Cites "To the soure Reader" to show the use of the word
      scab as a name for syphilis (p. 19).

4   LEEPER, ALEX. Note on Philostratus and Herrick. Notes and
    Queries, 8th ser. 8 (9 November):374.
        Quotes two passages from Philostratus' Love Letters
    which parallel Herrick's "Counsel to Girls" ("To the
    Virgins, to make much of Time").

5   MOREL, LÉON. James Thomson: Sa Vie et Ses Oeuvres. Paris
    and London: Librairie Hachette et Cie, pp. 238-39.
        Cites "To his Muse" (H-84), "Corinna's going a Maying,"
    and "To Perilla" as examples of Caroline poetry which ex-
    presses a love for the countryside coupled with a concern
    for pleasant literary effect; contrasts these poems with
    later descriptive poetry which is more satiric, thoughtful,
    and less naïvely joyful in tone.

                              1896

1   EDGAR, PELHAM. "Robert Herrick." Citizen 2 (December):
    332-36.
        Calls Herrick "the spiritual heir of Spenser," for
    beauty is the principal concern in both of their works.
    Divides Herrick's nature poetry into two classes: poems
    presenting delicate, rapidly changing "pictures" (the
    Oberon poems, for instance) and those (like "Corinna")
    that end with a hint of melancholy. Stresses Herrick's
    many moods, but finds his "spontaneity" a cause of tedious
    repetition.

2   Le GALLIENNE, RICHARD. "Robert Herrick: 'The Muses'
    Library.'" In Retrospective Reviews: A Literary Log.
    Vol. 1. New York: Dodd Mead & Co.; London: John Lane,
    the Bodley Head, pp. 1-3.
        Characterizes Hesperides as "a sort of Restoration
    Ecclesiastes" and defends Noble Numbers as "the result of
    real religious devotion."
        Excerpted: 1901.1.

3   _____. "Robert Herrick: His Editors." In Retrospective
    Reviews: A Literary Log. Vol. 2. New York: Dodd Mead
    & Co.; London: John Lane, the Bodley Head, pp. 19-24.
        Prefers Grosart's edition (even in spite of the length
    of its "Memorial-Introduction") (1876.1), yet praises
    Saintsbury's introduction to his edition (1893.1):
    Saintsbury has a "large inclusiveness of temperament and
    experience . . . that fits a man for the appreciation of
    such writers as Herrick and Fielding."

1896

4   SANDERS, H.M. "Robert Herrick." <u>Gentleman's Magazine</u> 280
     (June):590-611.
         An appreciative account of Herrick's times, life, and
     work. Sees his style as derived from Roman and Eliza-
     bethan models and stresses Jonson's lyrics as "the pre-
     dominating influence in his verse." Believes "every little
     incident" of his life in Devonshire "furnished him with ma-
     terial for a verse." Disputes Grosart's belief that the
     "curious arrangement or want of arrangement" of the 1648
     volume is due to the printer (1876.1): it shows "the
     actual purpose of the poet to mingle and blend the ideal
     and the real, and to avoid monotony by a succession of
     grateful [sic] contrasts." Sees the 1648 volume as
     Herrick's life work, which he knew would bring him eventual
     fame.
         Excerpted: 1901.1.

5   WRIGHT, W.H. KEARLEY. <u>West-Country Poets: Their Lives and
     Works</u>. London: Elliot Stock, pp. 244-45.
         Includes a brief sketch of Herrick's life and works,
     even though this poet is so well known as to make this
     summary unnecessary. Volume as a whole includes notice of
     some four hundred writers.

                                1897

1   <u>The Lyric Poems of Robert Herrick</u>. Edited by Ernest Rhys.
     The Lyric Poets. London: J.M. Dent & Co., xxiv + 181 pp.
         Introduction presents Herrick's poetry as the result of
     "a natural ear for music . . .; a lyrical fancy; a consum-
     mate sense of words; a fortunate schooling at the hands of
     Ben Jonson and certain Elizabethans, or of Catullus,
     Horace, and Martial; a congenial life for poetry, although
     in a London that was perhaps too lively, and a Devonshire
     that was too dull." Sees Herrick as one of England's fin-
     est lyrists.
         Introduction reprinted, with minor revisions, in
     <u>Herrick's Poems</u>, intro. Ernest Rhys, Everyman's Library
     (New York: E.P. Dutton & Co.; London: J.M. Dent & Co.,
     1908), xvi + 512 pp. (Some poems and parts of poems are
     replaced by asterisks in this edition.)

2   ANON. "Old-Time Christmas-Tide Poems." <u>Poet-lore: A Quar-
     terly Magazine of Letters</u> 9 (January, February, March):
     31-36.
         Prints "I sing of a maiden that is makeless," "The Con-
     test of the Ivy and the Holly," and Herrick's "A Christmas

Caroll, sung to the King in the Presence at White-Hall."
Describes Herrick's poem as "without pose or dogma or
sophistication"--as innocent as its medieval predecessors.

3   ANON. "A Poet of Spring." Temple Bar 111 (May):26-41.
        Presents Herrick as the last of an old generation,
    Milton the first of a new generation of English poets--even
    though "some of Herrick's work is in Milton's earlier man-
    ner." Sees Herrick as a political man who was not inter-
    ested in the doctrinal questions that intrigued writers of
    the latter half of the century. Argues that Herrick's mode
    of thought is "a gentle Horatian philosophy" expressed in
    an art of "light fancy, lyrical sweetness and purity" he
    learned from Jonson; Milton's lesson from Jonson was his
    "strong reasoning, classical learning, severe and stately
    verse." Maintains that the division of Herrick's poems
    into Hesperides and Noble Numbers is an index of the fact
    that in his mind secular and religious concerns are sepa-
    rate. Describes the lack of order of the poems in the 1648
    volume as similar to Jonson's Underwoods, but sees the
    quality of the poems as uneven--the epigrams in particular
    are "dead weight" in a volume generally characterized by a
    positive approach to his subject matter. Although Herrick's
    classical scholarship is not as profound as Jonson's,
    Herrick does exploit Roman and occasionally Greek poets--
    and also Elizabethan drama and song. Sees his talent as
    one that reshapes and reimagines his literary sources and
    presents the poems written about Devonshire life as his
    most successful. Expresses particular admiration for "The
    mad Maids song," which "could only have been sung by
    Ophelia."
        Reprinted: Eclectic Magazine 128 (June 1897):841-50.

4   ANON. Review of Flosculorem Fasciculus, by C.S. Jerram.
        Academy 52 (31 July):89.
        Includes a stanza from "His wish" (H-938) translated
    into Latin by Jerram.
        Responses: 1897.6-7.

5   CARPENTER, FREDERIC IVES, ed. English Lyric Poetry, 1500-
        1700. The Warwick Library. New York: Charles Scribner's
        Sons; London: Blackie & Son, pp. li-liv.
        In the introduction to his anthology, Carpenter de-
    scribes a shift from Elizabethan poetry "to the inimitable
    and indescribable 'seventeenth-century touch' of Jonson,
    Donne, and Herrick, uniting the common and the remote, the
    simple and the 'metaphysical' in the nearest and most un-
    common conjunctions of lyrical verse that English poetry

1897

has ever seen." Sees Herrick as one of several poets who
continue certain aspects of the Spenserian tradition; he
"is indeed the last expression of the pagan Renaissance"--
yet his verse and that of the other Cavaliers is modified
by "the quiddities of the metaphysics, the self-reproaches
of the mystics and the devotees, and the darkness of
Puritanism." Calls him "the most perfect specimen of a
minor poet that England has ever known." Prints twenty-
five Herrick poems on pp. 205-18.
  Excerpted: 1901.1.

6   COBB, W.F. "Herrick and Martial." Academy 52 (14 August):
    138.
      Responds to 1897.4 that Herrick's "His wish" (H-938) is
    derived from Martial's Epigrams, X, 47 and II, 90; in fact,
    some of Jerram's phraseology is also from Martial.
      Response: 1897.7.

7   JERRAM, C.S. "Herrick and Martial." Academy 52 (21 August):
    155.
      Responds to 1897.6 that he was not thinking of Martial
    when he translated "His wish" (H-938).

8   MASTERMAN, J. HOWARD B. "Caroline Lyrical Poets." In The Age
    of Milton. London: George Bell, pp. 94-121.
      Sees the Caroline poets as influenced by Donne and, to a
    lesser extent, Jonson. Presents their poetry as containing
    "an undercurrent of protest against that gloomy Puritan
    asceticism which seemed to eliminate joy from life, and
    beauty from worship." Devotes four pages (101-5) to
    Herrick, who now holds "the foremost place among Caroline
    lyrical poets." Suggests that the characterization of
    Herrick as the most excellent lyric poet before Shelley is
    not far wrong, even though his excellent craftsmanship is
    not matched by spontaneous feeling. Uses words like
    "delightful" to describe most of the love poems (some of
    which, however, he finds "indelicate"), objects to the
    epigrams as displaying "all Martial's unsavouriness, and
    none of his ingenuity," and recommends poems from Noble
    Numbers as "sincere and reverent expressions of religious
    feeling."
      Later editions and reprints. Excerpted: 1901.1.

9   MOORMAN, FREDERIC W. William Browne: His Britannia's Pas-
    torals and the Pastoral Poetry of the Elizabethan Age.
    Quellen und Forschungen zur Sprach- und Culturgeschichte
    der Germanischen Völker, 81. Strassburg: Karl J.
    Trübner, pp. 131-32, 145-50.

Contrasts Browne's love of Devonshire with Herrick's
preference for court life (pp. 131-32). Compares Browne's
description of the Fairies' Banquet in Book 3 of the
Pastorals (written between 1624 and 1628) with Herrick's
"A Description of his Dyet" and "Oberons Feast." Noting
details in "Oberons Feast" not in "A Description" but
paralleled in Browne's lines, claims "there can be no doubt
that the version of the Hesperides is posterior to Browne's
Third Book of Pastorals." Accounts for Herrick's knowledge
of Browne's unpublished work by noting both poets' friend-
ships with the Pembrokes and with John Seldon; believes
Browne would not have been imitating Herrick because in the
1620s, Browne was a poet with some reputation and Herrick
was unknown. Assumes Browne was influenced by Midsummer
Night's Dream and by Devonshire folklore (pp. 145-50).

1898

1   The Hesperides & Noble Numbers. Rev. ed. 2 vols. Edited by
    Alfred [W.] Pollard with a Preface by A.C. Swinburne. The
    Muses' Library. New York: Charles Scribner's Sons;
    London: Lawrence & Bullen, xxvi + 322 pp.; 420 pp.
    Reprint. 1905.
        Revision of 1891.1. "Note to Second Edition" announces
    that this edition includes the correction of "some trifling
    errors, which had crept into the text and the numeration of
    the poems" of the first edition and many additional notes
    to the poems--most of which were supplied by an anonymous
    scholar (C.P. Phinn; see 1876.1). Appendix 1 now lists two
    Herrick poems printed in the 1645 edition of Witt's Recrea-
    tions, seventy-three more in the 1650 edition, and ten
    additional poems in the 1654 edition.

2   ANON. "Anthologies in Little: II, Robert Herrick." Academy
    53 (5 March):257-58.
        Brief characterization of Herrick's life as "a budget of
    paradoxes" prefaces six lyrics from Hesperides.

3   GILSON, MARY. "The Inspiration of the Pastoral Element in
    Robert Herrick." Wellesley Magazine 7 (8 October):21-27.
        An appreciative account of Herrick's pastoralism, which
    Gilson sees as derived from his love of Devonshire and as
    similar in spirit to "the primitive, sweet simplicity" of
    Botticelli.

1898

4 POLLARD, A.W. "Herrick Sources and Illustrations." <u>Modern
   Quarterly of Language and Literature</u> 1 (November):175-84.
       A prefatory note suggests that Herrick "acquired a trick
   of throwing into verse the ideas which met with his ap-
   proval in his desultory reading"; he "often used italics to
   indicate a borrowed thought, and in the final edition of
   his works every italicised line will have to be traced to
   its original, together with numerous others, as to the
   source of which his memory must have failed him when he was
   seeing his book through the press." Observes that his 1891
   Muses' Library edition adds notes to Grosart's and that the
   1898 revision of that edition includes "a wealth of notes"
   provided by an anonymous scholar (Phinn; see 1876.1). Now
   lists 112 additional passages from Sallust, Tacitus, Seneca,
   Jonson, Spenser, Lyly, Burton, and others that may be
   sources for Herrick's poems.

1899

1 <u>Herrick's Women, Love, and Flowers</u>. Edited by J. Potter
   Briscoe. The Bibelots. New York: Truslove, Hanson, &
   Comba, x + 135 pp.
       Introduction presents Herrick as a "natural," "English"
   writer. Prints poems under nine headings such as "Verses
   to Julia," "Flowers, Trees, and Shrubs," and "Old Customs
   and Beliefs."

2 ANON. Note on Herrick's adaptations. <u>Bookman</u> (New York) 10
   (October):113-14.
       Prints Richard Allison's "There is a Garden in Her
   Face," which Herrick adapted in his "Cherrie-ripe," and six
   lines from John Suckling's "Ballad upon a Wedding," which
   Herrick used in writing "Upon her feet," addressed to
   Susanna Southwell. Both observations come from Walter
   Hamilton's <u>Parodies of the Works of English and American
   Authors</u> (1887.2).

3 SAINTSBURY, G[EORGE]. "Literature." In <u>Social England: A
   Record of the Progress of the People in Religion, Laws,
   Learning, Arts, Industry, Commerce, Science, Literature and
   Manners, from the Earliest Times to the Present Day</u>.
   Vol. 4. Edited by H[enry] D[uff] Traill. New York: G.P.
   Putnam's Sons; London: Cassell & Co., pp. 295-309.
       Presents <u>Hesperides</u> (pp. 300-301) as a "typical" book of
   its period: it is "largely affected by the 'metaphysical'
   touch," which when not carried to an extreme (as it is in
   Cowley) provides "the transformation of the hackneyed and

1900

familiar into the strange and high." The artificial meta-
phors used by Herrick and his contemporaries result in a
"strange freshness and simplicity of appeal."
Later editions and reprints, including New York:
Greenwood Press, 1969. Excerpted in 1901.1.

1900

1   ALDRICH, THOMAS BAILEY. "Robert Herrick. The Man and the
     Poet." Century Illustrated Monthly Magazine 59 (March):
     678-88.
        A genial, witty account of Herrick's life and works.
     Notes that "with all his show of candor Herrick really re-
     veals as little of himself as ever poet did." Yet draws
     some conclusions from the poems and imagines Herrick as "a
     sort of Samuel Pepys, with perhaps less quaintness, and the
     poetical temperament added. Like the prince of gossips,
     too, he somehow gets at your affections." Admires the
     "exquisite" poems describing country life and folk customs,
     noting that unlike poets like Shakespeare, Milton, and
     Keats, who drew their inspiration from the Continent,
     Herrick was inspired by what he saw in Devonshire and
     Middlesex. Maintains, therefore, "There is no English poet
     so thoroughly English as Herrick." Finds Noble Numbers
     less interesting than Hesperides, for he doubts the depth
     of Herrick's religious convictions and sees the religious
     poems as deficient in "inspiration and magic"--and some-
     times "so fantastical and grotesque as to stir a suspicion
     touching the absolute soundness of Herrick's mind at all
     times." Characterizes Herrick as "a great little poet.
     The brevity of his poems . . . would place him among the
     minor singers; his workmanship places him among the mas-
     ters." Relates his precision and fine use of detail to his
     background as a goldsmith and compares his innocent sim-
     plicity to Blake's. Maintains that his many loves were
     imaginary infatuations and closes, "As Shakespeare stands
     alone in his vast domain, so Herrick stands alone in his
     scanty plot of ground."
        Reprinted as the introduction to Aldrich's edition of
     Poems by Robert Herrick: A Selection from "Hesperides" and
     "Noble Numbers," Century Classics (New York: Century Co.,
     1900), pp. xv-l, and as "Robert Herrick" in his Ponkapog
     Papers (Boston: Houghton Mifflin & Co., 1903), pp. 153-95.
     Excerpted: 1901.1, and in Current Literature 28 (May
     1900):151-53.

1900

2   PHILLPOTTS, EDEN. "Where Herrick Lies." <u>Black and White</u> 20
(14 July):62.
Impressionistic piece on the graveyard at Dean Prior and
on Herrick, "our melodious Robin."
Excerpted: <u>Current Literature</u> 29 (September 1900):
298-99.

1901

1   MOULTON, CHARLES WELLS, ed. "Robert Herrick." In <u>The Library
of Literary Criticism of English and American Authors</u>.
Vol. 2, <u>1639-1729</u>. Buffalo, N.Y.: Moulton Publishing Co.,
pp. 233-41. Reprint. Gloucester, Mass.: Peter Smith,
1959.
Gives key dates in Herrick's life and lists editions of
poems through 1893; prints excerpts from Herrick criticism
under the following categories: "Personal," "<u>Hesperides</u>,"
"<u>Noble Numbers</u>," and "General."

2   SPURR, HARRY A. "Some Thoughts on Herrick." <u>Gentleman's
Magazine</u> 290 (March):270-79.
Declares intention of being more specific than earlier
writers in evaluating Herrick's work; will provide "personal and particular observations" about the poetry. Directs readers interested in his classical allusions to
Pollard (1891.1); notes the influences of Jonson on
Herrick's style; cites several echo allusions of <u>Hamlet</u>;
and gives examples of Herrick's imitations of Carew,
Suckling, and Waller to suggest that he "played the
'sedulous ape' to many of his contemporaries." Suggests
similarities between Herrick and Swinburne, William Watson,
and Omar Khayyam. Then turns to <u>Hesperides</u>, the "mirror"
of Herrick's thought and emotion, to show his patriotism,
his loyalty to the king, his sensuality and morality, and
his melancholy. Praises Herrick's "scope and variety,"
even while criticizing occasional coarseness and super-
ficiality.

3   THOMPSON, A. HAMILTON. "The Caroline Poets." In <u>A History of
English Literature and of the Chief English Writers,
Founded upon the Manual of Thomas B. Shaw</u>. London: John
Murray, pp. 251-62. Reprint. 1923.
Treats Herrick (pp. 255-56) as "a singular example of
that union of the earthly and the divine which is so char-
acteristic of a certain class of lyric poets." Stresses
his grace and sees him as a transitional figure between

Elizabethan eloquence and seventeenth-century "choiceness of finish and attention to form."

4   THOMSON, JOHN. <u>Indexes to the First Lines and to the Subjects of the Poems of Robert Herrick</u>. Bulletin of the Free Library of Philadelphia, no. 3 (August), 98 pp.
    Indices of first lines and subjects of poems by Herrick. Keyed to 1856.1. Glossary of words from <u>Abby-lubbers</u> ("idlers") to <u>Zonulet</u> ("a little girdle").

<u>1902</u>

1   ANON. "A Call on Robert Herrick." <u>Atlantic Monthly</u> 90 (October):574-75.
    Account of a visit to Dean Prior, where the writer discovers verification of his suspicion that "Parson Herrick's delicious pastoral pages are pure bluff"; this part of Devon and its people are "dull."

2   B., H.I. "Herrick's 'Hesperides': 'Lutes of Amber.'" <u>Notes and Queries</u>, 9th ser. 9 (24 May):408-9.
    Queries whether Herrick's use of <u>lutes of amber</u> in "Upon Julia's Voice" derives from his reading of Greek poetry.
    Responses: 1902.3-5, 7, 11.

3   DORMER, J. "Herrick's 'Hesperides': 'Lutes of Amber.'" <u>Notes and Queries</u>, 9th ser. 9 (14 June):471.
    Responds to 1902.2 that Herrick uses <u>amber</u> to mean a "shining" metal. Attributes that use of the word to a confusion between the fossil gum <u>amber</u> and the metallic alloy <u>electrum</u>, a confusion that dates back to Homer.
    Discussion continued: 1902.4-5, 7, 11.

4   ____. "Herrick's 'Hesperides': 'Lutes of Amber.'" <u>Notes and Queries</u>, 9th ser. 10 (2 August):95.
    Responding to 1902.11, reasserts his view presented in 1902.3.
    Discussion continued: 1902.5, 7.

5   ____. "Herrick's 'Hesperides': 'Lutes of Amber.'" <u>Notes and Queries</u>, 9th ser. 10 (27 December):511.
    Gives further reasons for view articulated in 1902.3 and 1902.4. Notes Herrick's use of <u>amber</u> in "A Nuptiall Song" --an echo allusion, evidently, of Homer's <u>Epigrams</u>, xv.10.

1902

6   L., P.L. "Herrick: Silver-Pence." <u>Notes and Queries</u>,
      9th ser. 9 (18 January):49.
         Asks meaning of <u>silver-pence</u> in "Oberons Palace."
      Response: 1902.12.

7   LEEPER, ALEX. "Herrick's 'Hesperides': 'Lutes of Amber.'"
      <u>Notes and Queries</u>, 9th ser. 10 (25 October):336.
         Responding to 1902.2-4, 11, notes an instance of amber
      as an ornament on a lyre in Aristophanes' <u>Equites</u>, 532.
      Discussion continued: 1902.5.

8   POLLARD, ALFRED W. "A Poet's Studies." In <u>Old Picture Books:
      With Other Essays on Bookish Subjects</u>. London: Methuen,
      pp. 216-26.
         Traces a number of Herrick's borrowings from Greek,
      Roman, and Renaissance sources, maintaining that he uses
      them to create his own individual perspective, for Herrick
      is "one of the most individual and original of poets."
      Observes that most of the italicized lines in the 1648
      volume are translations from Latin (other italics denote
      speeches or proverbs), but that there are many additional
      echoes of classical authors in Herrick's poetry. Specu-
      lates "that when preparing his poems for the press he
      underscored the passages of which he happened to recollect
      the original, but that his memory in many cases refused to
      serve him." Shows that Seneca, Sallust, and Tacitus are
      sources for some of the "cleaner" epigrams, "though for a
      considerable number he found his evil inspiration in
      Martial." Accounts for Herrick's "alternate leaning to
      absolutism and its reverse" in his political poems by
      maintaining that lines in those poems often derive from
      his commonplace book, rather than from his own philosophy
      of government. Similarly, <u>Noble Numbers</u> includes quota-
      tions and paraphrases from Augustine, Cassiodorus, Bernard,
      Basil, Ambrose, John of Damascus, Boethius, and Aquinas.
      Reports a few phrases from Catullus, Tibullus, Propertius,
      and Juvenal--none of whom are major sources for Herrick--
      and many lines from Horace, "whom he occasionally imi-
      tates." Finds yet more "phrases and turns of thought" from
      Ovid and maintains that it is to Martial that Herrick owes
      his "chief obligation" for the inspiration of many epigrams
      and also a number of poems, including "Goe happy Rose"
      ("To the Rose. Song"), and "The Lilly in a Christal."
      Suspects that Herrick's knowledge of Greek literature is
      generally by way of Latin translations, but points to the
      number of times Herrick approximates the spirit of Anacreon
      and to some few poems which are in fact translations of
      Greek poems. Observes how often Herrick borrows from

Jonson, Burton, and Montaigne and speculates that some of
his classical borrowing may in fact be from them rather
than from original sources. Concludes that the phrases
Herrick borrowed have no intrinsic worth: "He breathed
upon them and filled them with his music, so that they
assimilate so admirably with his verse, that even when he
printed them in italics the meaning of the change of type
has long remained a secret to his commentators." Herrick
"was really a conscious artist, and no mean one"--a fact
that could be further documented by a study of his skill in
translating his sources into apt English phrases. A note
indicates that the anonymous scholar to whom Pollard is
indebted is the Rev. C.P. Phinn.

9   REED, EDWARD B. "Herrick's Indebtedness to Ben Jonson."
    Modern Language Notes 17 (December):478-83.
        Remarks that the most outstanding "Son of Ben" is not a
    dramatist, but a lyric poet, and shows a number of signifi-
    cant imitations of Jonson from Herrick's work. Regards
    Jonson as providing meters, phrases, ideas, and--most
    important--poetic theory which Herrick emulated.

10 ROBERTSON, JOHN M. "Herrick." In Criticisms. Vol. 1.
    London: A. and H. Bradlaugh Bonner, pp. 1-12.
        First written as a response to Pollard's edition of The
    Complete Works (1891.1); objects to the choice of Swinburne,
    "the most cloying of sensuous verbalists," to write the
    preface. Argues that Herrick is not (as Swinburne thinks)
    principally a lyrist, but "an artist in verse." Compares
    Herrick's craftsmanship with Gautier's.

11 STEPHENS, F.G. "Herrick's 'Hesperides': 'Lutes of Amber.'"
    Notes and Queries, 9th ser. 10 (5 July):17.
        Responding to 1902.2-3, presents likelihood of a lute
    being inlaid with amber.
        Discussion continued: 1902.4-5, 7.

12 SWITHIN, St.; MAYALL, ARTHUR; and MATTHEW, JOHN HOBSON.
    "Herrick: Silver-Pence." Notes and Queries, 9th ser. 9
    (1 March):178.
        Responding to 1902.6, each of the three contributors
    proposes that Herrick is alluding to the practice of using
    a silver penny to cut the membrane of a tongue-tied child.
    (Matthew includes a note that Jews use a sharp flint for
    circumcision, and in Notes and Queries, 9th ser. 9
    [14 June]:478-79, M.L.R. Breslan objects to that concluding
    comment.)

1903

1   ALDEN, RAYMOND MACDONALD. English Verse: Specimens Illus-
    trating Its Principles and History. New York: Henry Holt
    & Co., pp. 25-27, 64, 90.
        Prints examples from Herrick to illustrate English use
    of one-stress iambic and two-stress iambic verses (Chap-
    ter 2: "The Foot and the Verse"), and of tercets and the
    combination of long and short lines (Chapter 3: "The
    Stanza").
        Several reprints.

2   BEECHING, H.C. "The Poetry of Herrick." National Review 40
    (January):788-99.
        Begins with a one-paragraph account of Herrick's life
    and offers an argument to verify earlier commentators'
    belief that the "best of the secular verse was written
    before 1629" and Pollard's dating "the last and worse six
    hundred of the poems later than the migration to Devon-
    shire" (1891.1). Believes, nevertheless, that there is
    little need to divide the poems into early and late works.
    Characterizes Herrick's poetry as concrete ("He moves about
    in a world that is very real, and which he thoroughly
    realizes"), as skillfully written ("Herrick is an artist
    to his fingertips"), and metrically interesting ("he left
    Jonson far behind"). Comments on his conscious naïveté, a
    quality "allied to his humour . . . [which] pervades much
    of his writing, even when the intention is not directly
    humorous." Categorizes the poems as having three principal
    subjects: nature, love, and religion. Disputes Gosse's
    view of Noble Numbers (1875.2), for Beeching sees the
    religious poems as more sincere than the love poems:
    "There are no raptures as with Crashaw, and no subtleties
    of thought as with Herbert, but a very genuine sort of
    practical religion . . . touched into grace by the poet's
    never-failing sense for style."
        Expanded as introduction to 1905.1.

3   COURTHOPE, W.J. A History of English Poetry. Vol. 3.
    London: Macmillan & Co., pp. 253-65. Reprint. New York:
    Russell & Russell, 1962.
        After a succinct survey of Herrick's life, considers him
    in terms of the influence of "the classical Renaissance."
    Sees his love songs in the tradition of Horace and Anacreon
    --with no Petrarchan influence whatsoever. Finds "nothing
    . . . of the solemn and sometimes Christian vein of re-
    flection" of Jonson's verse in Herrick's "restive dithyram-
    bic verse"; his "moralising rather resembles the philosophy

of Catullus and Horace: 'Let us eat and drink for tomorrow we die.'" Presents Herrick's country poems in a pastoral tradition descending from Sidney, Breton, Barnfield, and Browne, all of whom color their poetry "with a kind of ideal Arcadian atmosphere." Yet notes that Herrick's appreciation of "the high-days and holidays of the Catholic [sic] Church" is akin to Horace's delight in Roman ritual. Argues that the greatest influence of the Renaissance is in Noble Numbers, in which Herrick's "simple materialist" piety is displayed. Considers Herrick's craftsmanship that of a man living in an age "when the taste for Euphuism had blended with the critical appreciation of classical learning" and compares him with "the first classical Euphuists, particularly Greene and Lodge." Closes with an appreciation of his fairy poetry, speculating that Herrick knew a manuscript copy of Browne's description of a fairy feast in Britannia's Pastorals; praises Herrick's Oberon poems as masterpieces of Euphuism.

4   FISH, MATILDA. "The Pastoral Elements in English Poetry from Herrick to Burns." College Folio 12 (October):1-16.
      A Holden Prize Essay at the College for Women of Western Reserve University. Two paragraphs on Herrick present his verse as "thoroughly English"; Fish sees his work as midway between pastoral poets who idealize country life and those who describe their own lives in happy rural places (pp. 4-5).

5   GARSTANG, A.H. "The Love Songs of a Bygone Day." Fortnightly Review 74 (1 December):973-91.
      Treats love poetry of the Jacobean and Caroline periods, when--he claims--love poetry "attained a pitch of excellence never since excelled or equalled." Begins with Campion, Donne, and Jonson, and then turns to the Sons of Ben: Carew, Suckling, Lovelace, and (on pp. 984-90) Herrick. Sees the Hesperides poems as "the truest English expression of the Renaissance," which he defines as a time of delight in nature. Rejects the goal of finding a single classical poet to designate as Herrick's master, for he shares with all of nature's "chosen singers" an "intense love of earth and earthly pleasures." Believes Herrick to have been influenced by Campion as much as by Jonson or Donne, yet stresses his individuality as an impassioned lyrist who sings in "pure delight."

1903

6   GOSSE, EDMUND. "Herrick." In English Literature: An Illus-
     trated Record. Vol. 3, From Milton to Jonson. New York:
     Macmillan; London: William Heinemann, pp. 58-61.
         Presents Herrick in Chapter 1, "The Decline: 1630-
     1660." Sees him as one poet who avoids, almost entirely,
     the "complicated extravagance" in which both lyric poets
     and dramatists of his age indulged. Admires his pagan
     lyrics which offer "brilliant pictures" of Devonshire life;
     describes the 1648 volume as "a vast confused collection
     . . . [of poems] tossed together into a superficial like-
     ness to the collected poems of Martial"; and protests that
     Herrick's temperament is akin to Martial's, not to
     Catullus'. Illustrates his summary of Herrick's life with
     the frontispiece to the 1648 volume; assumes that Herrick
     generally delighted in Devonshire life, but is otherwise
     reluctant to speculate about his activities not documented
     in the life records.

7   [POLLARD, ALFRED W.] "A List of Variations in Three Copies of
     the Original Edition of Herrick's 'Hesperides' and 'Noble
     Numbers.'" Library 4 (April):206-12.
         Provides the results of C.P. Phinn's collation of three
     copies of the 1648 Hesperides. Observes two significantly
     different readings: the Thomason and Grenville copies
     (both owned by the British Museum) present "warty in-
     civility" in line 2 of "To Dean-bourn, a rude River in
     Devon, by which sometimes he lived," whereas Phinn's copy
     reads "watry incivility"; the Grenville copy gives "As if
     they started at Bo-peep" in line 4 of "Upon her feet,"
     whereas the Thomason and Phinn copies read "As if they
     played at Bo-peep." Although the three copies generally
     "agree absolutely, not merely as to the text, but in broken
     or misplaced letters and other peculiarities," there are a
     number of differences between them--all confined to eight
     sheets, "and only one or two pages in each sheet." After
     listing the variants, requests readers to contribute
     theories "as to what went on in the printing office to
     account for these variations."
         Continuation: 1903.8.

8   _____. "Notes on Books and Work." Library 4 (July):328-31.
         Adds eleven variants to the list in 1903.7 and reports
     the results of examining two more copies of the 1648 vol-
     ume: "The general result of the collation is fairly plain,
     and establishes the fact, which no editor of Herrick has
     hitherto noticed, that the leaves containing pp. 29, 30,
     175, 176, and 207, 208 in most copies are cancels." Notes
     that the question of whether it was Herrick who proofread

the cancels is relevant to the question of whether "warty"
or "watry" is Herrick's intention in "To Dean-bourn." Concludes that this is a case of "the author walking into the
printing-office and correcting misprints when sheets had
already been printed off."

*9   SPURR, H.A. "'Julia' in 'Hesperides.'" <u>Liberal Review</u> 6
      (August):86-94.
           Cited in Tannenbaum (1949.1), item 634.

*10 YOUNG, F. "The Mind of Robert Herrick." <u>Liberal Review</u> 5
      (March):189-96.
           Cited in Tannenbaum (1949.1), item 675.

<u>1904</u>

1   <u>Robert Herrick's Poems</u>. Introduction by Alice Meynell. Red
      Letter Library. London: Blackie & Sons, xvi + 373 pp.
           Meynell's introduction presents Herrick as a poet very
      much of his time--of the Elizabethan period and after.
      Allows he was probably a "poet of fancy," rather than "of
      imagination," but claims that of the poets of fancy,
      Herrick is the "sprightliest" and "noblest."
           Reissued in 1927.

2   BOAS, HENRIETTA O'BRIEN. <u>With Milton and the Cavaliers</u>.
      London: James Nisbet & Co., pp. 291-98. Reprint. New
      York: James Pott & Co., 1905.
           Presents the life and work of Herrick, whom she sees as
      "a lover of all that is joyous and beautiful."

3   COLSON, F.H. "Herrick and Dean Prior." In <u>Memorials of Old
      Devonshire</u>. Edited by F.J. Snell. London: Bemrose &
      Sons, pp. 141-54.
           Finds Dean Prior a "charming" place, but speculates that
      Herrick wrote most of his poems of country life before re-
      moving to Devonshire. Argues that the more sober poems,
      particularly those in <u>Noble Numbers</u>, were written while
      Herrick was in Devonshire; finds them to contain a "depth
      and fullness" not in the happier lyrics.

4   CORBETT, F. St. JOHN. "Rev. Robert Herrick." In <u>A History of
      British Poetry: From the Earliest Times to the Beginning
      of the Twentieth Century</u>. London: Gay & Bird, pp. 173-75.
           In the chapter entitled "Greater Poets of the Seventeenth
      Century," includes faint praise of Herrick and prints five
      "sweet and untainted" poems from <u>Hesperides</u>.

1904

5   GWYNN, STEPHEN. The Masters of English Literature. London and
       New York: Macmillan, pp. 76-82.
            Presents Herrick as a cavalier exiled to Devon, yet as a
       poet whose best work is derived from his life in Dean
       Prior. Observes Herrick's conscious imitation of Jonson
       and his unconscious kinship to Shakespeare's "fidelity to
       nature." Notes echoes of Donne's style in "His Winding-
       sheet" and of Ophelia in "The mad Maids song." Discounts
       Noble Numbers, for Herrick's paganism overrides his
       Christianity. Cites Palgrave's judgment that Herrick is
       the best English lyric poet before Burns (1877.2), even in
       spite of his "want of power and passion."
            Revised editions of 1908 and 1925 include only minor
       changes in wording.

6   SCOLLARD, CLINTON. "A Glimpse of Herrick's Devon." In
       Footfarings. [Clinton, N.Y.]: George William Browning,
       pp. 159-70.
            Brief account of the people and places Scollard saw on
       a brief visit to Dean Prior.

7   [WARRE, F. CORNISH.] "Robert Herrick." Edinburgh Review 199
       (January):109-27.
            Characterizes Herrick's verse as a seventeenth-century
       development of Elizabethan song; his style includes "the
       neatness and quaintness" of Herbert and "his own note and
       his own methods." Stresses Herrick's understanding of
       classical poetry, especially the influence of Horace and
       Jonson, and agrees with Swinburne's judgment (1891.1) that
       he surpasses his contemporaries--even Herbert and Donne.
       Finds Herrick's religious verse, however, inferior to
       Herbert's, Crashaw's, and Vaughan's, for "his religion was
       contemplative, not emotional." Objects to the epigrams as
       "blots on his page," but closes by acclaiming him a poet to
       whom his admirers "go back . . . with fresh pleasure again
       and again." (Helen Grant Cushing and Adah V. Morris,
       Nineteenth Century Readers' Guide to Periodical Literature,
       vol. 1 [New York: H.W. Wilson, 1944], p. 1260, attribute
       this article to Warre.)

8   WENDELL, BARRETT. The Temper of the Seventeenth Century in
       English Literature. New York: Charles Scribner's Sons;
       London: Macmillan & Co., pp. 146-53. Reprint. Freeport,
       N.Y.: Books for Libraries Press, 1967.
            After praising the delightful, fanciful tone of the most
       engaging and the most representative poet among the Tribe
       of Ben, contrasts stanza 1 of Herrick's "To the Virgins, to

make much of Time" with stanzas 74 and 75 of Spenser's
Faerie Queene, Book II, Canto 12, to show Herrick's
"exquisite harmony of spontaneity and intelligence."

1905

1 Poems of Herrick. Selected and with an Introduction by Canon
Henry C. Beeching. The Golden Poets. Edinburgh: T.C. &
E.C. Jack, xliv + 256 pp.
Introduction (pp. xvii-xliv) expands 1903.2. Presents
the life in somewhat more detail. Includes more examples
to show Herrick's artistry--"how he came back and back to
the same theme; trying the same thought in different
metres, trying the same effective word in a different place
in the line, and so on." Rewrites final paragraphs, omit-
ting references to Gosse, with whom Beeching disagrees
(1875.2), but still expressing the view that poems in Noble
Numbers have earned for Herrick "if not a high, yet a sure
place among our English religious poets."

2 ANON. "The Age of Song." Saturday Review of Politics, Literature, Science, and Art 100 (28 October):560-61.
Review of 1905 reprint of Pollard's edition (1898.1).
Accounts for Herrick's current popularity by saying the
present generation has no poets whatsoever; now English
readers look back to the great age of their poetry, the
Elizabethan and Caroline periods, "an England of the May-
pole and the parish church, where Catholic tradition lin-
gered unbroken in a thousand pleasing observances of rural
life, where religion and the human instincts went hand in
hand and no incongruity was felt between theological belief
and careless joy." Sees Herrick as the greatest lyrist of
that age.

3 NEWELL, CHARLOTTE. "A Seventeenth Century Singer." Sewanee
Review 13 (April):198-208.
Appreciative survey of Herrick's life and works, con-
centrating on Hesperides, whose poems she describes as
expressions of a "joyous nature." Believes Herrick "the
jolly Epicurean" can be seen behind the poems of Noble
Numbers, even in spite of Herrick's intention to write
serious pious pieces.

1905

4 PRIDEAUX, W.F. "Herrick's 'Hesperides,' 1648." Notes and
      Queries, 10th ser. 4 (16 December):482-83.
          Lists twenty differences between the original and cor-
      rected versions of pp. 207 and 208 of the 1648 volume to
      show that Grosart was mistaken in supposing "that the type
      may have been kept standing for awhile" (1876.1); the number
      of changes in the two pages points to the conclusion that
      the type had been redistributed before it was noticed that
      stanza 11 had been omitted from the original issue. Also
      notes the revision of stanza 3 in "Kissing Usurie" and
      shows that the revision necessitated the resetting of
      pp. 29 and 30. Believes that these two leaves were in-
      serted in unsold copies after a number of copies of issue
      A had been distributed and reveals that he owns "a
      copy of issue A with the substituted leaves pasted in at
      the end." Suggests that booksellers advertise their copies
      of the 1648 volume as either issue A or issue B.

5 W., M. "A Literary Causerie: Robert Herrick." Academy 68
      (25 March):334-35.
          An appreciation of Herrick, whom the author presents as
      a descendant of Catullus and a poet with "one foot in
      Elizabethan letters, and the other . . . in the literature
      of the Restoration."

                              1906

1 The Poems of Robert Herrick. The Chapbooks. Edited, with a
      Biographical Introduction, by John Masefield. London:
      E. Grant Richard, xxxiv + 313 pp.
          Masefield's survey of the life includes the speculation
      that Herrick's sermons were "rather short, probably, like
      the lyrics, rather delicate and sugary." Sees Herrick as
      "the one perfect artist whose art is perfectly spontaneous
      and light of heart." Stresses Herrick's love of dainty,
      delicate things and his delight in the fantastical. Index
      to first lines.

2 GRIERSON, HERBERT J.C. The First Half of the Seventeenth
      Century. Periods of European Literature, vol. 7. New
      York: Charles Scribner's Sons; Edinburgh and London:
      William Blackwood & Sons, pp. 177-78. Reprint. Folcroft,
      Pa.: Folcroft Press, 1969.
          On the grounds of Herrick's "technical perfection,"
      judges him "as an artist second to Milton only." Places
      both Milton and Herrick in traditions established by the
      French Pléiade, "Milton fulfilling as none of them had been
      able to do the bolder programme of epic and tragedy and

1907

ode, Herrick catching all the pagan grace and fancy of
their lighter Anacreontic strains to which he gave certainly no less of classical perfection of style."

3   MADDEN, CLARENCE La RUE. Robert Herrick: Pagan Priest: An
    Appreciation of a Seventeenth Century Master Lyrist.   Cedar
    Rapids, Iowa: Torch Press, 63 pp.
        Sees Herrick as "a queer, droll, genial, good-humored,
    old parson, as egotistical as Pepys, as naïve as Chaucer,
    as talkative as Dr. Johnson, and better beloved today by
    those who know him well than any of them."

4   MORTON, EDWARD PAYSON.   Correspondence [An Early Reference to
    Herrick].   Modern Language Notes 21 (March):96.
        Calls attention to "Upon the Infernal Shades of the
    Author's Poems; or, The Hooded Hawk" in Naps upon Parnassus
    (1658); stanza 5 includes the lines "There's but One to be
    found / In all English ground / Writes as well; who is
    hight Robert Herick." These lines by "P.Q." constitute
    one of the few contemporary references to Herrick that we
    have.

5   WYNDHAM, GEORGE, ed.   Introduction to Ronsard & la Pléiade,
    with selections from their poetry and some translations in
    the original metres.   New York: Macmillan Co.; London:
    Macmillan & Co., pp. 1-60.
        As he treats the most subtle influences of the Pléiade
    on English poetry, suggests that even while Herrick had
    probably read Anacreon in Greek, he could also have been
    influenced by French translations of Anacreon, for they
    were the first done in modern verse--and "on a model that
    could be, and was, easily reproduced in English." Notes
    that Herrick's writing "Charon and Phylomel, a Dialogue
    sung" after Olivier de Magny wrote a dialogue between
    Charon and a lover that was sung in the French court is
    probably not coincidental.
        Reprinted in George Wyndham, Essays in Romantic Litera-
    ture, ed. Charles Whibley (London: Macmillan & Co., 1919),
    pp. 65-113; and in the Essay Index Reprint Series
    (Freeport, N.Y.:   Books for Libraries, 1968).

1907

1   LOBBAN, J.H.   "The Choice of Books: Robert Herrick."   Bookman
    (London) 31 (March):253-54.
        Brief comment on life and works of Herrick, who "has the
    Elizabethan sweetness and the Jacobean conceit.   He is half

1907

Campion and half Donne, but the resultant is a thing unique
in English literature."

2 MacMICHAEL, J. HOLDEN. "George I: The Nightingale and
   Death." Notes and Queries, 10th ser. 8 (20 July):57.
        Notes that Herrick's and other poets' attributions of
   melancholy to the nightingale is founded in legend but not
   verified by nature, for in fact the nightingale's song is
   exultant.

1908

1 AXWORTHY, RICHARD. "Robert Herrick as a Folk-Lorist."
   Cornubian and West Country Annual 5 (1907-8):44-48.
        Appreciative notice of Herrick as a poet who recorded
   the happy village life of seventeenth-century England.

2 De la MARE, WALTER. "Robert Herrick." Bookman (London) 34
   (May):51-56.
        Surveys Herrick's life and works, quoting a number of
   the poems, which De la Mare generally admires, but which
   he finds lacking in depth.

3 HAYES, JOHN RUSSELL. "Poets of Country Life: Robert
   Herrick." Book News Monthly 27 (September):19-24.
        An appreciative account of the life and works of the
   "best-loved of English pastoral poets."

4 SAINTSBURY, GEORGE. A History of English Prosody from the
   Twelfth Century to the Present Day. Vol. 2, From
   Shakespeare to Crabbe. London: Macmillan & Co.,
   pp. 325-28. 2d ed. 1923. Reprint. New York: Russell &
   Russell, 1961.
        Expresses admiration of Herrick's prosody; brief exam-
   ples show he is a "master of harmony."

1909

1 FOX, ARTHUR W. "The Colour Sense in Poetry." Manchester
   Quarterly: An Illustrated Journal of Literature and Art
   28 (April):113-35.
        Includes Herrick (p. 127) in a series of poets from
   Homer to Tennyson who share a sense of color which "gives
   a living glory to [their] descriptive passages." Presents
   the color sense as analogous to the musical sense exhibited
   by other poets.

2   HOLMAN, EDNA BOURNE. "At Herrick's Home in Devon."
      Scribner's Magazine 45 (March):257-64.
        An account of an extended visit to Dean Prior; illus-
trated by sketches of the area and of Herrick memorabilia
by Louis A. Holman.

3   JONES, TOM. "Herrick on the Yew." Notes and Queries,
      10th ser. 12 (24 July):78.
        Responds to 1909.4 that Herrick's "crispèd yew" is "hale
and crisp, fresh and firm, as if it would last forever."

4   L., J.M. "Herrick on the Yew." Notes and Queries, 10th ser.
      12 (3 July):7.
        Asks whether by "crispèd yew" (in "Ceremonies for
Candlemasse Eve") Herrick meant "the general effect of a
yew tree . . . [which] is crinkley when battered by wind
and rain."
        Response: 1909.3.

1910

1   ANON. "Herrick and Suckling: A New Life of the Great Lyrist
      and a New Edition of the Writing of the Minor One." New
      York Times Saturday Review of Books, 14 May, pp. 269, 274.
        Reviews Moorman's Biographical and Critical Study
(1910.11) and A. Hamilton Thompson's edition of Suckling's
Works. Begins by agreeing with the current view of
Herrick as "the great artist of the Renaissance lyric in
England"; notes, however, the limitations in Moorman's
presenting Herrick only in the English tradition, for the
innovations of Englishmen like Donne and Jonson were part
and parcel of literary movements that went beyond national
boundaries. Cites Lee's and Wyndham's recent work on the
influence of the Pléiade on English literature (1910.9;
1906.5) to suggest that Herrick and his contemporaries were
likely to have known and discussed the experiments in
classicism of their French predecessors. Observes
Herrick's sharing with Ronsard a predilection for diminu-
tives; and suggests that a full comparison of "the qualities of imagination and emotion, [the] powers of expression, and [the] philosophic temper" of Herrick and Ronsard
would be valuable, for they are the two finest poets of the
Renaissance. Finds Ronsard "richer" than Herrick--to the
point that after a comparison of the two, "Herrick leaves
us cold."

1910

2 ANON. Review of <u>Biographical and Critical Study</u>, by Moorman.
    <u>Athenaeum</u>, 14 May, p. 576.
        Finds Moorman's biographical chapters "pleasant reading"
    (1910.11); points out one error of fact: Herrick's "An Ode
    to Master Endymion Porter" was written on the occasion of
    Herrick's, not Porter's, brother's death. Expresses dis-
    appointment in the critical chapters because they present
    "a mere traffic in obvious remarks." Concludes that
    Herrick may be "too subtle for Mr. Moorman. The qualities
    which are involved in the conscious refinement of his art
    and his impassioned devotion to it deserve closer attention
    than has yet been accorded to him."

3 ANON. Review of <u>Biographical and Critical Study</u>, by Moorman.
    <u>Nation</u> 91 (6 October):317-18.
        Praises Moorman's efforts in searching for additional
    information on Herrick's life (1910.11), but notes the
    "treacheries of time" have prevented his learning anything
    new. Finds the chapter on Elizabethan and Caroline poetry
    useful, but is dissatisfied with the chapters on Herrick in
    which Moorman overemphasizes Herrick's debt to Horace and
    overpraises Herrick when he calls him "the glorious con-
    summator of Renaissance song."

4 ANON. Review of <u>Biographical and Critical Study</u>, by Moorman.
    <u>Spectator</u> 104 (7 May):770.
        Finds Moorman's biography "a much too long but very
    readable book" (1910.11). Refutes his description of
    Herrick as a pagan, and insists that <u>Noble Numbers</u> are
    "the only poems that reveal his personality; they are
    almost the only poems, besides those upon country life,
    the sentiments of which are not borrowed from other
    sources." Discounts Moorman's extreme praise of Herrick's
    lyricism even while allowing him to be "a consummate
    artist."

*5 BETTANY, F.G. "Robert Herrick, The Master of the Lyric."
    <u>Sunday Times</u>, 4 April.
        Listed by Delattre (1911.2) in his bibliography as a
    review of Moorman (1910.11).

6 [CLUTTON-BROCK, ARTHUR.] "Herrick." <u>Times Literary Supple-
    ment</u> (London), 25 August, pp. 297-98.
        Review of Moorman's <u>Biographical and Critical Study</u>
    (1910.11). Finds the biography inadequate "because of the
    iniquity of oblivion" and dispraises the criticism as
    "scientific rather than aesthetic." Provides an appraisal
    of Herrick as a "Pepys who kept a versified diary, not in

chronological order and mainly about his sensations and
emotions." Sees him as surpassing the Elizabethan lyrists,
who tend to be empty and monotonous, and praises his "remarkable sincerity" as the quality that saves Herrick "from
disaster"--especially in Noble Numbers. Maintains that in
the religious verse Herrick "writes like a layman, not like
a parson. . . . religion to him is only a means of living
happily." Suggests if Herrick had been an Italian Catholic,
he could have written verses to "a multitude of saints" as
he writes to "his multitude of imaginary mistresses."
   Reprinted, with first paragraph (comments on Moorman's
work) excised, as "The Rev. Robert Herrick," in Arthur
Clutton-Brock, More Essays on Religion (London: Methuen,
1927), pp. 24-34.

7   EDGAR, PELHAM. Review of Biographical and Critical Study, by
    Moorman. Sewanee Review 18 (October):503-7.
       A "hearty commendation" of Moorman's work (1910.11),
    using Moorman's treatment of the question of the reality
    of Herrick's mistresses as an example of his good sense.

8   GRIFFENHOOFE, C.G. Celebrated Cambridge Men, A.D. 1390-1908.
    Cambridge: A.P. Dixon; London: James Nisbet, p. 71.
       Brief paragraph on Herrick, noting his poems which were
    "favorably received at the time." Says many of them are
    appropriate for musical settings and that they "bear the
    stamp of fresh country life."

9   LEE, SIDNEY. The French Renaissance in England: An Account
    of the Literary Relations of England and France in the
    Sixteenth Century. New York: Charles Scribner's Sons,
    p. 211.
       Passing reference to Herrick in the section on "The
    Pléiade in England": "The inspiration of the Pléiade was
    more penetrating than that of any other school, and it left
    on English song a mark which was more lasting. . . . The
    French airs are echoed in the poetry of Wither and Herrick;
    even the lyres of Charles II's day were attuned to them."

10 MAGNUS, LAURIE. Review of Biographical and Critical Study, by
    Moorman. Bookman 38 (May):89-90.
       Criticizes Moorman (1910.11) for wordiness, for neglect-
    ing to provide a bibliography, for neglecting textual prob-
    lems, and for popularizing his subject matter. Sees the
    chapter on "The Lyric of the English Renaissance" as most
    interesting for the background it provides and laments the
    fact that Moorman did not treat the historical questions

1910

that would help determine real distinctions between the
apolitical Herrick and John Milton, his political contemporary.

11 MOORMAN, F.W. Robert Herrick: A Biographical and Critical
Study. London: John Lane, the Bodley Head; New York:
John Lane, 357 pp. Reprints. London, Edinburgh, and New
York: Thomas Nelson & Sons, n.d. [1910?], 261 pp. New
York: Russell & Russell, 1962.
Part 1 (five chapters) presents the "Life," Part 2 (four
chapters), the "Works." Appendix 1 prints Herrick's inden-
ture of apprenticeship from the Herrick papers at Beaumanor,
Appendix 2, a translation of "The Dirge of Eric Blood-axe,"
a poem about one of Herrick's distant ancestors.
Biographical chapters trace Herrick's family from their
ancestor Eric the Forester, who settled in Leicestershire
where much of the family has continued to live. Presents
the known facts of Herrick's life against a background of
late sixteenth- and seventeenth-century events which may
have shaped his experience; includes speculation, usually
from internal evidence, for the dating of some of the
poems. Finding no data as to Herrick's employment during
the twelve years after his departure from Cambridge, speculates that he relied on friendly patrons: "His open sesame
to this society was, of course, his poetry." Counters
Gosse's belief in the reality of Julia (1875.2) with the
observation that "she leaves upon the mind a very shadowy
impression"; suggests that Herrick wrote Julia poems both
before and after his removal to Dean Prior. Doubts
Hazlitt's suggestion that Herrick held a position at
Whitehall (1890.1) and accepts Grosart's theory that
"Master Herrick's Farewell unto Poetry" expresses his real
frame of mind as he left London for a new life in Devonshire (1876.1).
Describes Dean Prior as a place Herrick generally en-
joyed--noting, however, that poems written just before
leaving Dartmoor express discontent, as do a few other
verses written there. Imagines Herrick, "The Anacreon of
the Devil Tavern, the courtier-lyrist, the poet of perfumes
and millinery, [seeking] amid his new surroundings new
themes for poetic handling, and [finding] them close at
hand in the rustic sports, junketings and superstitions of
his parishioners." Cites the anecdotes recounted by Barron
Field (1810.2) as evidence that Herrick was remembered in
Dean Prior long after his death. Treatment of the publication of Hesperides includes the supposition that the title
indicates that the poems are "children of the West Country," in the sense that most of them (including Noble

Numbers) were written there. Argues that the apparent lack
of interest in the 1648 volume was caused by his kind of
"delicate and imperishable" verse being out of style by
mid-century, but points to the inclusion of "The New
Charon" in a volume with verses by Denham, Marvell, and
Dryden as a hint that Herrick was a respected poet in 1649.
    Part 2 surveys "The Lyric of the English Renaissance"
(Chapter 1) and then treats "The Lyrical Poems of the
Hesperides" (Chapter 2) in terms of Herrick's debt to Greek
and Latin poets (especially Anacreon, Catullus, and--most
of all--Horace), his reaction against Petrarchanism, and
his following Jonson in "structural form . . . precision of
style, and . . . fastidious sense of artistic treatment."
Focuses on love as the central theme of the secular poems.
Chapter 3, "The Non-Lyrical Poems of the Hesperides,"
treats the Oberon poems in the context of the fashion of
fairy poetry in the 1620s, ceremonial verses celebrating
Christian holidays in the context of Devonshire customs,
and the epigrams in the context of Elizabethan and Jacobean
collections of epigrams. Chapter 4, "The Noble Numbers,"
presents the religious poems as orthodox statements of
religious faith: "his conception of religion . . . [is]
scarcely more mature than that of a child of eight." Ends
by contrasting Herrick's happy lyricism with the mature
(and often troubled) songs of modern poets like Burns,
Shelley, and Heine.

12   NIXON, PAUL. "Herrick and Martial." Classical Philology 5
      (April):189-202.
          Cites numerous parallels between Martial's epigrams and
      Herrick's verses on his poetry and his epigrams; but ob-
      serves that whereas satiric wit is one of Martial's defin-
      ing characteristics, Herrick consistently fails at his
      attempts at sarcastic humor. Herrick's best poems, his
      excellent trifling verses about his mistresses, are in a
      poetic mode altogether different from anything to be found
      in Martial. "The vital difference [between the two poets]
      is that the one is as much a love-poet and moralist as the
      other is a wit. . . . Of the three Latin poets whom Herrick
      most frequently imitates, Martial is certainly the one whom
      he least desired to rival."

13   [THOMAS, EDWARD.] "Herrick Man and Poet." Saturday Review
      of Politics, Literature, Science, and Art 109 (16 April):
      498-99.
          Review of Moorman's Biographical and Critical Study
      (1910.11). Criticizes Moorman for not going beyond
      Grosart, Hazlitt, and Gosse in his biography. Praises the

1910

critical chapters, but objects that Moorman has not come to
an adequate understanding of Herrick the man and the poet,
whom the reviewer imagines to be "a little big man, a
coarse man with a shrill voice and moist lips, smiling much
and liking to talk about women but caring little about
them." Stresses a mingling of "coarseness and delicacy" in
Herrick's poems.

    Reprinted as "Robert Herrick" in Edward Thomas, The
Tenth Muse (London: Martin Secker, 1911), pp. 28-35.
Several reprints.

14   TUPPER, JAMES W. "The Greatest of the Seventeenth Century
      Lyrists." Dial 49 (16 August):87-89.
      Agrees with Moorman (1910.11) that Herrick differs "only
in kind and not in degree from the Elizabethans"--even
though the very excellence of Herrick's artistry is a
symptom of the "waning" of a great age of English lyricism.

15   WARD, Rev. J. HEALD. "Counsellor John Were of Silverton, and
      the Siege of Exeter, with Notices of the Poet Herrick and
      his Devonshire Friends." Transactions of the Devonshire
      Association for the Advancement of Science, Literature, and
      Art 42:383-90.
      Account of the Siege of Exeter (1645-46), during which
time most of Fairfax's army was quartered at Silverton,
Were's home. Associates Were with Herrick by way of several of Herrick's "heroes" and friends whom Were must have
known: Sir John Berkley, Sir George Parry, Thomas Shapcott,
and others. Speculates that "King Oberon's Apparel" is
partly or totally by Herrick. Prints "To the King, Upon
his comming with his Army into the West" and "To his
honoured friend, Master John Weare, Councellour"; in the
latter, Herrick praises Were's talents as a lawyer.

1911

1   BUTLER, H.B., and FLETCHER, C.R.L. Historical Portraits,
      1600-1700. Vol. 2. Oxford: Clarendon Press, p. 65.
      Brief biographical sketch closes with comments on
Herrick's "lighthearted paganism," occasional "frank
coarseness," the "neatness and easy flow of his lyrics,"
and his kinship to Catullus.

2   DELATTRE, FLORIS. Robert Herrick: Contribution à l'étude de
     la poésie lyrique en Angleterre au dix-septième siècle.
     Paris: Félix Alcan, 585 pp. Reprint. 1912.
        Presents Herrick's poetry both as representative of the
     age of Charles I and as the work of an exceptional poet.
     Book 1, "L'Homme," presents chapters on Herrick's family
     and childhood; his apprentice and student years; his time
     as "le 'fils' de Ben Jonson"; his life in Dean Prior; and a
     summary chapter on his character. The latter concludes
     that "L'homme ainsi, en Herrick est inférieur a l'oeuvre."
     Attributes the excellence of the poetry to Herrick's abil-
     ity to transform the ordinary with a "lumière mystérieux"--
     not to his being an original or enlightened thinker. In-
     formed throughout by extensive research in England. Book 2,
     "Le Poète," presents Herrick as primarily an urbane poet of
     society. Divides the poems into thematic groups: the king
     and court, folklore and fairy lore, and so on.
        Book 3 treats "L'Ecrivain" in four chapters. "L'imita-
     tion chez Herrick" treats the poetry in the context of
     Renaissance theories of imitation of the classics and the
     popularity of classical poetry in Herrick's age: examines
     the influence of Greek and (especially) Latin poets on
     Herrick, for "'Grécanisseur' d'occasion, Herrick est un
     'latiniseur' de tous les instants." "Le style" treats the
     combination of artifice and spontaneity that gives the work
     qualities both of direct familiarity and of stylish and un-
     involved negligence not found in any of his contemporaries
     and analyzes such aspects of his vocabulary as inkhorn
     terms, Anglo-Saxon words, diminutives, and classical allu-
     sions. "La metrique" examines various combinations of
     vowels and consonants and rhythmical patterns in the poems.
     "L'ordre et la chronologie des Hesperides" argues that
     although the order of poems within the 1648 volume is
     generally chronological, Herrick makes many exceptions to
     that rule--probably to introduce into the book all the
     variety and contrasts of life itself. Agrees with Pollard
     (1891.1) that the manuscript poems which circulated in
     London and appear in the first part of the volume probably
     were written before Herrick moved to Devonshire and that
     the more melancholy poems were written later--perhaps while
     he was feeling isolated in Devon. Believes that during his
     Cambridge and London years, Herrick wrote jovial poems,
     sumptuous epithalamia, and most of the love lyrics; in
     1629, he turned to Anthea rather than Julia, rural England
     rather than bookish pastoralism, folklore and country peo-
     ple rather than fantastic fairies. Believes that when war
     was declared, Herrick became increasingly sober and wrote
     the royalist poems and compliments to his friends; in a

sense of dismay, then, he turned toward moral and religious wisdom. In the concluding chapter, traces Herrick's reputation to 1911 and presents him as representative of his age. Appendices print life records, edit Herrick's "Upon a Carved Cherrystone Sent to Wear in the Tip of the Lady Jemmonia Walgrave's Ear," list poems set to music through the nineteenth century, tabulate metrical patterns in the poems, and provide a bibliography.

3   FEHR, BERNHARD. Review of Biographical and Critical Study, by Moorman. Beiblatt zur Anglia. Mitteilungen über englische Sprache und Literatur und über englischen Unterricht 22 (August):225-28.
     A favorable review of 1910.11, which includes new information on Herrick from the State Papers. Extends Moorman's comparison of Herrick and Wordsworth, and notes the significance of Catullus and (especially) Horace in Herrick's poetic: "Like the poetry, the man is a harmonius blend of classic and romantic."

4   HAIGHT, ELIZABETH HAZELTON. "Robert Herrick: The English Horace." Classical Weekly 4 (8 April):178-81; (22 April): 186-89.
     Dismisses arguments that Herrick is closely akin to Catullus, Martial, Anacreon, or Virgil and demonstrates similarities between Herrick and Horace, two poets "whose broad tastes . . . gave room for country and for city life, for living and for philosophizing, for the goblet and for the lyre." Begins by paralleling their lives, noting a significant difference in that Horace loved his life in the country, whereas Herrick disparages Devonshire; yet both poets were intrigued by their country neighbors and both wrote "exquisite" love poems devoid of real passion ("Herrick in these gay trifles to many maids is more of a philandering Horace than an ardent Catullus who poured out his heart to one name"). Suggests parallels in their attitudes toward politics, toward religion, and in the genres in which they wrote. Closes part 1 of the article by reminding her reader of Herrick's version of "A Dialogue betwixt Horace and Lydia" and by showing that the first six stanzas of "His age, dedicated to his peculiar friend, Master John Wickes, under the name of Posthumus" contain seven quotations from or allusions to Horace.
     Part 2 treats topoi Herrick shares with Horace: "the stoic hero, Epicurean verses, poems on a simple life in the country. . . . poems on poetry." Quotes a number of Herrick's poems, including a few from Noble Numbers, to

show how often they "are full of the spirit of Horace as
well as of quotations from him."

5   HOLLIDAY, CARL. The Cavalier Poets: Their Lives, Their Day,
and Their Poetry. New York: Neale Publishing Co., 320 pp.
Treats Herrick, Quarles, Herbert, and others as "metaphysicals" or "cavaliers"--for Holliday, the terms are
synonymous. Discusses Herrick (pp. 31-45) as a genial,
lighthearted songster. Prints twenty-three of his poems
(pp. 161-81).

6   O'CONNOR, JOSEPH. "Notes on Literature." In The Rochesterian.
Vol. 1. Rochester, N.Y.: Genesee Press, pp. 93-256.
Includes three pages (pp. 175-77) on the life and works
of Herrick, whom he sees as "the laureate of epicureanism
in England."

7   WADDY, REGINALD. "Elizabethan Lyrics and Love-Songs."
Proceedings of the Musical Association, 1911-1912,
5 December, pp. 21-39.
Traces the Elizabethan song beginning with Nicholas
Yonge's 1588 Musica Transalpina. Notes that "To the
Virgins, to make much of Time" had been set to music some
twenty-eight times; observes that many of Herrick's lyrics
would make successful song-texts (pp. 28-29).

1912

1   AYNARD, JOSEPH. "Robert Herrick." Journal des débats, April,
pp. 685-87.
Review of Delattre's Robert Herrick (1911.2), which
Aynard sees as "un livre charmant, un vrai livre de
jeunesse et de printemps." Sees Delattre as a rigorous
critic whose aim is to make his readers enjoy and under-
stand a man and his age.

2   BOAS, F.S. Review of Biographical and Critical Study, by
Moorman. Modern Language Review 7 (July):381-83.
Offers praise of Moorman's "Life"--excepting only a few
details: Moorman omits some footnotes that would indicate
his reliance on others' research; he is sometimes too
speculative about what Herrick may have seen or done; and
he mistakenly uses "warty" for "watery" in line 2 of "To
Dean-bourn." Prefers the second part of the volume, "The
Works," in which Moorman presents "the width and amplitude
of Herrick's art"; wishes only for a more detailed account

of Herrick's debts to Seneca and Tacitus (and for correction of the error of mistaking John for Jasper Heywood).
Response: 1912.7.

3   CAZAMIAN, L[OUIS].   Review of Robert Herrick, by Delattre.
    Revue critique des livres nouveaux 7 (15 November):178-79.
         Presents Delattre's thesis (1911.2) as "un exemple
    achevé de recherche littéraire utile non moins que distin-
    guée"; the work is informed by "un esprit très scrupuleux,
    à la curiosité très large." Notes, however, a tendency on
    Delattre's part to rely on intuition and assertion rather
    than on documentation as he presents Herrick and his time.

4   DELATTRE, FLORIS.   "From Drayton to Herrick."   In English
    Fairy Poetry from the Origins to the Seventeenth Century.
    London: Henry Frowde; Paris: Henri Didier, pp. 147-87.
         Traces the evolution of fairy poetry from 1620 to 1650,
    a time when "it was not yet past its vogue, though altered
    and degraded." After treating Drayton, William Browne,
    Milton, and Randolph, turns to Herrick in whose work "fairy
    themes reached the height of elaborateness." Describes the
    pamphlet A Description of the King and Queene of Fayries,
    their habit, fare, their abode, pompe and state (1635),
    which contains Herrick's "A Description of his Dyet" (an
    early, incomplete version of "Oberons Feast") and forty-
    four lines of "A Description of the King of Fayries
    Clothes, brought to him on New-yeares day in the morning,
    1626, by his Queenes chamber-maids" (ascribed to Sir Simeon
    Steward in several seventeenth-century manuscripts), and
    two other fairy poems. Notes that the four poems are so
    similar that Hazlitt questions whether the "Steward" poem
    ("King Oberon's Apparel") might be by Herrick (1869.1);
    believes, however, that "Steward was merely the happy imi-
    tator of his talented friend. Examines similarities be-
    tween "Oberons Feast" and the presentation of Oberon's
    banquet in Browne's Pastorals, speculating that Moorman and
    Courthope may be wrong in suggesting that Herrick is imi-
    tating Browne (1897.9 and 1903.3); the opposite may be true.
    Contrasts Herrick's fairyland with Shakespeare's; whereas
    the playwright presents a place in which "the country is
    all aglow with the last rays of the departing sun," Herrick
    offers "brisk and witty puppets, and the play they are act-
    ing is but a sort of ingenious peepshow." Concludes that
    with some minor exceptions, Herrick is, as Gosse called
    him, "the last Laureate of Fairyland" (1875.2). Appendix 1
    (pp. 195-200) prints the poems from A Description of the
    King and Queene of Fayries . . . .

5   LANG, ANDREW. "Herrick." In <u>History of English Literature</u>
     <u>from "Beowulf" to Swinburne</u>. London: Longmans, Green, &
     Co., pp. 334-35.
          Paragraph on Herrick's life followed by brief charac-
     terization of his poems--including those in <u>Noble Numbers</u>--
     as "full of the country life, they smell of April and May."
     Closes with a comment on the epigrams, of which "there is
     no good to be said."
          Several later editions and reprints.

6   LEGOUIS, ÉMILE. "Robert Herrick (1591-1674)." <u>Revue des</u>
     <u>cours et conférences</u>, 14 January, pp. 361-67, and
     25 January, pp. 490-501.
          Summary, by "R.P.," of lectures given by Professor
     Legouis at the University of Paris. Part 1 treats the
     life, Part 2 the work of a poet who, a century after his
     death, was recognized as "le premier lyrique anglais de la
     Renaissance." Describes the 1648 volume as a presentation
     of a great number of poems in a "sweet disorder" of genres
     and moods: "Cet homme chante tout ce qui lui passe par la
     tête et par le coeur." Notes, however, that Herrick's
     spontaneity is more apparent than real, for many of his
     poems are imitations of classical and English Renaissance
     works. Sees some analogues with Ronsard and Belleau, but
     finds them coincidences, for Herrick "ne connaît rien de
     notre Renaissance."

7   MOORMAN, F.W. "A Herrick Reading." <u>Modern Language Review</u> 7
     (October):519.
          Defends the printing of "warty" rather than "watery" in
     line two of "To Dean-bourn, a rude River in Devon, by which
     sometimes he lived" (1910.11) against Boas's objection
     (1912.2): Herrick has used "warty" in the sense of
     "rocky"--an attribute that is true of Dean Bourn.
          Response: 1913.2.

8   M[ORE], P[AUL] E[LMER]. "Herrick." <u>Nation</u> 95 (24 October):
     378-81.
          Essay on Herrick's life and works occasioned by the
     appearance of Moorman's and Delattre's biographies (1910.11
     and 1911.2). Sees Herrick's lyric poetry as "marked by
     three characteristics: the repetition of conventional
     themes, a general amateurishness of execution, with the
     occasional elevation to supreme beauty of form and inten-
     sity of emotion."

1912

9   REED, EDWARD BLISS. <u>English Lyrical Poetry: From its Origins</u>
    <u>to the Present Time</u>. New Haven: Yale University Press;
    London: Henry Frowde, Oxford University Press, pp. 263-73
    and passim. Reprint. 1914.
        After brief outline of Herrick's life and reputation,
    in which Reed notes that Herrick's work did not influence
    his successors, treats Herrick's classicism--especially his
    debt to Jonson. Sees Herrick's avoiding the "influence" of
    Donne as fortunate, and judges Herrick "one of our foremost
    artists." Finds the <u>Hesperides</u> poems more successful than
    those in <u>Noble Numbers</u>, for Herrick's real interests lay in
    "material loveliness," rather than in "mysticism." Agrees,
    then, with Gosse's judgment that Herrick's best religious
    poems are those that are most secular (1880.1). (For a
    more extensive treatment of Herrick's debt to Jonson, see
    Reed, 1902.9.)

10 TALLENTYRE, S.G. "The Parson-Poets." <u>North American Review</u>
    195 (January):84-88.
        Brief essays on the life and works of Herrick, Herbert,
    and Richard Barnham (1788-1845). Concludes, "One sees
    Herrick's muse as the loveliest of country girls . . .
    whispering her amorous message in her parson's ear";
    Herbert's "has something of the naïve and grave-eyed sim-
    plicity of a child-saint listening, rapt and innocent, for
    a heavenly music"; Barnham had no muse at all: he was a
    "white-tied, sensible round-faced parson . . . not at all
    unlike the good and jolly monks he depicted."

1913

1   ANON. "In England with the Poet Herrick." <u>Book News Monthly</u>
    32 (November):148-49.
        Brief comments on Herrick's life and works, accompanied
    by pictures of Dean Prior by Louis A. Holman.

2   BOAS, F.S. "A Herrick Reading." <u>Modern Language Review</u> 8
    (January):92-93.
        Withdraws his objection (1912.2) to Moorman's preference
    for "warty incivility" in "To Dean-bourn," but calls atten-
    tion to 1903.7 and 1903.8, in which Pollard notes that
    pages containing the reading "warty" have "two obviously
    wrong readings" on the opposite side of the leaf (p. 30).
    Concludes that the matter is still open to question.

3   CHEMIN, CAMILLE. "Robert Herrick (1591-1674)." Revue
        pédagogique 63 (July):54-72.
            Follows Delattre (1911.2; 1912.4) in presenting
        Herrick's life and works. Notes that the man whose biog-
        raphy Delattre presents in 1911.2 is a complex person and
        poet and stresses the variety of genres Herrick placed to-
        gether in "sweet disorder."

4   HILLS, MYRA E. "The Beauty, Variety, and Sources of Inspira-
        tion of Herrick's Poetry." Bulletin of Western Reserve
        University 16 (May):56-69.
            A Holden Prize essay for 1911-12; presents Herrick as
        an English pastoral poet. An appreciative survey of the
        poems, stressing their variety "within a narrow range, as
        though he had made a thousand sketches of a thousand charm-
        ing aspects of one garden."

5   RHYS, ERNEST. Lyric Poetry. Channels of English Literature.
        New York: E.P. Dutton & Co.; London and Toronto: J.M.
        Dent & Sons, pp. 203-9.
            Sees Herrick's poems as combining Jonsonian classicism
        and English straightforwardness. Contrasts Cowley's im-
        mediate success at mid-century with Herrick's volume's
        going unnoticed in the seventeenth century; observes that
        Herrick is now one of England's best-known poets.

6   SCHELLING, FELIX E. The English Lyric. Types of English
        Literature. Boston and New York: Houghton Mifflin Co.,
        Riverside Press, pp. 88-91 and passim. Reprint. 1918.
            After discussing Carew, turns to "Our other English
        poetical hedonist, Robert Herrick." Finds his work uneven,
        but maintains that in some of his lyrics he "equalled the
        best of the Elizabethan lyrists; and in general, his tech-
        nique is more perfect than theirs."

7   SMITH, KIRBY FLOWER, ed. The Elegies of Albius Tibullus.
        New York: American Book Co., p. 63.
            Discounts the influence of Tibullus on English Renais-
        sance literature in general and on Herrick in particular.
        "Robert Herrick has been called the 'English Tibullus.'
        He mentions Tibullus once, and has the same genuine love
        for the country, but does not imitate him, and it would be
        difficult to find two writers more unlike in their ideas of
        poetic art."

1914

1914

1   BOAS, F.S. Review of <u>Robert Herrick</u>, by Delattre. <u>Modern</u>
     <u>Language Review</u> 9 (October):530-33.
          Describes Delattre's work (1911.2) as more "comprehen-
     sive" than Moorman's similar study (1910.11). Praises
     Delattre's precise and diligent scholarship; finds his
     literary analyses penetrating; commends the chapter on
     "L'imitation chez Herrick," but opines that Delattre under-
     estimates his audience's prior knowledge when he provides
     so many background details about seventeenth-century
     England.

2   KEENE, H.G. "The Transition Age: Herrick, Jonson, Fletcher,
     Bacon, Hooker, etc." <u>East and West</u> 13 (December):1130-41.
          Brief mention of Herrick as one of several early
     seventeenth-century poets known for pleasing but slight
     verses; notes that many of his "exquisite" poems were
     written before the political disturbances that, after 1640,
     diverted England's attention away from poetry.

3   PHELPS, WILLIAM LYON. "The Poet Herrick." In <u>Essays on Books</u>.
     New York: Macmillan Co., pp. 255-64. Reprint. 1922.
          Essay occasioned by Moorman's <u>Biographical and Critical</u>
     <u>Study</u> (1910.11). Stresses Herrick as a lyric poet, and
     notes, "Lyrical poetry does not betray the character of its
     author, it simply reveals his moods." Judges the 1648 vol-
     ume to be a "slender" book of "exquisite" poems.

4   SMITH, G.C. MOORE. "Herrick's 'Hesperides.'" <u>Modern</u>
     <u>Language Review</u> 9 (July):373-74.
          Suggests possible meanings for Herrick's title
     <u>Hesperides</u>: "Children of the West Country" (from Moorman,
     1910.11); "Poems of Later Life" or "Poems of youth and of
     old age"; "the islands or gardens of the west."

1915

1   <u>The Poetical Works of Robert Herrick</u>. Edited by F.W. Moorman.
     Oxford English Texts. Oxford: Clarendon Press, xxiii +
     492 pp. Reissued. London: Humphrey Milford, 1935,
     2 vols., 486 pp.
          Introduction (pp. v-xxiii) explains that Moorman intends
     "to furnish a reproduction of the original text of the
     <u>Hesperides</u> and <u>Noble Numbers</u> published in 1648, and,
     secondly, to collate this text with that of those poems of
     Herrick which exist in manuscript, or which were printed

1915

in Playford's music-books, or in anthologies of verse, during the poet's lifetime." Refers to work by Grosart; Phinn
and Pollard; and Prideaux (1876.1; 1903.7-8; 1905.4) on
divergencies between various copies of the 1648 volume and
states that his text is based on a copy of Hesperides which
"gives us the text as revised by Herrick in the printing-
office." Argues that line 2 of "To Dean-bourn, a rude
River in Devon" properly includes the phrase "warty incivility," rather than "watry incivility." Lists manuscript
and early printed versions of the poems and examines some
of Herrick's revisions to show that they reveal "a thorough,
and at times relentless, revision of his verses" as he
readied them for the 1648 volume. Prints ten additional
poems not included in Hesperides or Noble Numbers. The
critical appendix (pp. 421-53), which prints variants from
manuscript and printed sources listed in the introduction,
closes with three pages of readings of the Firth Manuscript,
which Moorman received after the appendix was completed.
Indices of titles and first lines.
Revised edition: 1921.1.

2   ANON. "The Muses' Martyrdom." Littell's Living Age 286
    (25 September):802-7.
        Essay on Herrick and his critics occasioned by the
    publication of Moorman's edition of The Poetical Works
    (1915.1). Sees Herrick as a master craftsman and therefore
    welcomes Moorman's printing of manuscript versions of the
    poems from which we can learn how carefully and how suc-
    cessfully Herrick rewrote them.

3   ANON. "A New Edition of Herrick." Nation 101 (12 August):
    206.
        Praise of Moorman's edition (1915.1), especially of his
    demonstration that "generally Herrick's self-criticism was
    in the direction of brevity and precision." Suggests that
    "To his Mistress, objecting his age" in Playford's 1653
    Ayres and Dialogues is a later revision of "To a Gentle-
    woman objecting to him his gray haires," "printed in
    accordance with alterations marked by the author in a copy
    of the 1648 edition." Calls attention to the additional
    poems at the end of Moorman's volume.

4   ANON. Review of Poetical Works, by Moorman. Saturday Review
    of Politics, Literature, Science, and Art 119 (5 June):583.
        A notice of "a fine and conscientious piece of work we
    can entirely commend" (1915.1).

1915

5   ANON. "Vaughan and Herrick." Athenaeum, 12 June, pp. 521-22.
        Review of L.C. Martin's edition of Vaughan's Works and
     of Moorman's edition of Herrick's Poetical Works (1915.1).
     Notes some inconsistencies in Moorman's editorial practices
     which the reviewer sees as a failure to differentiate be-
     tween the printer of Hesperides and the poet.

6   FEHR, BERNHARD. Review of Robert Herrick, by Delattre.
     Beiblatt zur Anglia. Mitteilungen über englische Sprache
     und Literatur und über englischen Unterricht 26 (February):
     55-59.
        Finds Delattre's study (1911.2) more rigorous than
     Moorman's parallel work (1910.11). Delattre is particu-
     larly helpful in placing Herrick in his appropriate liter-
     ary contexts and in providing interesting parallels:
     Herrick's aestheticism with Oscar Wilde's, for example.
     Maintains that Herrick achieves a kind of "naturalism."

7   LODGE, OLIVER W.F. "The Text of Herrick." Times Literary
     Supplement (London), 17 June, p. 206.
        Disputes Moorman's emendation of line 15 of "His
     Letanie, to the Holy Spirit" (1915.1), for His modifies
     skill later in the line.

8   MOORMAN, F.W. "The Text of Herrick." Times Literary Supple-
     ment (London), 24 June, p. 214.
        Thanks Lodge for his correction of his emendation of
     line 15 of "His Letanie, to the Holy Spirit" (1915.7).

9   [SQUIRE, JOHN COLLINS.] Review of Poetical Works, by Moorman.
     New Statesman 5 (10 July):330.
        Review of Moorman's edition (1915.1); notes that the
     variants printed there show that Herrick "blotted, filed,
     and pumice-stoned as much as any English poet. . . . [He]
     was above all else a craftsman and a connoisseur." Does
     not find Herrick to be a profound writer, but notes his
     ability to provide a "keene" picture of the physical world.
     Accounts for both his "offensive epigrams" and Noble
     Numbers by pointing to Herrick's "sheer virtuosity."
     Finds the latter unsuccessful, but praises Herrick for
     having been "one of the greatest small masters in the
     history of verse."
        Reprinted in John Collins Squire, Books in General by
     Solomon Eagle, first series (New York: A.A. Knopf; London:
     Heinemann, 1919), pp. 121-26.

1916

10 VIZETELLY, ERNEST ALFRED. "Some English Poets of Tudor and
Stuart Days." In Loves of the Poets. London: Holden &
Hardingham, pp. 53-87.
Paragraph on Herrick (p. 72) as a "confirmed bachelor"
whose love poetry is unrelated to his life.

1916

1 HEARN, LAFCADIO. "Notes on Herrick." In Interpretations of
Literature. Vol. 2. Edited by John Erskine. New York:
Dodd, Mead, & Co.; London: William Heinemann, pp. 118-38.
Evaluates Herrick as a man who "must have had a good
heart." Concentrates on the "true poems" (as opposed to
the epigrams, which are "simply worthless"), quoting a number to show their "graceful charm." Sees Herrick's style
and content as more like Japanese poets' than other English
writers' are, but notes that his melancholy is Roman in
that he seeks to assuage it by enjoying life. Calls his
paganism the "healthy" paganism of the Renaissance. Presents him as "the only Caroline poet worthy of close study
by Japanese students"; by contrast, "A careful study of
Milton would be likely to do you more harm than good."
Reprinted: Port Washington, N.Y.: Kennikat Press,
1965, 1968. Also in Lafcadio Hearn, Complete Lectures on
Poets, ed. Ryuji Tanabé, Teisaburo Ochiai, and Ichiro
Nishizakir (Tokyo: Hukuseido Press, 1934); several reprints.

2 SHAFER, ROBERT. "The English Ode to 1660: An Essay in Literary History." Ph.D. dissertation, Princeton University,
173 pp.
Includes a brief examination (pp. 117-19) of the five
poems Herrick named odes, finding that the three secular
odes ("An Ode to Master Endymion Porter," "An Ode to Sir
Clipsebie Crew," and "An Ode for him" addressed to Ben
Jonson) combine a Horatian familiar geniality with a sense
of stately formality; the two sacred odes ("Ode of the
Birth of our Saviour" and "An Ode, or Psalme, to God") are
also addresses and written in complex stanza forms. Suggests that Herrick's not calling others of his poems odes
is due either to carelessness or to caprice.
Published: Princeton University Press, 1918, 173 pp.;
reprinted: New York: Gordian Press, 1966.

1916

3   SMITH, G.C. MOORE. "Some Notes on Herrick." <u>Notes and</u>
      <u>Queries</u>, 12th ser. 1 (11 March):205.
           Twelve annotations to add to Grosart's, Pollard's, and
      Moorman's (1876.1; 1891.1; 1915.1).

                              1917

1   BOAS, F.S. Review of <u>Poetical Works</u>, by Moorman. <u>Modern</u>
      <u>Language Review</u> 12 (January):89-93.
           Welcomes Moorman's text (1915.1) because of its format
      and because it takes advantage of Pollard and Phinn's and
      Prideaux's work on the revisions within the 1648 volume
      (1903.7-8; 1905.4). Notes, however, that Moorman's failure
      to give a complete list of variants leads to some confusion,
      for there are some differences between copies within the
      two categories of revised and unrevised texts. Praises
      Moorman's collations of manuscript poems and of poems in
      anthologies printed during Herrick's lifetime; notes that
      Moorman's analyses of revisions of poems as they passed
      through several stages show how carefully Herrick prepared
      the 1648 volume. Closes by suggesting that Herrick's pair-
      ing Beaumont and Fletcher in line 51 of "The Apparition of
      his Mistresse calling him to Elizium" is due not to his
      seeing Fletcher as more significant than Shakespeare (whose
      name Herrick used in the earlier version of the poem,
      called "His Mistris Shade"), but to the 1647 publication of
      the first folio of Beaumont and Fletcher's works--a volume
      to which Herrick had contributed "Upon Master Fletchers
      Incomparable Playes."

2   COX, E. MARION. "Notes on the Bibliography of Herrick."
      <u>Library</u> 8 (April):105-19.
           Surveys the publishing history of Herrick's poems and
      his reputation from near obscurity to the point that he now
      has a permanent place in English literary history. (Con-
      tains some errors.)

3   HALLSTRÖM, PER. "Robert Herrick." In <u>Essayer</u>. Stockholm:
      Föreningen för Bokhandtverk, pp. 77-111.
           An appreciative account of Herrick's life and work,
      stressing his lighthearted verse. Presents translations
      of poems, most about flowers and/or love, into Swedish.
      Comments on the influence of other poets, especially
      Jonson, on Herrick.

4   MELLOR, H.C.F. "Herrick's Name." Times Literary Supplement
     (London), 3 May, p. 214.
          Observes that Herrick's surname is spelled six different
     ways in seventeenth-century manuscripts; his Christian name
     is contracted in various ways and appears as Rog. in one
     manuscript and Rich. in another.
          Response by Martin Conway, Times Literary Supplement
     (London), 10 May, p. 225, asserts that modern proponents of
     standardized spelling would do well to remember that it
     does not matter if names are spelled in various ways.

5   MOORMAN, F.W. "Cavalier Lyrists." In The Cambridge History
     of English Literature. Vol. 7. Edited by A.W. Ward and
     A.R. Waller. New York: Macmillan Co.; Cambridge:
     University Press, pp. 1-29.
          Account of Herrick's life and work (pp. 5-18) assumes
     that most of his songs about the countryside were written
     during his years at Dean Prior. Sees Hesperides as "the
     supreme achievement of renascence song," for even though
     Herrick followed Jonson in his classicism, he "entered into
     that heritage of song that has come down from the homelier
     strains of the Elizabethan song-books and miscellanies."
     Traces influences of Marlowe, Catullus, and Horace, and
     says Herrick is "the most Anacreontic of all English
     poets." Believes even Noble Numbers is infused with "the
     atmosphere of a remote Roman world," for Herrick "is one
     of the most pagan of English poets." Refers to early
     manuscript versions of some of the poems as evidence that
     "he was a careful and deliberate artist who practiced with
     unfailing assiduity the labor of the file." Observes his
     lyric range, disliking only those epigrams "which reflect
     the nastiness of Martial without his wit." Accounts for
     Herrick's "lack of intensity" with the theory that his
     song is that of "a nation still in its childhood. . . .
     among all these singers of a day when England was a nest
     of singing-birds, Herrick reigns as king."
          Several reprints.

6   THOMAS, EDWARD. "Herrick." In A Literary Pilgrim in England.
     New York: Dodd, Mead, & Co.; London: Methuen & Co.,
     pp. 163-74. Reprints. Essay Index Reprint Series,
     Freeport, N.Y.: Books for Libraries Press, 1969; and
     Oxford and New York: Oxford University Press, 1980.
          An appreciative presentation of Herrick's biography.
     Suggests that his early delight in nature was derived from
     literature on the golden age; notes that Herrick continued
     to praise country life even while he lived in Dean Prior,
     which must have been "rude and inconvenient." Since

1917

Herrick describes no specific scenes in Dartmoor, his
associations with the area must be intuited by visitors.

1919

1   BAYFIELD, M.A. The Measures of the Poets: A New System of
English Prosody. Cambridge: University Press, pp. 69-70.
Prints Herrick's "Anacreontike" (H-540) as "perhaps a
unique instance" of a poem in which the odd-numbered lines
begin with a "double upbeat." (See pp. 34-35 for a defi-
nition of this phrase, which is used by analogy with a
musical conductor's anacrasis, or upbeat.)

*2 HALLSTRÖM, PER. Konst och Liv: Litterara och Politiska
Essayer [Art and life: Literary and political essays].
Stockholm: Albert Bonniers, pp. 65-97.
Cited in Tannenbaum (1949.1), item 478. Pebworth
(1978.28), p. 260, describes as a "Brief biography and
appreciative comments stressing Herrick's lighthearted love
of nature and the musicality, freshness, and warmth of his
verse."

3   SMITH, G. GREGORY. "Influence." In Ben Jonson. English Men
of Letters. London: Macmillan & Co., pp. 272-302.
Cites "An Ode for him" and "To live merrily, and to
trust to Good Verses" to show the "subtler meaning" of the
kinship between Jonson and his followers. Discounts, however, the extent of Jonson's influence on later seventeenth-
century poets, even on Herrick.

4   WARD, JOSEPH HEALD. "Herrick's Debt to Andrew Willet." Notes
and Queries, 12th ser. 5 (February):37.
Gives an example of Herrick's translating a quotation by
Willet from Augustine (Noble Numbers, 250: "Hardning of
hearts") and claims that he "could give many instances" of
Herrick's use of Willet.

1920

1   CABELL, JAMES BRANCH. "Concerning Corinna." In The Certain
Hour (Dizain des Poëtes). New York: Robert M. McBride &
Co., pp. 107-24.
A fictional story of Herrick's death.

1921

2   JUDSON, A.C.   "Robert Herrick's Pillar of Fame." <u>Texas Review</u>
5 (July):262-74.
     Surveys editions of Herrick's poems and Moorman's and
Delattre's biographical and critical studies (1910.11 and
1911.2). Accounts for Herrick's present popularity by
citing three "personal qualities" of his verse: "first of
all, its personal note, secondly, its variety, and, finally,
its exquisite simplicity and melody and grace." Sees
Herrick as the seventeenth-century poet who reveals most
about himself in his verse; believes the contrast between
his early and late poetry results from his being, early in
his career, a "politicking student" and, later, "a country
parson," and also from his failing to truly assimilate what
he had absorbed of Christianity and classicism; sees his
artful artlessness as unique in the seventeenth century of
Donne, Herbert, and Milton.

3   TODHUNTER, JOHN.   "Murmers from the <u>Hesperides</u>."   In <u>Essays</u>.
London: Elkin Mathews, pp. 112-29.
     Account of the work of "that most dainty of English
rhymers" includes a picture of Herrick's life and character
derived from the poems.

<u>1921</u>

1   <u>The Poetical Works of Robert Herrick</u>. Rev. ed.   Edited by
F.W. Moorman with a Prefatory Note by Percy Simpson.
Oxford English Poets. London, New York, etc.: Oxford
University Press, vii + 446 pp.
     The preface provides a brief description of the printing
and publishing of the 1648 volume and explains that this
edition differs from Moorman's 1915 edition (1915.1):
"First, it confines itself to the text of 1648, noting only
the variants of that issue. Secondly, as it has been pre-
pared, not for the scholar, but for the lover of poetry, it
omits almost entirely the 'Epigrams' of the <u>Hesperides</u>."
Also excludes Moorman's introduction and his critical
appendix. Indices of titles and first lines.

2   ANON.   "From Heat to Herrick."   <u>Nation</u> 113 (3 August):114.
     Brief piece recommending Herrick's poetry as an antidote
to August heat.

1921

3 ANON. Review of Moorman's 1921 edition of The Poetical Works.
Observer (London), 4 September, p. 4.
Appreciates the omission of "almost all the coarse and
clownish epigrams" in this new edition for the general
reader. Comments on the contradictions to be found in the
work of "our greatest, most genuine pastoral poet" who was
an unhappy exile from the city.

4 [BLUNDEN, EDMUND.] Review of Moorman's 1921 edition of The
Poetical Works. Times Literary Supplement (London),
18 August, p. 528.
Suggests that Southey went too far in calling Herrick "a
coarse-minded and beastly writer" (1831.1), but disparages
Herrick's poetry as often "dull, tasteless, and unneces-
sary." Grants that Herrick "is often in his best vein when
he writes of ceremonies" and notes that it is "poetic
pageantry," rather than the events themselves, that in-
spires him. Praises his lyric talents and finds the fairy
poems "delightful." Closes with the wish that Moorman's
editorial principles had been flexible enough to allow him
to include twenty-three lines inserted in manuscript copies
of "Oberons Palace" but not in the 1648 edition.
Reprinted as "Herrick" in Edmund Blunden, Votive Tab-
lets: Studies Chiefly Appreciative of English Authors and
Books (London: Cobden-Sanderson, 1931), pp. 70-76.

5 HEWLETT, MAURICE. "Pretty Witchcrafts." In Wiltshire Essays.
London, etc.: Humphrey Milford for Oxford University
Press, pp. 107-13.
Examines Herrick's poems for clues about his ladies--
especially Julia, whom Hewlett believes was uniquely im-
portant to Herrick.

1922

1 CARTER, G.E.L. "Some Folklore from Herrick." In Devonian
Year Book: 1922, pp. 66-68.
Prints eight Herrick poems under the headings
"Christmas," "Twelfth Night," and "Candlemas."

2 DUCKETT, ELEANOR S. "Some English Echoes of Catullus."
Classical Weekly 15 (24 April):177-80.
Presents a series of quotations from English poetry in
the mode of Catullus, including eight passages from or
references to Herrick.

3   JUDSON, A.C. "Robert Herrick's Grave." Notes and Queries,
     12th ser. 10 (3 June):426-27.
         Speculates that Herrick may have been buried within the
     church at Dean Prior, for in 1917 workmen uncovered four
     gravestones--two of which they did not investigate before
     covering them over--under the floor of the choir. One of
     them might be Herrick's.
         Response: 1922.5.

4   LYND, ROBERT. "Herrick." In Books and Authors. London:
     Richard Cobden-Sanderson, pp. 11-18.
         Sketches Herrick's accomplishments; concludes, "It is
     absurd to speak of Herrick as though he were a great lyric
     poet. He is not with Shakespeare. He is not with Campion.
     But he is a master of light poetry--of poetry under the
     rose."
         Several reprints.

5   M. "Robert Herrick's Grave." Notes and Queries, 12th ser. 10
     (24 June):487.
         Responding to 1922.3, notes that usually only incumbents
     are buried within the church. That rule might be broken if
     a former incumbent requested burial indoors; but in "The
     Bed-man, or Grave-maker" and "To Robin Red-brest," Herrick
     expressed a desire to be buried outside.

                              1923

1   Robert Herrick. Selected and Edited by Henry Newbolt.
     Nelson's Classics. London: Thomas Nelson & Sons, xii +
     478 pp. Reprint. 1926.
         Introduction by J.C. Squire presents Herrick as "one of
     the most laborious and conscientious of all English
     artists." Argues that although the religious verses are
     "flat" and the satires "mostly silly and even clumsy,"
     Herrick's light verses offer a kind of delight found no-
     where else in English literature.

2   HARRINGTON, KARL POMEROY. Catullus and His Influence. Our
     Debt to Greece and Rome. Norwood, Mass.: Plimpton Press
     for George G. Harrap & Co., pp. 85, 150, 157, 177-85.
     Reprint. N.Y.: Cooper Square Publishers, 1963.
         In Chapter 6, "Catullus in England," presents Herrick as
     "the seventeenth-century poet who drank deepest at the
     fount of Catullus. . . . In his spontaneity, his mastery
     of a wide range of metrical forms, as well as of poetic
     types, and his lyrical intensity," he is like Catullus.

Yet quotes Moorman's statement that Herrick "lacks the
passion of the Veronese lyrist." Cites a number of echoes
of Catullus in Herrick's verses. Other chapters treat
Catullus himself (Chapters 1 through 3), "Catullus in the
Middle Ages and the Renaissance" (Chapter 4), and "Catullus
on the Continent Since the Renaissance" (Chapter 5).

1924

1   LEGOUIS, ÉMILE, and CAZAMIAN, LOUIS. Histoire de la littéra-
    ture anglaise. Paris: Hachette, 1325 pp.
       See 1926.2 for English translation.

1925

1   DUCKETT, ELEANOR SHIPLEY. Catullus in English Poetry. Smith
    College Classical Studies, no. 6 (June). Northampton,
    Mass.: Smith College, 199 pp.
       Prints a number of the Carmina followed by English poems
    derived from them. Includes twenty poems or excerpts from
    poems by Herrick.

2   FORSYTHE, R.S. "The Passionate Shepherd; and English Poetry."
    Publications of the Modern Language Association of America
    40 (September):692-742.
       After identifying Theocritus' Idyll XI as the "ultimate
    source," Ovid's Metamorphoses, Book XIII, as a "more im-
    mediate classical source," and a number of English Renais-
    sance poems as predecessors of Marlowe's invitations to
    love in Tamberlaine, Part 1, and "The Passionate Shepherd
    to his Love," treats Herrick as one of Marlowe's many
    successors. Cites "To Phillis to love, and live with him,"
    "The Wake," "To the Maids to walke abroad," and "The
    Apparition of his Mistresse calling him to Elizium"
    (pp. 704-6) among Renaissance lyrics using topoi popular-
    ized by Marlowe's poem.

3   HAYNES, FRENCH. "A Study of Robert Herrick." Howard College
    Bulletin (Birmingham, Ala.) 83 (December):18-45.
       A general survey of the poems, stressing their range and
    variety.

1926

1 HOPKINS, R. THURSTON. "Dean Prior and Herrick." In The
     Literary Landmarks of Devon and Cornwall. London: Cecil
     Palmer, pp. 113-27.
         Disputes the idea that Herrick ever came to enjoy Devon:
     "There is not a line in his work to prove that he ever
     found the spirit of the land, that unsubstantial something
     which gives each stretch of country its personality, its
     character." Notes two poems that do relate to life at Dean
     Prior: "The Entertainment: or, Porch-verse, at the Mar-
     riage of Master Henry Northly, and the most witty Mistresse
     Lettice Yard" and "The good-night or Blessing." Prints
     "Graces for Children" and "Another Grace for a Child" to
     show "the fresh and childlike grace" of Noble Numbers, "To
     Daffadills" to demonstrate his "supreme and overwhelming
     passion" for flowers, and "A Thanksgiving to God, for his
     House" as a poem presenting "a simple, genial appreciation
     of little items of good cheer and comfort" at Dean Prior.
     Presents a letter from the incumbent at Dean Prior, the
     Reverend Perry-Keene, who describes the vicarage where
     Herrick lived and Dean Comb, the valley of Dean Bourn.

2 LEGOUIS, ÉMILE. "Robert Herrick." In A History of English
     Literature, by Émile Legouis and Louis Cazamian. Vol. 1,
     The Middle Ages and the Renaissance. Translated by Helen
     Douglas Irvine, pp. 349-51.
         Translation of 1924.1. Presents Herrick as "Midway be-
     tween the Cavaliers and the Anglicans"; calls him "the per-
     fect artist in slight verse, while Milton, with his sov-
     ereign art, reigned over grander poetry."

3 NEWBOLT, HENRY. "Some Devotional Poets of the Seventeenth
     Century." In Studies Green and Gray. London, Edinburgh,
     and New York: Thomas Nelson & Sons, pp. 277-88. Reprint.
     Essay Index Reprint Series, Freeport, N.Y.: Books for
     Libraries Press, 1968.
         Treats six poets whose religion is lost to the modern
     world, but whose sincerity and artistic integrity are
     appealing to a twentieth-century reader; sees Noble Numbers
     as "a volume of consummate verse" (pp. 284-85).

1927

1   MANDEL, LEON, II. Robert Herrick: The Last Elizabethan.
Chicago: Argus Press, 71 pp.
Foreword by Joseph Quincy Adams maintains that Herrick's
"classicism is one of form rather than content: his Roman
toga covered an English heart."
After a biographical sketch (pp. 21-39), Mandel presents
four chapters on the poetry. Finds the love lyrics pleasant but inconsequential poems written when "Herrick was
living at Dean Prior alone with his memories"; the epigrams
"are ugly in their stark reality" and Noble Numbers,
"equally ugly in their stiff unreality." Admires Herrick's
ability to write lyrics that could be set to music.
Praises "The mad Maids song" as nearly as excellent a
presentation of pathetic madness as Shakespeare's lines
for Ophelia.

2   SCHELLING, FELIX E. "Devotional Poetry in the Reign of
Charles I." In Shakespeare and "Demi-Science": Papers on
Elizabethan Topics. Philadelphia: University of Pennsyl-
vania Press; London: Oxford University Press, pp. 138-57.
Contrasts Herrick's devotional poetry with that of
Quarles, Herbert, Sandys, Crashaw, and Vaughan--all of whom
he sees as more deeply devout than Herrick. Even his best
religious poems "are as ripples on a shallow lake to the
crested waves of Crashaw or the deep sea stirrings of
Vaughan."

3   VAN STONE, ETHEL G. "Herrick's Ladies." Tuftonian, n.s. 2
(October):10-12.
Notes how Herrick "turns to" various ladies who suit his
various moods; Julia is the one who means the most to him.

1928

1   The Poetical Works of Robert Herrick. With a Preface by
Humbert Wolfe and Decorations by Albert Rutherston.
4 vols. London: Cresset Press, lxxxix + 90 pp.; 175 pp.;
179 pp.; 144 pp.
Draws material for the preface from Moorman (1910.11)
and from the poems themselves; writes as though recreating
a casual conversation by an American journalist, who maintains Herrick's excellence: even though none of his work
is profound, it "lighten[s] and irradiate[s]" the heart.
Index of first lines at end of vol. 4.

1929

2   EMPEROR, JOHN BERNARD. The Catullian Influence in English
     Lyric Poetry, Circa 1600-1650. University of Missouri
     Studies, vol. 3, no. 3 (July). Columbia: University of
     Missouri, 133 pp. Reprint: N.Y.: Octagon Books, 1933.
         After introductory comments defining the major charac-
     teristics of Catullus' poetry, categorizing it, and gen-
     eralizing that "although English love poetry of the seven-
     teenth century drew heavily upon Catullus, it was indebted
     rather to the body and substance of his work than to its
     spirit," comments on Catullus' influence on thirty-seven
     poets. Devotes the most pages (pp. 100-112) to Herrick,
     who "is more thoroughly acquainted with Catullus and more
     fully endowed with the superficial graces of Catullus" than
     any other English poet of any century. Yet "Herrick is not
     'Catullian' in the more important sense which we attach to
     the word, that is, in the sense of possessing fiery earnest-
     ness and passionate ardor." Gives forty-two instances of
     Herrick's echoing Catullus.

3   NAYLOR, E[DWARD] W. "Three Seventeenth Century Poet-Parsons
     and Music." Proceedings of the Musical Association
     (27 March):93-113.
         Discusses Traherne's, Herbert's, and Herrick's poetic
     references to music and notes evidence that Herrick
     counted a number of musicians among his friends. Prints
     several examples of seventeenth-century songs, some ar-
     ranged by Naylor.
         Reprinted, without musical examples: Edward W. Naylor,
     "Three Seventeenth-Century Poet-Parsons--and Music," in
     The Poets and Music (London: J.M. Dent & Sons, 1928),
     pp. 71-85.

4   WIDDOWS, MARGHARITA. English Literature. New York: E.P.
     Dutton & Co.; London: Chatto & Windus, pp. 153-55.
         Presents Herrick's poems as those of "irresponsible
     youth" and more melancholy poems of maturity. Praises his
     "economy of words" and his ability to match content and
     form.

1929

1   BOTTING, ROLAND B. "Herrick's Epigram 'Upon Spur.'" Modern
     Language Notes 44 (February):106-7.
         Rejects Grosart's annotation of lines 5-6 of "Upon
     Spur" (1876.1) and proposes an emblem from Henry Peacham's
     Complete Gentleman (1634) or its source, Alciatus'

1929

Emblemata, as the original for Herrick's image of an ass
that thought it was being worshiped when it carried a
goddess upon its back.

1930

1   DELATTRE, FLORIS. "La chanson amoureuse de Robert Herrick."
    Echanges 3 (June):108-21.
        Surveys Herrick's treatment of love, the theme most
    often found in his work. Finds him combining imitation
    and invention, classical themes and personal sentiment, a
    sense of dream and one of reality as he sings to his
    "fresh and fragrant" mistresses.

2   EMPSON, WILLIAM. Seven Types of Ambiguity. London: Chatto
    & Windus, pp. 204-5.
        Includes two paragraphs on "The Funerall Rites of the
    Rose" in his chapter on the fifth type of ambiguity, "a
    fortunate confusion, as when an author is discovering his
    idea in the act of writing . . . or not holding it all in
    the mind at once." Sees the pun on "spring" (line 6) as
    an "odd and delicious example" of the type: Herrick pre-
    sents "a conscious pun as if it was an accident, and
    leaves piled up in a 'sweet disorder' what the conceit
    would have found it hard to enclose."
        Various reprints and later editions.

3   HAMER, ENID. The Metres of English Poetry. London: Methuen
    & Co.; New York: Macmillan Co., 351 pp., passim.
        Uses quotations from Herrick in her chapters on "Iambic
    Stanza Forms" ("Gather ye Rose-buds" ["To the Virgins, to
    make much of Time"], "A Ring presented to Julia," "To
    Violets," "His Grange, or private wealth," and "Upon
    Julia's Clothes"); "The English Ode" ("An Ode to Master
    Endymion Porter, upon his Brothers death"); and "Tri-
    syllabic Metres" ("To his Mistresse").

4   LATHAM, MINOR WHITE. The Elizabethan Fairies: The Fairies
    of Folklore and the Fairies of Shakespeare. Columbia
    University Studies in English and Comparative Literature.
    New York: Columbia University Press, 322 pp. passim.
        Quotes Herrick, Drayton, Jonson, and others as he de-
    scribes fairy lore of the sixteenth and seventeenth cen-
    turies, particularly as it appears in Shakespeare's plays.

5   NEWTON, A. EDWARD. "In Dimpled Devonshire." Yale Review 19
    (June):762-72.
        An account of an extremely pleasant day spent in
    Herrick's vicarage and parish church in Dean Prior.

1931

1   ANON. Review of Der Nachruhm Herricks und Wallers, by
    Roeckerath. Times Literary Supplement (London), 30 April,
    p. 347.
        Qualifies Roeckerath's thesis (1931.5) by noting that
    Herrick's reputation is now higher than Waller's. Finds
    her analysis of the causes for their respective critical
    fortunes otherwise convincing and praises her careful
    study.

2   BROADUS, EDMUND KEMPER. The Story of English Literature.
    New York: Macmillan Co., pp. 158, 160, 179-81. Reprint.
    1932. Revision. 1936.
        Uses "To the Virgins, to make much of Time" and
    "Corinna's going a Maying" as two of a number of instances
    of Renaissance poets' poignant awareness of the brevity of
    life. Presents Herrick as the best poet and the most loyal
    of the Sons of Ben. Believes that Noble Numbers actually
    appeared in 1647. Enjoys Herrick's "sheer impishness" and
    admires his ability to express a variety of moods.

3   LEWIS, B. ROLAND. Creative Poetry: A Study of Its Organic
    Principles. Palo Alto, Calif.: Stanford University
    Press, 409 pp.
        Includes examples from Herrick in his chapters, "The
    Theme of a Poem" (in which he maintains that every poem
    represents a dominant emotion--that of "To the Virgins, to
    make much of Time" is playfulness), "The Organic Rhythm of
    a Poem," and "The Organic Pattern of a Poem."

4   MACAULAY, [DAME EMILY] ROSE. Some Religious Elements in
    English Literature. London: Hogarth Press, pp. 85, 102-4,
    117.
        Includes Herrick in Chapter 4, "Anglican and Puritan,"
    where she presents him as a neo-pagan lyrist. Brief com-
    ment on Noble Numbers, "with its variety of religious ex-
    perience, its devoutness, its fear of hell, its gratitude
    for the blessings of life, its burst of presumably well-
    earned penitence." Believes that Herrick's "mystic sense,
    his joy in unseen words, magic and myth" is directed
    mainly to his fairy poetry, rather than to his religious
    verse.

1931

5   ROECKERATH, NETTY. <u>Der Nachruhm Herricks und Wallers</u>. Kölner
     Anglistische Arbeiten, vol. 13. Leipzig: Bernhard
     Tauchnitz; London: Williams & Norgate, 115 pp.
         Provides extensive quotations in their original lan-
     guages (generally English) from editions, critical studies,
     reviews, and so on, to show the changing critical fortunes
     of Herrick and Waller. Sees Waller's early success as a
     result of his having political backing, of his being per-
     ceived as a refiner of the language, and of his avoiding
     the "coarseness" that characterizes some of Herrick's
     verse. A chart of editions of Herrick's and Waller's works
     illustrates Waller's popularity declining as Herrick's rose
     in the nineteenth and early twentieth centuries (pp. 98-
     100).

6   SALOMON, LOUIS B. <u>The Devil Take Her: A Study of the Rebel-</u>
     <u>lious Lover in English Poetry</u>. Philadelphia: University
     of Pennsylvania Press, 359 pp. passim.
         Refers to Herrick throughout this survey of poetry of
     "the revolt against the traditions of courtly love."
     Stresses the uniformity of poems using this topos: "Such
     a survey might almost be called a study in masculine un-
     originality, so marked a resemblance do most of these
     verses show to other examples that have gone before them,
     and so noticeable is the influence of fashion on their
     manner and matter. . . . Hardly any of [the poems quoted
     in this book] rank high as poetic productions, though the
     light-hearted ones may occupy a fairly honorable place
     among <u>vers</u> <u>de</u> <u>société</u>."

                              1932

1   AIKEN, PAULINE. <u>The Influence of the Latin Elegists on</u>
     <u>English Lyric Poetry, 1600-1650, with Particular Reference</u>
     <u>to the Works of Robert Herrick</u>. University of Maine
     Studies, Second Series, no. 22 (February). Orono:
     University of Maine Press, 115 pp. Reprint. New York:
     Phaeton Press, 1970.
         Demonstrates the pervasive influence of the Latin love
     elegy on Cavalier poetry. Chapter 1 traces the elegy from
     Greek songs of the eighth century B.C. and characterizes
     the Roman elegists Gallus, Tibullus, Propertius, Ovid, and
     Catullus (whose work is sometimes elegiac). Chapter 2
     shows their influence on three groups of English Renais-
     sance writers: "In the school of Spenser it is present,
     but for the most part subordinate to courtly or pseudo-
     Platonic love; in the verse of Donne's followers it forces

                              94

its way to the surface . . .; in the school of Jonson it
flows openly to the surface, but is slender in volume until
it rises like a fountain in the poetry of Herrick." Chapter 3 maintains that "the influence of the elegists is the
strongest classical element" in Herrick's work. Herrick's
approach, however, is not to adopt his Latin sources: "He
prefers to adapt, to echo, to vary, at times even to
parody. . . . Herrick's poetry with all that is Latin
removed would be rather thoroly [sic] dehydrated." The
greatest influence on Herrick's nonerotic verse is Tibullus,
with whom he shares an interest in the countryside. Chapter 4 includes parallel passages from Ovid's Amores and
Herrick's verses to show that Ovid is the predominant influence in the amatory poetry. Concludes that "the elegiac
revival under the Stuarts seems to be the last free flower-
ing of the Renaissance. . . . it forms the logical transition from the courtly and Platonic love conventions to the
refined immorality of the Restoration."

2   BUSH, DOUGLAS. Mythology and the Renaissance Tradition in
     English Poetry. Minneapolis: University of Minnesota
     Press; London: Humphrey Milford, Oxford University Press,
     pp. 217-18.
        Sees Herrick's use of myth as decorative: "To read
     Herrick after Marlowe or Spenser is to turn from the
     Italian painters to Watteau."
        Revised edition (New York: W.W. Norton & Co., 1963)
     includes further comments reflecting the same expansion of
     Bush's opinion of Herrick evident in the second edition of
     his English Literature in the Earlier Seventeenth Century
     (1962.2): "Yet in that pagan-Christian masterpiece,
     'Corinna's going a Maying,' the opening and later allusions
     link Corinna and other budding boys and girls with pagan
     rituals and cosmic process . . ." (p. 231).

3   FRIEDERICH, WERNER P. Spiritualismus und Sensualismus in der
     englischen Barocklyrik. Wiener Beiträge zur englischen
     Philologie, vol. 57. Vienna and Leipzig: William
     Braumüller, 311 pp.
        Treats Carew, Crashaw, Donne, Herbert, Herrick,
     Suckling, and Vaughan throughout this three-part study:
     Part 1, "Sensualismus"; Part 2, "Spiritualismus"; and
     Part 3, "Die Folgen dieses inneren Konfliktes." Argues
     that, in the baroque, the spiritual and the sensual are in
     conflict rather than resolution.

4   HOOKER, EDWARD NILES. Review of Der Nachruhm Herricks und
    Wallers, by Roeckerath. Modern Language Notes 47
    (February):138.
        Sees 1931.5 as inadequate: objects to Roeckerath's
    treatment of Waller on several grounds and notes that she
    fails to see that the new interest in Herrick is related
    to the lyric revival of the nineteenth century.

5   MACAULAY, ROSE. The Shadow Flies [British title: They Were
    Defeated]. New York and London: Harper & Brothers, 476 pp.
    Reprint. St. Clair Shores, Mich.: Scholarly Press, 1971.
        A novel based on Herrick's life; likely to please and/or
    amuse readers knowledgeable about the factual and legendary
    stories associated with the poet. Begins on the Sunday
    that Herrick, "a burly, Roman-headed figure," throws his
    sermon at the congregation (earlier, he and they "had
    spent a happy Saturday" decorating the church with pumpkins,
    wheat sheaves, and other harvest decorations). Ends on
    Midsummer Day, 1647, when Herrick, "seditiously, defiantly,
    and for the last time," reads the Evening Service and
    thinks of leaving Dean Prior for London.

6   PRESCOTT, HENRY W. Review of Influence of the Latin Elegists,
    by Aiken. Modern Philology 30 (August):109-10.
        Takes Aiken (1932.1) to task for the "ignorance" that
    informs her chapter purporting to define the Greek and
    Roman elegy and for her three-chapter presentation of "a
    mass of loose and general correspondences" between Herrick
    and his classical predecessors. Adds the opinion that
    Propertius is "second only to Tibullus" as a classical
    poet who influenced Herrick.

1933

1   AULT, NORMAN. "Herrick and the Song-Books." Times Literary
    Supplement (London), 20 April, p. 276.
        In response to 1933.5, examines the printing history of
    Herrick poems in seventeenth- and eighteenth-century
    anthologies to show that although some of the lyrics were
    reprinted, neither Herrick's name nor his book were known
    until the 1790s.
        Response: 1933.6; rejoinder: 1933.2.

2   _____. "Herrick and the Song-Books." <u>Times Literary Supple-</u>
         <u>ment</u> (London), 22 June, p. 428.
                 Suggests that Hooker make known the manuscript discover-
         ies to which he alludes in 1933.6, for nothing yet known
         points to Herrick's being well-known in the eighteenth
         century.

3   DEARMER, PERCY. <u>Songs of Praise Discussed: A Handbook to the</u>
         <u>Best-Known Hymns and to Others Recently Introduced</u>. London:
         Oxford University Press, Humphrey Milford, pp. 21-22,
         191-92, 220, 440.
                 Briefly characterizes hymns based on Herrick poems:
         "When virgin morn doth call thee to arise" (based on
         "Mattens, or morning Prayer"), "In this world, the Isle of
         Dreams" ("The white Island: or place of the Blest"), and
         "Here a little child I stand" ("Another Grace for a
         Child"). (These hymns may be found in <u>Songs of Praise</u>,
         Enlarged ed. Words edited by Percy Dearmer; music edited
         by Ralph Vaughan Williams and Martin Shaw [London: Oxford
         University Press, 1931].) Brief biographical statement
         includes Moorman's judgment of Herrick as a primary lyrist
         in the time when England was "a nest of singing birds"
         (1917.4).

4   ELTON, OLIVER. "Herrick." In <u>The English Muse: A Sketch</u>.
         London: G. Bell & Sons, pp. 223-25 and passim.
                 Presents Herrick as "essentially a singer of the private
         life," a poet whose craftsmanship makes him "pre-eminent in
         his own time for his sense of artistic rightness." Stresses
         the variety in Herrick's verse and says he "is one of the
         <u>calculating</u> poets--and hence his air of spontaneity." Sees
         Herrick as the "last Elizabethan."
                 Several reprints.

5   HOOKER, EDWARD NILES. "Herrick and the Song Books." <u>Times</u>
         <u>Literary Supplement</u> (London), 2 March, p. 147.
                 Lists various printings of poems by Herrick in the
         seventeenth and eighteenth centuries to show that Herrick's
         work was "available and known" to the eighteenth century.
                 Response: 1933.1; rejoinder: 1933.6; reply: 1933.2.

6   _____. "Herrick and the Song Books." <u>Times Literary Supple-</u>
         <u>ment</u> (London), 1 June, p. 380.
                 In answer to Ault (1933.1), argues that Herrick poems
         "both published and unpublished in seventeenth-century
         commonplace books" show that they were circulated then;
         Hooker's intention in 1933.5 was to suggest that Herrick

1933

poems, but not necessarily their author's name, "were
available and known" in the eighteenth century.
Ault's reply: 1933.2.

7   LOSSING, M.L.S. "Herrick: His Epigrams and Lyrics."
University of Toronto Quarterly 2 (January):239-54.
Disputes the idea that one can read Herrick's poems
without considering the "coarse" epigrams and the "puerile
and dull" Noble Numbers and attempts to define Herrick's
total poetic sensibility. Sees Herrick as a master craftsman: his lyrics are subtly refined; the "rough coarseness"
of his satiric epigrams is "in the classical tradition";
the "simple actuality" of Noble Numbers is appropriate for
poems written by a clergyman "for the people." When we see
that all three kinds of poems share "an immediate presentation of sensation . . . we do full justice to Herrick and
the lyrics."

8   POWYS, LLEWELYN. "Herrick's Fairies." Spectator 151
(21 July):77-78.
Brief account of Herrick's "cobweb mythology."

9   WOOD, FREDERICK T. Review of Der Nachruhm Herricks und
Wallers, by Roeckerath. English Studies 15 (October):
197-98.
Criticizes Roeckerath (1931.5) for judging Herrick and
Waller by twentieth-century standards, but sees her study
as otherwise "competent and illuminating."

1934

1   ANTHONY, EDWARD. "Robert Herrick and Dean Prior." Saturday
Review of Literature 10 (31 March):588.
Provides a letter from James Thorpe, vicar of Dean
Prior, requesting contributions to aid in the restoration
of the bell tower at Dean Prior. (Same letter printed in
1934.9.)

2   BATESON, F.W. "Elizabethans, Metaphysicals, and Augustans."
In English Poetry and the English Language: An Experiment
in Literary History. Oxford: Clarendon Press, pp. 26-64.
2d ed. New York: Russell & Russell, 1961.
Attributes the "richness" of "Delight in Disorder" to
Herrick's skill at "exploit[ing] the ambiguous associations
of the epithets." Believes that the state of the English
language in the seventeenth century allowed him to use

ambiguity to give the poem a "tantalizing quality" and to
unite the poem's three themes (untidiness is becoming, the
clothes are the woman, anti-Puritanism) into a single
argument for paganism (pp. 42-43). Presents "The Primrose"
as similar in its use of words for their associative value
(pp. 44-45).

3   EASTON, EMILY. Youth Immortal: A Life of Robert Herrick.
    Boston and New York: Houghton Mifflin Co., Riverside
    Press, 234 pp.
        A sympathetic biography of a genial poet; places Herrick
    in an Elizabethan golden age--imagining, for example, "the
    Herrick children [finding] many tiny animal pets . . . and,
    best of all, faeries" as they played "In the woods, beyond
    the flowery meadows of Hampton." Refers throughout to
    judgments by Palgrave, Beeching, and others. Notes sim-
    ilarities between Herbert and Herrick, but sees Herrick's
    poems growing out of a more "simple childlike" faith.

4   GRIERSON, H.J.C., and BULLOUGH, G., eds. The Oxford Book of
    Seventeenth Century Verse. Oxford: Clarendon Press,
    988 pp.
        Preface lists Herrick in a group of seventeenth-century
    poets whose work is "troubled . . . by the intrusion of the
    intellect, a spirit of inquiry impatient of traditional,
    conventional sentiment" (p. vi) and speaks of "the playful
    and serious fancies of Herrick and Marvell" (p. ix). In-
    cludes forty-three poems by Herrick (pp. 299-331).
        For F.R. Leavis's response, see 1935.3.

5   LEWIS, C.S. "The Personal Heresy in Criticism." In Essays
    and Studies by Members of the English Association.
    Vol. 19. Oxford: Clarendon Press, pp. 7-28.
        As part of his argument that poetry is not an expression
    of the poet's personality, argues that when one reads
    "Upon Julia's Clothes," "The only experience which can lay
    any claim to be poetical experience is an apprehension, not
    of the poet, but of silk. Perception of the poet's skill
    comes later."
        Tillyard's rejoinder: 1935.7; Lewis's response:
    1936.6; controversy reprinted: 1939.6.

6   MILLER, FRANCES SCHOULER. "Cherry Pit." Times Literary
    Supplement (London), 27 December, p. 921.
        Calls attention to a rewritten version of Herrick's
    "Cherry-pit" in the August 1734 issue of The Gentleman's
    Magazine as an instance of the currency of Herrick's verse
    in the eighteenth century.

1934

7   P., R. "Herrick the Fanciful." <u>Christian Science Monitor</u>,
15 August, Weekly Magazine Section, p. 10.
    Criticizes Easton for writing a book appropriate neither
for the scholar nor for the general reader (1934.3).

8   SITWELL, EDITH. <u>The Pleasure of Poetry: A Critical Anthology</u>.
First Series. New York: W.W. Norton & Co., pp. 35-40,
93-111.
    Introduction presents Herrick as a minor poet, that is,
as "a poet meant to conceive short, small and exquisite
things." Stresses sound patterns in the shorter poems, for
they are generally his "best" works. Prints thirteen poems.

9   THORPE, JAMES. "Robert Herrick and Dean Prior." <u>Observer</u>
(London), 28 January, p. 11.
    Letter to the editor appealing for money to aid in the
restoration of the church bells at Dean Prior. (Same
letter as in 1934.1.)

10   YOUNG, STARK. "Ring around the Roses." <u>New Republic</u> 79
(25 July):290-91.
    Summarizes the contents of Easton's <u>Youth Immortal</u>
(1934.3) and suggests that Easton could have offered a
sharper judgment of Herrick's work had she discussed it in
the contexts of seventeenth-century critical theory and of
contemporary paintings whose style and subject matter is
analogous to his.

1935

1   HOPKINS, GERARD MANLEY. <u>The Correspondence of Gerard Manley</u>
<u>Hopkins and Richard Watson Dixon</u>. Edited by Claude Colleer
Abbott. London: Oxford University Press, p. 98.
    Writing about "schools" of poets, says, "Schools are
very difficult to class: the best guide, I think, are
keepings. Keats's school chooses medieval keepings, not
pure nor drawn from the middle ages direct but as brought
down through that Elizabethan tradition of Shakspere [sic]
and his contemporaries which died out in such men as
Herbert and Herrick."

2   _____. <u>The Letters of Gerard Manley Hopkins to Robert</u>
<u>Bridges</u>. Edited by Claude Colleer Abbott. London: Oxford
University Press, p. 88.
    Writing about William Barnes, says, "His poems use [sic]
to charm me also by their Westcountry 'instress,' a most
peculiar product of England, which I associate with airs

like Weeping Winefred, Polly Oliver, or Poor Mary Ann, with Herrick and Herbert, with the Worchestershire, Hereford-shire, and the Welsh landscape. . . ."

3 LEAVIS, F.R. "English Poetry in the Seventeenth Century." Scrutiny 4 (December):236-56.
    Review essay occasioned by the publication of The Oxford Book of Seventeenth Century Verse (1934.4) and Vivian de Sola Pinto's Rochester: Portrait of a Restoration Poet (London: Bodley Head Press, 1935). Focuses on the "line of wit" from Donne to Dryden; penultimate paragraph closes by commenting on Herrick: "Without Jonson behind him what would Herrick (still an overrated figure) have been? The point of the instance lies in the very triviality of Herrick's talent, which yet produced something not alto-gether negligible (beside him Carew looks like a major poet). Herrick, too, in his trivially charming way, il-lustrates the advantages poetry enjoyed in an age in which a poet could be 'classical' and in touch with a living popular culture at the same time." In a note (pp. 254-56), defends the phrase "trivially charming" by contrasting "The Funerall Rites of the Rose" with lines 309-28 of Marvell's "Upon Appleton House" to show that Herrick is "solemn" without being "serious"; lacking Marvell's wit, he presents a "game [which] . . . does not refer us outside itself. . . . 'Let us,' he virtually says, 'be sweetly and deliciously sad,' and we are to be absorbed in the game, the 'solemn' rite."
    Reprinted, with additional notes on Carew and Cowley, as "The Line of Wit" in F.R. Leavis, Revaluation: Tradi-tion and Development in English Poetry (London: Chatto & Windus, 1936); several reprints.

4 RICHARDS, IRVING T. "A Note on Source Influences in Shelley's 'Cloud' and 'Skylark.'" Publications of the Modern Lan-guage Association 50 (June):562-67.
    Suggests Herrick's "The Hag" as a source for Shelley's "The Cloud" and Marvell's "On Paradise Lost" as a source for his "To a Skylark."

5 SHARP, ROBERT LATHROP. "Observations on Metaphysical Imagery." Sewanee Review 43 (October-December):464-78.
    Analysis of "The far-fetched figure" of metaphysical poetry; includes three quotations from Herrick to show that he "often shows something like the metaphysical touch."

1935

6   THOMPSON, W. MEREDITH. Der Tod in der englischen Lyrik des
     siebzehnten Jahrhunderts. Sprache und Kultur der Ger-
     manischen und Romanischen Völker. Anglistische Reihe,
     vol. 20. Breslau: Verlag Priebatschs Buchhandlung,
     pp. 17-20, 50-53.
         Focuses on Herrick's epicureanism, which allows him to
     take pleasure in things of this world even while mutability
     is his central concern. Sees the aging Herrick taking
     pleasure in the prospect of death, in the transformation
     of beauty afforded by his belief. His poems are squarely
     of the age--bridging the Cavaliers and the Anglicans and
     sometimes approaching the methods and preoccupations of
     Donne.

7   TILLYARD, E.M.W. "The Personal Heresy in Criticism: A
     Rejoinder." In Essays and Studies by Members of the
     English Association. Vol. 20. Oxford: Clarendon Press,
     pp. 7-20.
         Concludes his rejoinder to Lewis (1934.5) by observing
     that Lewis is mistaken in assuming that "Upon Julia's
     Clothes" is about silk; the poem represents the speaker's
     state of mind when he apprehends Julia in silks. The
     poem's rhythm, vocabulary, syntax, and structure lead to
     the reader's awareness of the poet's "unaffected sensual-
     ity, keen observation, sophistication, and sense of
     decorum."
         Lewis's response: 1936.6; controversy reprinted:
     1939.6.

8   WESTERBERG, ARNOLD G. "Herrick's Lyrics." English Journal 24
     (June):499-502.
         Surveys Herrick's "lyric world," which Westerberg sees
     as an apolitical, passionless place of pastoral, and some-
     times London, pleasures.

                              1936

*1   BAKER, E.L. "Robert Herrick's Poetry as Poetry of Wit."
     University Bulletin of Louisiana State University 30
     (March):105-6.
         Cited in Tannenbaum (1949.1), item 381.

2   BRISCOE, JOHN D'AUBY; SHARP, ROBERT LATHROP; and BORISH,
     MURRAY EUGENE. A Mapbook of English Literature, pp. 7, 9,
     11, 26.
         Labels Dean Prior, Westminster School, and Trinity Hall
     on maps of England, London, and Cambridge.

1936

3   GAERTNER, ADELHEID. "Robert Herrick." In Die englishe
    Epithalamienliteratur im siebzehnten Jahrhundert und ihre
    Vorbilder. Coburg: A. Druck, pp. 56-66.
         Parallels lines from Herrick's epithalamia with passages
    from Catullus, and Spenser, Jonson, and Donne to show that
    although Herrick borrows from earlier epithalamia, his "A
    Nuptiall Song" is entirely original.

4   JORDAN, W[ILBUR] K[ITCHNER]. "Robert Herrick, 1591-1674."
    In The Development of Religious Toleration in England, From
    the Accession of James I to the Convention of the Long
    Parliament (1603-1640). Cambridge, Mass.: Harvard
    University Press; London: G. Allen & Unwin, pp. 432-35.
         Presents Herrick's religious poetry as different from
    the doctrinal piety more typical of his age, for he was a
    skeptical, materialistic, and rational man. Sees Herrick
    as a "sensitive and reasonably intelligent" person who
    ignored the religious and political conflicts of his time.

*5 KERR, MARGARET M. "A Bibliography of Robert Herrick."
         T.H. Howard-Hill, comp., Bibliography of British Liter-
    ary Bibliographies (Oxford: Clarendon Press, 1969), item
    155, lists this as a thesis accepted for Part 3 of the
    University of London Diploma in librarianship.

6   LEWIS, C.S. "Open Letter to Dr. Tillyard." In Essays and
    Studies by Members of the English Association. Vol. 21.
    Oxford: Clarendon Press, pp. 153-68.
         Responds to 1935.7. Reiterates his position that "the
    end attained by reading ["Upon Julia's Clothes"] is a
    heightened perception of the charm of a woman beautifully
    dressed" and expresses astonishment that Tillyard should
    think that Herrick's interest is in himself, rather than
    in Julia.
         Reprinted: 1939.6.

7   LYDE, L.W. "Herrick's Violets." Observer (London),
    22 March, p. 13.
         A letter to the editor observes that Herrick's and
    Shakespeare's "association of the violet with the idea of
    renewal" is derived from a tradition dating from before
    the time of Pindar, who wrote of Athens as "a radiant city
    with violet crown."

1936

8   MacLEOD, MALCOLM L. A Concordance to the Poems of Robert
    Herrick. New York: Oxford University Press, 317 pp.
    Reprints. New York: Haskell House, 1971; Folcroft, Pa.:
    Folcroft Library Editions, 1977; Norwood, Pa.: Norwood
    Editions, 1978.
        A Ph.D. dissertation, University of Virginia, 1936.
    Concordance keyed to Moorman's edition (1915.1); may also
    be used with Martin's and Patrick's texts (1956.1 and
    1963.1).

9   PICKEL, MARGARET BARNARD. Charles I as Patron of Poetry and
    Drama. London: Frederick Muller, pp. 72-74.
        Presents Herrick in Chapter 5, which treats "Other
    Royalist Poets" (Richard Corbett, Henry King, Herrick,
    George Herbert, William Cartwright, John Cleveland, Sir
    Henry Wotton, etc.), noting that Herrick "began his career
    as a courtier and accompanied the Duke of Buckingham as
    chaplain on the expedition to the Isle of Rhé in 1627";
    before 1627, he may have held a post in the Royal Chapel at
    Whitehall. Calls attention to the number of complimentary
    poems he wrote to the royal family. Suggests that
    Herrick's dispraise of "dull Devonshire" should not be
    overemphasized, for the State Papers include his petition
    that the grant of his place in Dean Prior "may be des-
    patched"; in his own hand are the words "caetera mando
    Deo." Moreover, Herrick did return to Devonshire after
    the Restoration.

10 POWYS, LLEWELYN. "Robert Herrick: Minister of Grace."
    Saturday Review of Literature 13 (8 February):3-4, 12.
        Argues that Herrick "was religious as are those who
    venerate the tradition and usages of antiquity," but that
    sometimes he reveals "a pagan heartlessness to suffering
    and a pagan contempt for all that is uncomely or old."
    Describes Dean Prior as it was in the seventeenth century,
    imagines Herrick's life there, and quotes Domestic State
    Paper. Charles I. 1640 (vol. cccclxxiv. no. 77), which
    names Herrick as the father of Thomsen Parsons's child.
    Quotes throughout from Hesperides to substantiate his
    thesis that Herrick's "religion is to worship life."

11 RUGGLES, MELVILLE J. "Horace and Herrick." Classical
    Journal 31 (January):223-34.
        Prints parallel passages from Herrick's Hesperides and
    Horace's Odes to show that "though Herrick's epigrams
    resemble those of Martial or Catullus, most of his poems--
    especially those in a graver mood--are steeped in Horatian

color." Sees similarities in themes and sensibilities and
presents a number of instances of Herrick's translating
lines from Horace or using his poems as models.

1938

1   BROOKS, CLEANTH, and WARREN, ROBERT PENN. Understanding
    Poetry: An Anthology for College Students. New York:
    Henry Holt & Co., pp. 367-74.
        Contrasts "To Blossoms" with Donne's "The Blossom" to
    show the difference between two "good" poems--one simple,
    the other (Donne's) complex.
        Several later editions.

2   HOWARTH, R.G. "A Song of Herrick's Altered by Burns." Notes
    and Queries 175 (27 August):153.
        Points out that an "old English song" Robert Burns men-
    tions in a letter to George Thomson is Herrick's "The
    Primrose," which appears as one of Carew's poems in an
    edition of 1772 that Burns could have seen.

1939

1   BROOKS, CLEANTH. "Notes for a Revised History of English
    Poetry." In Modern Poetry and the Tradition. Chapel Hill:
    University of North Carolina Press, pp. 219-44. Published
    in London: Poetry, 1948. Reprint. New York: Oxford
    University Press, 1965.
        Uses two of Herrick's lyrics as examples to show that,
    except for the Spenserians', seventeenth-century poetry,
    "whether dramatic or nondramatic, secular or religious,
    light or serious, successful or unsuccessful, is basically
    and generally a poetry of wit." After citing the use of
    "sinceritie" in line 4 of "Upon Julia's Fall" and of
    "supremest" in "To Perilla" as two instances of his many
    conceits which are "of a piece" with the metaphysicals,
    shows similar tendencies in seventeenth-century prose
    writers and contrasts them with neo-classical poets, who
    "[tend] to use poetic materials . . . to decorate or dig-
    nify" their subjects, and pre-Romantics, who are "often
    content merely to point to the objects themselves."
    Carries his history up to Hardy and Yeats.

1939

2   DELATTRE, FLORIS. La littérature de l'angleterre puritaine,
     1603-1660. Études d'aujourd'hui, 6. [Cahors]: Didier,
     pp. 42-43.
         Sees Herrick's poems as "sur les sujets les plus divers,
     les poèmes les plus prestes, les plus caressantes chansons
     que nous présente la langue anglaise." Believes the poems
     in Noble Numbers are informed by a simple, but strong
     faith.

3   McEUEN, KATHRYN ANDERSON. Classical Influence upon the Tribe
     of Ben: A Study of Classical Elements in the Non-Dramatic
     Poetry of Ben Jonson and His Circle. Cedar Rapids, Iowa:
     Torch Press, 335 pp. Reprint. New York: Octagon Books,
     1968.
         Aims "to show the amount and the kind of influence ex-
     erted by certain of the classical poets upon the non-
     dramatic verse" of a number of poets, including Herrick,
     who is "the truest and greatest poetical Son of Jonson."
     Includes comments on Herrick in discussions of "Martial"
     (Chapter 2); "The Roman Satirists: Juvenal, Persius, and
     Horace" (Chapter 3: "Satire, in its real sense of giving
     instruction by ridiculing or castigating persons guilty of
     infraction of moral, social, or literary laws, is not
     found in Herrick's poetry"); "Horace" (Chapter 4); "The
     Latin Elegists" (Chapter 5: "Herrick, whose verse con-
     tains almost innumerable elegiac conventions, wrote no
     erotic elegies"); "The Pastoral: Theocritus and Virgil"
     (Chapter 6: here the influence is "extensive"); "Anacreon
     and the Anacreontea" (Chapter 7); and "The Greek Anthology"
     (Chapter 8). Concludes "that the influence exerted by the
     classics upon the non-dramatic poetry of the Tribe of Ben
     was extensive, but that it was limited to the lighter
     genres." Designates no one Latin source as most signifi-
     cant for Herrick.

4   McPEEK, JAMES A. Catullus in Strange and Distant Britain.
     Harvard Studies in Comparative Literature, 15. Cambridge,
     Mass.: Harvard University Press, 411 pp. passim. Reprint.
     New York: Russell & Russell, 1972.
         Mentions Herrick some thirty times, but sees him as
     using themes from the Carmina with only moderate success.
     Prefers "his original bright-eyed lines on tempestuous
     petticoats."

5   THOMPSON, ELBERT N.S. "The Octosyllabic Couplet." Philologi-
    cal Quarterly 18 (July):257-68.
        Brief mention of Herrick as an example of a poet whose
    couplets employ "irregular and complex" rhythmic patterns
    (p. 261).

6   TILLYARD, E.M.W., and LEWIS, C.S. The Personal Heresy: A
    Controversy. London and New York: Oxford University
    Press, 156 pp.
        Three essays by each author; the first three appeared in
    Essays and Studies by Members of the English Association
    (1934.5, 1935.7, and 1936.6). In the fourth essay,
    Tillyard continues to argue that to discuss "Upon Julia's
    Clothes" purely in terms of "things" (Julia or her clothes)
    is fruitless, for they are "vehicles for some emotion not
    usually or at first sight attached to them." Claims that
    Herrick's own "personal triumph" was in adjusting himself
    to life in Devon and that one great value we receive from
    his poetry is the vision of that self-adjustment. Essays 5
    and 6, by Lewis and Tillyard, respectively, do not use
    Herrick as examples within their arguments.

                              1940

1   JONAS, LEAH. "Robert Herrick and Thomas Carew." In The
    Divine Science: The Aesthetic of Some Representative
    Seventeenth-Century English Poets. Columbia University
    Studies in English and Comparative Literature, no. 151.
    New York: Columbia University Press, pp. 228-49.
        One chapter in a series on seventeenth-century poets
    from Jonson to Denham. Treats Herrick and Carew as men
    whose "obvious love of the poetic art for itself and its
    secular possibilities is . . . their most significant
    common quality. Their methodical approach, restraint,
    clarity, and faith in the self-sufficiency of art all
    herald the later half of the century." Quotes a number of
    the poems to show Herrick's interest in style, his aware-
    ness that his audience consists of educated readers, his
    "delicate rather than deep sensitivity," and his debt to
    Jonson for the "idea of formulating a lyric style on
    selective imitation of the classics." Sees the order of
    poems within the 1648 Hesperides as a result of the desire
    to separate, in order to create a sense of variety, the
    approximately fourteen different types of poetry it con-
    tains. Presents the "sententious couplets" and the epi-
    grams as early examples of "two strains . . . that were to
    reach their full flowering in the next century--common

1940

sense and satire" and treats the epigrams as a part of the
Renaissance tradition that Scaliger defines when he dis-
tinguishes between mel ("honey") and fel ("gall"), acetum
("vinegar"), and sal ("salt") epigrams. Accounts for their
appearance in the volume, in part, by postulating "Herrick's
apparent unwillingness to leave even the least of his writings unpublished." Explains that Noble Numbers presents
"religious ideas [which] are those of a man of the eighteenth century," rather than seventeenth-century emotions.

2   LOANE, G.G. "Herrick's Sources." Notes and Queries, 178
      (30 March):224-25.
        Lists sources for some of Herrick's poems from Seneca,
      Chapman, Shakespeare, The Greek Anthology, Jonson, Homer,
      Horace, and the Bible to supplement the notes in the Muses'
      Library edition (1898.1).

3   WELLS, HENRY W. New Poets from Old: A Study in Literary
      Genetics. New York: Columbia University Press, 366 pp.
        Argues that modern poets--despite popular opinion--
      "stand greatly indebted in their own art and thought to
      poetry of earlier periods"; refers to Herrick in chapters
      on "The Heritage of Technique" (2), "The Heritage of Form"
      (3), and "The Heritage of Spirit" (4). Stresses Herrick's
      influence on W.H. Davies (pp. 241-43).

                              1941

1   BATESON, F.W., ed. The Cambridge Bibliography of English
      Literature. Vol. 1. New York: Macmillan Co.; Cambridge:
      Cambridge University Press, pp. 448-50.
        The Herrick entry is divided into four categories:
      "Original Edition" (the 1648 volume); "Collected Poems"
      (eleven editions); "Selected Poems" (seven editions, in-
      cluding Witt's Recreations, 1650); and "Biography and
      Criticism" (fourteen items).
        See Watson, 1957.7, for the Supplement to CBEL, and
      Watson, 1974.18, for The New Cambridge Bibliography of
      English Literature.

2   EVANS, WILLA McCLUNG. Henry Lawes: Musician and Friend of
      Poets. New York: Modern Language Association of America;
      London: Oxford University Press, 266 pp. Reprint.
      Milwood, N.Y.: Kraus Reprint Corp., 1966.
        In addition to a number of brief mentions of Herrick,
      includes four pages (154-58) on his special relationship
      with Lawes. Notes that Herrick's "The Curse. A Song" and

                              108

Lawes's "No Constancy in Man" are "inspired by the same
event" or "one influenced the other." Notices that the
music Lawes wrote for Herrick's poems is qualitatively
different from the settings he composed for other poets.
At a loss to account for the difference, she characterizes
the music for Herrick's poems as having "a peculiar delicacy and daintiness" that "[seems] so expressive of that
personal charm associated with the poet." Tentatively
identifies "My mistress blushed" preserved by Lawes in
B.M. Add. MS 53723 as a poem by Herrick. (Martin, 1956.1,
prints as "The Showre of Roses.")

3   HUTTON, JAMES. "The Cupid and the Bee." Publications of the
     Modern Language Association of America 56 (December):
     1036-57.
         Traces the history of translations of the Theocritean
     and Anacreontic versions of the story of Cupid and the bee
     from the Renaissance to the end of the eighteenth century.
     Believes that Herrick translated his version of Anacreon
     ("The wounded Cupid. Song") from the Greek, but probably
     used Estienne's or André's Latin text as well. Observes
     that Thomas Stanley, who published his version in 1649,
     "has taken Herrick's poem of the year before, and corrected
     it to the Greek text, also regularizing the trochaic metre.
     It is very successfully done."

4   THOMAS, WRIGHT, and BROWN, STUART GERRY. Reading Poems: An
     Introduction to Critical Study. New York: Oxford Univer-
     sity Press, pp. 650-51, 695-97.
         Argues that in "To Daffadills" Herrick conflates two
     "time-senses" so the reader feels "the sweet-sadness of all
     quick deaths" (pp. 650-51). Compares "To Daffadills" to a
     stanza by Louis MacNeice to define wit as the presentation
     of comparisons that cannot be made in the imagination
     (pp. 695-97).

1942

1   ANON. "Herrick's 'To the Virgins.'" Explicator 1 (October):
     Item 2.
         Calls attention to the change in tone from pagan phrases
     early in the poem to the "pious (and priestly) exhortation
     to marry" at the end and suggests the parable of the wise
     and foolish virgins (Matthew 25:1-13) as a source for words
     like lamp and tarry.

1943

1 DANIELS, EARL. Herrick's 'Upon Julia's Clothes.'" Explicator
   1 (March): Item 35.
   Notes that the poem shows the response of a man struck
   by beauty; that beauty is symbolized not by Julia's
   clothes, but by Julia herself.
   Responses: 1947.2; 1955.8.

2 HIRSH, EDWARD L. "Herrick's 'The Argument of His Book.'"
   Explicator 2 (November): Item 11.
   Responds to L.V.T. (1943.7) by suggesting that Herrick's
   alternations between sing and write in "The Argument"
   create a pattern which is reversed in the poem's final
   couplet; the reversal points the reader toward the "pur-
   poseful seriousness" of the poem's last clause.

3 MIZENER, ARTHUR. "Some Notes on the Nature of English
   Poetry." Sewanee Review 51 (January):27-51.
   Cites "To Dianeme" (H-160) as an example of a poem containing a "carefully hedged dependence on the validity of
   an analogy" as opposed--on the one hand--to Elizabethan
   poets' casual assumptions of correspondences between the
   human, natural, and supernatural realms and--on the other
   hand--to the metaphysicals' overtly bold assertions of
   likenesses (pp. 37-38).

4 O'CONNOR, WILLIAM VAN. "Tension and Structure of Poetry."
   Sewanee Review 51 (October):555-73.
   Contrasts "The mad Maids song" and a lyric from Wallace
   Stevens's "Peter Quince at the Clavier" with Sonnet 72
   from Spenser's Amoretti to show the distinction between
   "poetry of exploration" (Herrick and Stevens) and "poetry
   of exposition" (Spenser). Maintains that the reader must
   "work through" the first two poems; the reader is asked
   only to accept the statement that Spenser presents. Argues
   that the absence of tension in Spenser's poem--and in the
   poetry of O'Connor's own age--leads to poetry which is inferior because it does not engage the imagination.

*5 RAU, FRITZ. "Verweltlichte religiöse Begriffe und Formen in
   Robert Herricks Hesperides." Ph.D. dissertation, Univer-
   sity of Göttingen.
   Cited in 1955.6, p. 360n.

6   SITWELL, EDITH. "Notes on Herrick." In A Poet's Notebook.
     London: Macmillan, pp. 35-90.
          Appreciation of patterns of sound in a number of
     Herrick's lyrics: "The poems are as subtle, and as deli-
     cate, as the warm airs that awaken those little birds
     'whose feathers be greatly esteemed to work gold with',--
     they are faint as the breaths of air and perfume wafting
     through the branches of the flowering plum, or the still-
     ness of a sweet night."

7   T., L.V. "Herrick's 'The Argument of His Book.'" Explicator
     1 (April): Query 28.
          Asks whether write and sing are meant to be synonymous
     throughout the poem.
          Response: 1943.2.

                        1944

1   ELIOT, T.S. "What Is Minor Poetry?" Welsh Review 3
     (December):256-67.
          The text of an address delivered before the Association
     of Bookmen of Swansea and West Wales, at Swansea, on
     26 September 1944. Explores the question of how one might
     define the distinction between "major" and "minor" poetry.
     Includes a two-page discussion of the difference between
     Herbert, on the one hand, and Herrick and Campion, on the
     other. Whereas Herbert's Temple is "a continued religious
     meditation with an intellectual framework," Herrick's vol-
     ume lacks a "continuous conscious purpose . . . he is more
     the purely natural and un-selfconscious man, writing his
     poems as the fancy seizes him." Herrick's personality is
     less interesting than Herbert's; "in fact, it is its honest
     ordinariness which gives the charm." Campion, too, is
     less significant than Herbert, but his superb craftsmanship
     makes him "more important" than Herrick.
          Reprinted: Sewanee Review 54 (Winter 1946):1-18, and in
     On Poetry and Poets (London: Faber & Faber, 1957), pp. 39-
     52; and (New York: Farrar, Straus & Cudahy, 1957), pp. 34-
     51. Various later reprints.

2   GILBERT, ALLAN H. "Robert Herrick on Death." Modern Language
     Quarterly 5 (March):61-67.
          Counters the false view of Herrick as "chiefly a fairy
     poet" by pointing out how many poems in Hesperides (even
     more than in Noble Numbers) comment on death. Noting,
     however, that Herrick's tone is often determined by his
     dramatic qualities, rather than by his expressing personal

1944

beliefs, qualifies Walker's notion of Herrick as "a Sober
and Learned man" (1714.1). Concludes that the wisest path
might be to consider Herrick as "aided by two muses, one
jocund, the other diviner, inspiring him to sing of 'death
accursed,' and of the victory over death."

3 GRIERSON, HERBERT J.C., and SMITH, J.C. A Critical History of
   English Poetry. London: Chatto & Windus, pp. 146-49.
   Rev. ed. 1947.
       Begins chapter on "The Carolines" with Herrick. Surveys
   his life and works and then concludes that "if allowance be
   made for the different levels on which they moved, he may
   claim with Milton and Gray the merit, which Pattison would
   allow no other English poet, of being a poet and a careful
   artist, sweeter and fresher than his master Jonson and no
   less clear and terse."

4 Le COMTE, EDWARD S. Endymion in England: The Literary History of a Greek Myth. New York: King's Crown Press,
   pp. 114-15.
       Notes that both Herrick and D'Avenant make use of the
   Greek myth suggested by Endymion Porter's Christian name--
   Herrick in "An Eclogue, or Pastorall between Endimion
   Porter and Lycidas Herrick, set and sung," and D'Avenant
   in addressing Olivia Porter as "Endymion's love."

1945

1 BUSH, DOUGLAS. English Literature in the Earlier Seventeenth
   Century, 1600-1660. Oxford History of English Literature.
   Oxford: Clarendon Press, pp. 111-16 and passim.
       Presents Herrick as "The most versatile, the most clas-
   sical (in a limited sense), and the least metaphysical" of
   Jonson's successors. Accounts for his lack of popularity
   in the seventeenth century by pointing to the "Elizabethan"
   qualities of his verse--its sensuousness and its metrical
   regularity.
       Revised edition: 1962.2.

2 C., T.S. "Herrick's 'Another Grace for a Child.'" Explicator
   3 (February): Query 11.
       Asks the significance of the phrase "Cold as paddocks."
   Response: 1945.3.

3   MILL, ANNA JEAN. "Herrick's 'Another Grace for a Child.'"
      Explicator 3 (June): Item 61.
          Responds to T.S.C. (1945.2) that for a child of
      Devonshire paddocks ("frogs") are "the essence of cold
      clamminess"; the word, therefore, is apt, not quaint.

4   WILKINSON, L.P. Horace & His Lyric Poetry. Cambridge:
      University Press, pp. 149, 165, 167f. Reprint. 1946.
      Rev. ed. 1951.
          Mentions Herrick as a poet whose sensibility was com-
      patible with Horace's: like Petrarch and Ronsard, Herrick
      "found in him the best expression of what [he] already
      felt."

1946

1   BELGION, MONTGOMERY. "The Poet's Name." Sewanee Review 54
      (October-December):635-49.
          As a part of his argument that the proper function of
      literary criticism is discussion of poets' works, not of
      poets themselves, maintains that both Lewis and Tillyard
      are mistaken in their comments on "Upon Julia's Clothes"
      (1939.6); when one reads such a poem, one responds to the
      way "some one else has chosen, used, and arranged words
      which have for us meanings and associations, and an infi-
      nite power of suggestion. . . . But we are not having any
      new experience concerning silk."

2   FROST, ROBERT. "The Constant Symbol." Introductory essay to
      The Poems of Robert Frost. Modern Library Edition. New
      York: Random House, p. 46.
          In a discussion of poets' uses of various verse forms,
      cites Herrick's "To Daffadills" as a poem using an unusual
      stanza form: "Not that he is running wild. His intention
      is of course a particular mood that won't be satisfied with
      anything less than its own fulfillment."

3   HESS, M. WHITCOMB. "Nature and Spirit in Herrick's Poetry."
      Personalist 27 (July):299-305.
          An appreciative essay presenting Herrick as a genial
      country vicar, beloved by his parishioners and remembered
      fondly by their descendants for 150 years after his death.
      Goes so far as to suggest that Herrick may have published
      Hesperides as an expression of his "unshakable faith" in
      Charles I and that a knowledge of the poems may have "sus-
      tained" the king in his "calm way to the scaffold in 1648
      and his dignity up to the moment of execution." Believes

1946

that Herrick's excellence lies in "the powerful pulse of
the supernatural that beats in his poetry. Nature in his
hands is always informed and usually, if not always, ele-
vated by spirit."

4   MAXWELL, SUE. "Robert Herrick, the Metrician." Poet Lore 52
(October):353-59.
Examines the "unusual" metrical effects of poems from
both Hesperides and Noble Numbers, showing that Herrick's
versification often mirrors his theme of "order in sweet
neglect"; suggesting that the effects of his apprenticeship as a goldsmith can be seen in "the wording and work-
manship" of "hundreds" of the poems; and admitting that
"the poet was master of the metrician at times, but at
other periods the metrist has supplanted the artist."

5   MILES, JOSEPHINE. Major Adjectives in English Poetry from
Wyatt to Auden. University of California Publications in
English, vol. 12, no. 3. Berkeley and Los Angeles:
University of California Press, pp. 305-426.
In Part 1, "Introduction: Glass to Pattern," pp. 305-21,
tabulates and discusses adjectives and other words used by
twenty-five poets, including Herrick. (The two adjectives
he uses most often are good and sweet; the words he uses
most often are love (500 times), make and see (350), come
(330), and die, give, know, live, Man, and sweet (250 times
each). Part 2 discusses Wyatt, Donne, Pope, and Wordsworth
in an attempt to define changes in the poetic vocabularies
of poets of various historical periods.

6   STAUFFER, DONALD A. The Nature of Poetry. New York: W.W.
Norton & Co., pp. 162-63.
Includes an analysis of "Upon Julia's Clothes" to show
that a poet can be complex without being profound.

1947

1   BROOKS, CLEANTH. "What Does Poetry Communicate?" In The Well
Wrought Urn: Studies in the Structure of Poetry. New
York: Reynal & Hitchcock; New York: Harcourt, Brace, &
Co., pp. 62-73.
Uses "Corinna's going a Maying" to show that one re-
duces a poem if one treats it as though it were "an idea
or set of ideas which the poet has communicated with certain appropriate decorations." In the course of his
examination of "Corinna," notes that "the poem is obviously
not a brief for the acceptance of the pagan ethic so much

as it is a statement that the claims of the pagan ethic--
however much they may be overlaid--exist, and on occasion
merge, as on this day." Stresses, however, that the relationship of the claims of paganism and Christianity are
only "part of what the poem communicates"; "the poem is not
only the linguistic vehicle which conveys the thing communicated most 'poetically,' but . . . it is also the sole
linguistic vehicle which conveys the things communicated
accurately . . . the poem says what the poem says." Goes
on to explain that a person searching for poems' para-
phrasable contents will have particular trouble with modern
poetry, which works even more by "suggestion" and "indirec-
tion" than does Herrick's verse. In a postscript, refers
the reader to 1943.3.
   Volume reprinted several times; essay reprinted in
Essays in Modern Literary Criticism, ed. Ray B. West, Jr.
(New York and Toronto: Rinehart & Co., 1952), pp. 327-35.

2 HENRY, NAT. "Herrick's 'Upon Julia's Clothes.'" Explicator
   5 (April): Item 46.
      Agrees with Daniels (1943.1) that the poem records the
   author's response to Julia, but argues that his excitement
   is not symbolic but "literally sensual."

3 HUDSON, HOYT HOPEWELL. The Epigram in the English Renaissance.
   Princeton: Princeton University Press, pp. 20, 101.
      Prints the opening poem from Thomas Bastard's
   Chrestoleros (1598), which Herrick imitated in "The Argu-
   ment of his Book," and suggests that "Gather ye Rose-buds"
   ("To the Virgins, to make much of Time") may echo John
   Parkhurst's "In Quasdam Eximia Forma Puellas, / Niue
   Lusitantes" or Timothe Kendall's or Edward May's versions
   of Parkhurst's poem.

4 KIRBY, THOMAS A. "The Triple Tun." Modern Language Notes 62
   (March):191-92.
      Identifies the Triple Tun, the tavern Herrick mentions
   in "An Ode for him," as the Three Tuns, Bankside, since
   that is an area of London frequented by literary people of
   Herrick's and Jonson's time.

5 McNEAL, THOMAS H. "How Old Was Prudence Baldwin?" Notes and
   Queries 192 (26 July):324.
      Asks whether anyone actually knows the birth date of
   Herrick's servant.
      Reprinted: 1948.9.

115

1947

6   REGENOS, GRAYDON W.   "The Influence of Horace on Robert
    Herrick."   Philological Quarterly 26 (July):268-84.
        After summarizing earlier studies indicating that
    Herrick's debt to Martial and Catullus is inconsequential,
    shows the extent of Herrick's imitations of Horace (whom
    he names six times in Hesperides).   Uses parallel passages
    to document both the similarity between the two poets'
    philosophies of life and Herrick's direct imitations of
    lines from Horace.   Notes that Herrick borrows "from about
    forty percent of the Odes as well as from the Epodes,
    Satires, Epistles, and the Ars Poetica," and concludes that
    Herrick's most characteristic traits are those he shares
    with Horace.
        Abstracted: Transactions and Proceedings of the Ameri-
    can Philological Association 72 (1941):xl-xli.

7   TUVE, ROSEMOND.   Elizabethan and Metaphysical Imagery:
    Renaissance Poetics and Twentieth-Century Critics.   Chicago:
    University of Chicago Press, pp. 147-50 and passim.   Re-
    print.   Chicago: University of Chicago Press, Phoenix
    Books, 1961.
        Passing references to Herrick illustrate several kinds
    of Renaissance figures and tropes; on pp. 147-50, uses
    "Upon Julia's Voice" as an example of a poem whose images
    are "embellishments of nature . . . to make [nature's] own
    effects appear more strange and miraculous."   Julia's
    voice, then, is "the distilled quintessence of sweetness"--
    not merely an extraordinarily sweet voice.

8   WALLIS, LAWRENCE B.   Fletcher, Beaumont & Co.:   Entertainers
    to the Jacobean Gentry.   New York: King's Crown Press,
    327 pp. passim.
        Herrick mentioned as one of thirty-six writers contrib-
    uting commendatory verses to the Folio of 1647; explains
    his interest in Beaumont and Fletcher by pointing to the
    emotional impact of their "melting numbers."   Cites lines
    13-14 of "Upon Master Fletchers Incomparable Playes" as
    evidence that Fletcher devised the plot for A King and No
    King; assumes that Herrick's place as a "Son of Ben" gave
    him ample opportunity to know this fact (p. 195).

9   WASSERMAN, EARL R.   Elizabethan Poetry in the Eighteenth
    Century.   Illinois Studies in Language and Literature,
    vol. 32, no. 2.   Urbana: University of Illinois Press,
    291 pp.
        Treats Herrick in Chapters 4 and 5, "The Elizabethan
    Lyric" and "The Elizabethan Revival."   The former chapter
    treats Renaissance song-texts published in later

anthologies; the latter notes Drake's praise of Herrick and
other Caroline poets (1804.1) and Mary Robinson's imitation
of "the pattern of Herrick's 'Bid me to live'" ("To Anthea,
who may command him any thing").

1948

1   The Love Poems of Robert Herrick and John Donne. Edited with
    an Introduction by Louis Untermeyer. Brunswick, N.J.:
    Rutgers University Press, 251 pp.
        Introduction justifies pairing Herrick and Donne by
    noting that although they were contemporaries, "no two men
    ever wrote more directly and yet more diversely on the same
    subject." In a brief survey of the life and works, indi-
    cates that Devonshire "directed and almost dictated"
    Herrick's poems. Sees his accomplishment as "a triumph of
    tiny significances. . . . It may be said that Herrick
    trifled his way from light verse into lasting poetry."
    Herrick's poems--categorized by the mistresses they cele-
    brate--appear on pp. 13-155.

2   BROOKE, TUCKER. "Seventeenth-Century Poetry: III. The Aca-
    demic and Courtly Tradition." In A Literary History of
    England. Edited by Albert C. Baugh. New York: Appleton-
    Century-Crofts, pp. 651-64.
        Pp. 661-64 devoted to Herrick, "the delight and justi-
    fication of the anthologist. Some twenty easily selected
    lyrics have made him immortal; the rest are not so much
    inferior as repetitive of his themes." Sees Herrick's
    craftsmanship and his irony saving him from disaster as he
    creates fine poems; "Corinna," especially, is superb.
        Second edition, 1967, adds a brief bibliographical
    supplement.

3   COOK, REGINALD L. "Robert Frost's Asides on His Poetry."
    American Literature 19 (January):354.
        Cites Frost's praise of Herrick's "To Daffadills"
    (1946.2) "as an example of a poet fulfilling the obligation
    of his commitment as an artist. He says, 'I always mar-
    veled how the second stanza is just as perfect as the
    first.'"

4   DAICHES, DAVID. A Study of Literature for Readers and Critics.
    Ithaca, N.Y.: Cornell University Press, pp. 148-51.
        In Chapter 7, "The Nature of Poetry," explicates
    "Cherrie-ripe" to show the complexity of an apparently

simple poem; goes on to note the qualitative distinction between a poem by Edgar Guest and the "simplest trifle" by Herrick.

5   HESS, M. WHITCOMB. "Herrick's Golden Apples: The 'Hesperides': 1648." Catholic World 167 (May):140-45.
       An essay written on the tercentenary of the publication of the 1648 volume, claiming that even in the years when Herrick was all but unknown, his poetry was influencing the course of English literature and politics. Believes that the picture of merry England that Herrick created influenced eighteenth- and nineteenth-century poets: "almost concomitantly with the growth of imperialist, commercialist England, her pastoral lyrist gave his nation a dream to be possessed by. . . . That bright arcadian landscape where in her meadows sits eternal May made perfect propaganda material for the empire builders." Believes that Herrick is England's "finest pastoral poet" and admires his "irrepressible" cheerfulness. Does not blame Herrick for any ill that may have come from others using his vision to "make [England's] imperialism palatable to how many otherwise just Britishers and other peoples."

6   HOWARTH, R.G. "Notes on Skelton." Notes and Queries 193 (1 May):186.
       Note 3 questions Dyce's listing of Herrick as an imitator of Skelton (1843.1), for Howarth can find no Skeltonics in Moorman's edition of Herrick.

7   LODGE, OLIVER. "Herrick's Tercentenary." Book Handbook: An Illustrated Quarterly 1, no. 5:273-81.
       Presents Hesperides as a celebration of "English country life before the puritan revolt cut down the Maypoles, and broke the village crosses, and took the colour out of life and dress." Sees poems in Noble Numbers as evidence of "an innocent, almost a child-like faith." Lists thirteen editions of Herrick.

8   M., P.D. "Robert Herrick." Notes and Queries 193 (30 October):479.
       Queries whether the links between Robert Herrick's family, the Heyricks or Eyricks of Leicestershire, have been traced. (See index, under Herrick family, for relevant items.)

9   McNEAL, THOMAS H.   "How Old Was Prudence Baldwin?" <u>Notes and</u>
     <u>Queries</u> 193 (16 October):456.
          Reprint--with one additional sentence--of 1947.5.

10 MATTHEWS, A.G. <u>Walker Revised: Being a Revision of John</u>
     <u>Walker's Sufferings of the Clergy during the Grand Rebel-</u>
     <u>lion, 1642-60.</u> Oxford: Clarendon Press, p. 114.
          Adds to Walker (1714.1) the information that Herrick was
     sequestered before March 1646, that he was one of Lord
     Scudamore's pensioners, and that he was restored to his
     parish in 1660. Observes that Herrick's poetry is not
     mentioned by Walker.

11 PATTISON, BRUCE. <u>Music and Poetry of the English Renaissance.</u>
     London: Methuen & Co., pp. 177, 200. 2d. ed. 1970.
          Briefly mentions Herrick as a seventeenth-century suc-
     cessor of Campion. Also says, "Many of Herrick's lyrics
     suggest a background of popular song and dance."

12 PEARCE, ROY HARVEY. "'Pure' Criticism and the History of
     Ideas." <u>Journal of Aesthetics and Art Criticism</u> 7
     (December):122-32.
          Calls for literary criticism that combines the sensi-
     tivity to language of the New Critics and the techniques
     of the historians of ideas. Uses Brooks's analysis of
     "Corinna's going a Maying" (1947.1) as an example of an
     incomplete essay, for even though Brooks is right in point-
     ing out that Herrick "is actually attempting to reconcile
     'the conflicting claims of paganism and Christianity,'" he
     neglects "the core of the whole matter. . . . Herrick's
     perception of the resemblance between May-rite and
     Christian-rite . . . stems out of the larger awareness of
     the naturalistic challenge to absolute Christianity. And
     Herrick assumes this awareness . . . on the part of his
     audience." Since twentieth-century readers will not share
     a seventeenth-century perception of the significance of
     that challenge, they need "a semantics of relevant ideas"
     if they are to perceive the tone of the poem. Cites
     Merritt Hughes's essay on <u>Faerie Queene</u>, II, xii (<u>Journal</u>
     <u>of the History of Ideas</u> 4 [1943]:381-99) as a piece pre-
     senting appropriate historical analysis without moving on
     to relate that analysis to aesthetic qualities of the poem
     and Elizabeth Pope's <u>Paradise Regained: The Tradition and</u>
     <u>the Poem</u> (Baltimore: Johns Hopkins Press, 1947) as a book
     that combines historical and aesthetic approaches.

1948

13   WING, DONALD, comp. <u>Short-Title Catalogue of Books Printed in</u>
     <u>England, Scotland, Ireland, Wales, and British America and</u>
     <u>of English Books Printed in Other Countries, 1641-1700</u>.
     Vol. 2. New York: Columbia University Press for the Index
     Society, p. 179.
         Under "Herrick," lists two editions of <u>Hesperides</u>, 1648;
     one of <u>Noble Numbers</u>, 1647; <u>Poor Robin's Visions</u>, 1677; and
     "A song for two voices" [1700?]. (<u>Poor Robin's Visions</u>
     should be attributed to Robert Winstanley [1883.4] or
     William Winstanley [Sidney Lee, "William Winstanley," in
     <u>Dictionary of National Biography</u>, vol. 62, ed. Sidney Lee
     (New York: Macmillan Co.; London: Smith, Elder, & Co.,
     1900), pp. 209-11].)

<u>1949</u>

1   TANNENBAUM, SAMUEL A., and DOROTHY R., comps. <u>Robert Herrick</u>
     <u>(a Concise Bibliography)</u>. Elizabethan Bibliographies,
     no. 40. New York: Elizabethan Bibliographies, 58 leaves.
         Lists 860 items under the following categories: "Works,"
     "Selections," "Commentary," "Music," "Manuscripts," "In
     Praise of Herrick," "Bibliography," and "Addenda Not
     Indexed." Provides an index of names and subjects included
     in the bibliography. (Items 375 and 526 are about the
     American novelist Robert Herrick. Item 430 is about
     Richard Hooker, and the page numbers in Item 420 refer to
     Hooker [see 1837.1 for correct pages for Herrick].)
         Reprinted: <u>Elizabethan Bibliographies</u>, vol. 3, <u>Robert</u>
     <u>Greene, George Herbert, Robert Herrick, John Heywood</u> (Port
     Washington, N.Y.: Kennikat Press, 1967), 40 pp. Reprint
     corrects Item 430.

<u>1950</u>

1   ARMS, GEORGE, and KUNTZ, JOSEPH M., comps. <u>Poetry Explica-</u>
     <u>tion: A Checklist of Interpretations since 1925 of British</u>
     <u>and American Poems Past and Present</u>. [New York]: Swallow
     Press; William Morrow & Co., pp. 84-86.
         Lists twenty-three explications of Herrick poems.
     Revised edition by Joseph M. Kuntz (Denver: Alan
     Swallow, 1962) lists thirty-nine explications, pp. 137-39.
     See also new edition by Joseph M. Kuntz and Nancy C.
     Martinez (Boston: G.K. Hall & Co., 1980), pp. 226-32.

1951

2   BATESON, F.W. English Poetry: A Critical Introduction.
    London, New York, and Toronto: Longmans, Green & Co.,
    pp. 20, 46, 82f. 247n.
        Shows that in the first stanza of "Upon Julia's
    Clothes," Herrick's "sensuous paganism . . . makes its
    impact through verbal wit" (p. 46).
        In the chapter "Poetry and Society," contrasts "The
    comming of good luck" with four lines from Landor to il-
    lustrate his point that "no poem can be considered a good
    one unless the basic social attitudes implied or expressed
    are genuinely 'opposite' or 'discordant.'" Admires two
    contrasts in Herrick's poem: one between the genial
    clergyman-poet and Good Luck and one composed of "the
    complexities of Good Luck's own make-up" (pp. 82-83).

3   CRONIN, JAMES E. "'The Hag' in 'The Cloud.'" Notes and
    Queries 195 (5 August):341-42.
        Observes four similarities between Shelley's "The Cloud"
    and Herrick's "The Hag" and suggests that "The Hag" served
    as an unconscious source for Shelley's poem. See 1935.4.

4   MUSGROVE, S[YDNEY]. The Universe of Robert Herrick.
    Auckland University College Bulletin, no. 38; English
    Series, no. 4. Auckland: Pelorus Press, 34 pp. Reprints.
    Folcroft, Pa.: Folcroft Library Editions, 1967, 1971;
    Norwood, Pa.: Norwood Editions, 1973.
        Redeems Herrick from the labels "trivial" and "pagan" by
    demonstrating that he is a "considerable poet" whose vision
    depends on the world view of seventeenth-century Chris-
    tianity. Beginning with "The Argument of his Book,"
    examines a number of the poems to show that "Herrick's
    entry to the system of the world lies . . . through the
    gate of nature." Shows that his "view of nature is a
    sacramental one"; he "moves from the temple of the Muses
    to the temple of God easily and naturally, and with no
    sense of any incompatibility between the two." Refuses to
    categorize Renaissance poetry, for the significant fact is
    that poets like Herrick, Marvell, and Shakespeare lived in
    a world lost by the time of Dryden, whose imagination
    "distinguishes and divides," rather than "unites."

                            1951

1   ANON. "Caroline Poet." Times Literary Supplement (London),
    10 August, p. 501.
        Review of Musgrove (1950.4), noting that he provides a
    persuasive argument that Herrick was more than a writer of
    fanciful lyrics.

1951

2   Van DOREN, MARK.   Introduction to Poetry: Commentaries on
     Thirty Poems. New York: Hill & Wang, pp. 65-69. Reprint.
     1968.
        A close reading of "To Meddowes" shows how dramatic
     Herrick's lyric art is: "Lyric art, like any art, moves
     in the direction of drama--toward excitement--into it, and
     then away."

1952

1   CAZAMIAN, LOUIS. The Development of English Humor.   Durham,
     N.C.: Duke University Press, p. 372.
        Comments on Herrick's importance as a poet who inte-
     grates humor "with a mode of poetry that had been generally
     alien to it--the lyrical. . . . No less interesting is the
     admixture of humor with love poetry, shorn of all its con-
     ventional trappings." Notes Herrick's "good humor," his
     "raciness and realism," and his occasional satiric wit.

2   CUTTS, JOHN P. "British Museum Additional MS. 31432: William
     Lawes' Writing for the Theatre and the Court." Library,
     5th ser. 7 (December):225-34.
        Lists the songs in B.M. Add. MS. 31432 in the order in
     which they appear (using titles as Lawes gives them), fol-
     lowed by notes. Song numbers 38 through 44 are by Herrick.
     Observes that since Lawes died in 1645, his versions pre-
     date Hesperides's texts. Prints a second stanza of "Per-
     suasions not to love" (called "On the Vicissitudes of Love"
     in John Playford's Select Ayres and Dialogues [1659] and
     "Not to love" in Hesperides), which appears neither in
     Playford nor in the 1648 volume, and notes that Lawes's
     stanza 1 is six lines shorter than the version in
     Hesperides, for Lawes "omits lines 7-8 and 13-16" (see
     1976.14 for the theory that Herrick added those lines when
     he revised the songs for Hesperides). Suggests that the
     popularity of "Gather ye Rose-buds" ("To the Virgins, to
     make much of Time") was due, at least in part, to Lawes's
     excellent setting. Proposes that the manuscript is "in
     part a leisure Commonplace Book made by the author of his
     own settings of poems which he personally liked . . . and
     in part also a record of dramatical activity" on Lawes's
     part between 1631 and 1641.

1953

1 ABRAMS, M.H. The Mirror and the Lamp: Romantic Theory and the Critical Tradition. New York: Oxford University Press, p. 190.
    Quotes "Not every day fit for Verse," which "neatly summarizes the facts claimed [by Renaissance writers] for inspired composition."

2 ARCHIBALD, R.C. "There is a Lady Sweet and Kind." Notes and Queries 198 (August):357-58.
    Asks whether compilers of "various song collections" and "many gramophone records" could be correct in ascribing "There is a Lady Sweet and Kind" to Herrick.

3 CUTTS, JOHN P. "A Bodleian Song-Book: Don. C.57." Music and Letters 34 (July):192-211.
    Lists the contents of Bodleian MS. Don. C.57; of the 160 songs therein, some 12 are by Herrick. Provides variants from Moorman's edition of Herrick's 1648 volume and, because they differ in major ways from the printed versions, offers the manuscript versions of song-texts for "To a Gentlewoman, objecting to him his gray haires," "To Musick. A Song," and "Upon Mistresse Elizabeth Wheeler, under the name of Amarillis." Notes that the setting for "To Musick. A Song" is the only one rediscovered to date.

4 DUFF, J. WIGHT. A Literary History of Rome: From the Origins to the Close of the Golden Age. Edited by A.M. Duff. London: Ernest Benn, pp. 239-40.
    Compares Catullus to Herrick: "Each is a prince among songsters. Each unites artificiality and simplicity. Herrick's 'blossoms, birds, and bowers' are present in the Latin poet, though Alexandrianism left him freer from conceits than the 'metaphysical school' left Herrick." Yet sees Catullus as more like Burns than like Herrick, for the Roman poet is not "so affected and cold" as the seventeenth-century lyrist and, unlike Herrick, he never rejects nature in favor of art.

5 W., G. Review of Universe of Robert Herrick, by Musgrove. Southerly 14, no. 1:60.
    Admires Musgrove's individual perceptions about the poems, but believes he goes too far in alleging that Herrick's delicate lyrics treat a theme as significant as that of Paradise Lost.

1954

1   CRUM, M[ARGARET] C. "Notes on the Texts of William Lawes's
    Songs in B.M. MS. ADD. 31432." Library, 5th ser. 9 (June):
    122-27.
        Quotes E.H. Fellowes's caution that song-texts may not
    reflect early versions of poems published elsewhere, for
    the composer either may have erred in making his copy or
    may have altered a word or phrase to fit his music (English
    Madrigal Verse, 1588-1632 [Oxford: Clarendon Press, 1920],
    pp. xvii-xviii). Lists differences between "Charon and
    Phylomel, a Dialogue sung" as it appears in Herrick's 1648
    volume and in Lawes's manuscript, suggesting that most of
    the variants in the latter seem to be "changes made for
    musical reasons." Believes that Lawes supplied the addi-
    tional stanzas in "Ah Cruell Love" ("To Pansies") and "He
    that will not love" ("Not to love"), for those two stanzas
    "have the appearance of unskillful parodies, and if they
    are really Herrick's there is cause to be grateful for the
    later judgment which directed his choice of poems for
    printing in Hesperides." Also comments on Lawes's settings
    of verses by other poets, including Shirley and Carew.

2   HOWARTH, R.G. "Verses in Herrick's Church." Notes and
    Queries, n.s. 1 (April):177.
        Quotes four lines of verse inscribed on a flagstone in
    Herrick's church in Dean Prior and requests information
    about their source.

3   RØSTVIG, MAREN-SOFIE. The Happy Man: Studies in the Meta-
    morphoses of a Classical Ideal, 1600-1700. Oslo Studies in
    English, no. 2. Oslo: Akademisk Forlag; Oxford: Basil
    Blackwell, pp. 139-42 and passim.
        Presents Herrick as combining "the neo-Stoicism of the
    beatus ille-motif," "the carpe diem-motif of the Anacreon-
    tic tradition," and "appreciation of the pure enjoyments of
    country life." Notes that poems in Mildmay Fane's Otia
    Sacra (1648) contain echoes of Herrick.
        Revised: 1962.6.

4   UPDIKE, JOHN HOYER. "Non-Horatian Elements in Herrick's
    Echoes of Horace." Undergraduate honors thesis, Harvard
    University, 53 pp.
        Argues that in his echoes of Horace "Herrick reveals
    himself as out of sympathy with the ethical assumptions at
    the center of Horace's world," but that Herrick imitates
    Horace in his "artistic restraint."

1955

1   HENRY, NAT. "Herrick's 'Upon Julia's Clothes.'" <u>Explicator</u>
    14 (December): Item 15.
        Objects to Schneider's reading (1955.8) and argues that,
    as its title suggests, the poem is about Julia dressed.

2   HOWARTH, R.G. "An Early Elevation of Herrick." <u>Notes and</u>
    <u>Queries</u>, n.s. 2 (August):341.
        Cites Richard James's listing of Herrick with Jonson and
    Drayton in <u>The Muses Dirge</u> (1625) as evidence of Herrick's
    having a significant reputation in the second decade of the
    century.
        See Patrick, 1978.27, for a different analysis of
    James's comment on Herrick.

3   _____. "Herrick's Epitaph on His Niece Elizabeth." <u>Notes and</u>
    <u>Queries</u>, n.s. 2 (August):341-42.
        Establishes that the Elizabeth whose epitaph is in St.
    Margaret's Church, Westminster, was the child of Herrick's
    brother, William, and guesses that Herrick was still living
    in Westminster with William and his family when she died in
    May 1630. The epitaph, which is listed in the 1633 con-
    tinuation of Stow's <u>Survey of London</u>, was revised for
    Herrick's 1648 volume; it appears there as "Upon his kins-
    woman Mistris Elizabeth Herrick." Believes that the memo-
    rial tablet now in St. Margaret's Church is recently
    "restored" after having been taken to America during the
    last war.
        Continuation: 1956.7.

4   _____. "Two Poems by Herrick?" <u>Notes and Queries</u>, n.s. 2
    (September):380-81.
        Speculates that an eight-line fragment under the heading
    "Glad" on signature Bb[v] of <u>The English Parnassus</u>, compiled
    by Joshua Poole (1657), is a part of a companion poem to
    Herrick's "Master Herrick's Farewell unto Poetry" and that
    a fragment under the heading "Blush" on S4 (repeated, in
    part, on T4[v]) may also be by Herrick.
        Responses: 1955.5; 1956.8; 1962.5; 1978.32.

5   MAXWELL, J.C. "Two Poems of Herrick?" <u>Notes and Queries</u>,
    n.s. 2 (November):500.
        Responding to Howarth, 1955.4, observes that the first
    of the two poems Howarth suggests are Herrick's are in fact
    lines from the beginning of Jonson's <u>Sejanus</u>, Act V.
        Discussion continued: 1956.8; 1962.5; 1978.32.

6   RAU, FRITZ. "Kleine Beiträge: Robert Herrick." <u>Die Neueren</u>
      <u>Sprachen</u> 4, no. 8:357-63.
         A general presentation of Herrick's work and reputation.

7   ROSENTHAL, M.L., and SMITH, A.J.M. <u>Exploring Poetry</u>. New
      York: Macmillan Co., pp. 251-52.
         Explicates ten lines of "The Apparition of his Mistresse
      calling him to Elizium" to show that the combination of wit
      and seriousness characteristic of much modern poetry is not
      unique to the twentieth century.

8   SCHNEIDER, ELISABETH. "Herrick's 'Upon Julia's Clothes.'"
      <u>Explicator</u> 13 (March): Item 30.
         Responds to Daniels (1943.1) that the first stanza of
      the poem presents Julia dressed; the second, Julia un-
      dressed. Notes that because <u>liquefaction</u> in stanza 1 and
      <u>vibration</u> in stanza 2 are scientific words neatly applied
      to Herrick's "wholly unscientific, mildly erotic theme,"
      they provide an "ironic flavor" to the poem. Response:
      1955.1.

9   SMYTH, CHARLES. "A Herrick Epitaph." <u>Times Literary Supple-</u>
      <u>ment</u> (London), 13 May, p. 253.
         Announces that in memory of James Ramsey, an American
      buried in St. Margaret's Church, Westminster, citizens of
      West Virginia have restored Herrick's epitaph for his
      niece, Elizabeth Herrick, to the church. Basil Willey will
      speak on the occasion of the unveiling. (See 1955.11 for
      his address.)

10 WHITAKER, THOMAS R. "Herrick and the Fruits of the Garden."
      <u>English Literary History</u> 22 (March):16-33.
         Explores the seriousness of Herrick's verse by treating
      "the imaginative world of <u>Hesperides</u>." Believes that a
      selection of approximately fifty of the poems would create
      a volume with the "poise and wit" that Leavis misses in
      Herrick (1935.3). Quotes a number of the poems, including
      "The Funerall Rites of the Rose" (which Leavis disparaged),
      to show that Herrick's ceremonial poems are "placed" in the
      sense that Leavis says Marvell's are; Herrick, too, is
      serious, rather than solemn--the better poems are not
      "indulgences." Treats the "Christian-Dionysian ambiguity
      [which] runs through Herrick's symbolism" as a sign that
      Herrick's paganism is a significant part of his poetic:
      "Herrick's verse moves in two worlds, which are imperfectly
      coordinated." Argues that Herrick sees a "middle realm,
      'Part Pagan, part Papisticall'"; at its best, Herrick's art
      achieves the goal of "momentary imaginative transcendence

of the temporal--that life may spring again. The escape of
art leads back to the world of nature."

11   WILLEY, BASIL. "Robert Herrick: 1591-1674." <u>Church Quar-
     terly Review</u> 156 (July-September):248-55.
          The address delivered by Willey on 18 May 1955, on the
     occasion of the unveiling of a tablet restoring Herrick's
     epitaph on his niece, Elizabeth Herrick, in St. Margaret's
     Church, Westminster (see 1955.9). Expresses mild enthu-
     siasm for Herrick's art: "His best lyrics . . . are like
     diamonds, exquisitely cut and set, and have the same en-
     during quality."

                              <u>1956</u>

1   <u>The Poetical Works of Robert Herrick</u>. Edited by L.C. Martin.
     Oxford English Texts. Oxford: Clarendon Press, xl +
     632 pp.
          Introduction provides an outline of Herrick's life and
     reputation (pp. xi-xxi), analysis of the text and canon
     (pp. xxi-xxxvi), and comments on the chronology of the
     poems (pp. xxxvi-xl). Believes that although the 1648
     volume does not present poems in the order of their compo-
     sition, "that order, intentionally or not, seems to have
     had some effect on the arrangement." Cites suggestions by
     Hale, Pollard, and Delattre on the order of the poems
     (1892.8; 1891.1; 1911.2); considers the places of datable
     poems within the volume, suggests that poems now available
     in manuscript sources are likely to have been written be-
     fore Herrick moved to Devonshire; speculates that of the
     Devonshire poems, those that are optimistic were probably
     written before the beginning of the Civil War; sees the
     influence of Horace and Ovid in poems early in <u>Hesperides</u>,
     of Martial and Tacitus in later poems; and notes that poems
     seeming to have been influenced by Burton (whose <u>Anatomy of
     Melancholy</u> was published in 1621) appear most often in the
     latter part of <u>Hesperides</u>.
          Retains Moorman's pagination (1915.1) for pp. 1-419 of
     the text of the poems and then adds twenty-five pages of
     poems not included in previous editions (pp. 419-44). In
     appendices, prints letters from Robert Herrick to Sir
     William Herrick and variant versions of three Herrick
     poems. Critical notes (pp. 463-97) and a commentary
     (pp. 498-585, incorporating many of Phinn's notes: see
     1876.1) are followed by indices of titles and first lines.
          Reprinted, from corrected sheets of the first edition,
     in 1963. Revised edition: 1965.1.

1956

2   ANON. Review of Poetical Works, by Martin. Listener 55
    (31 May):727.
        Traces Herrick's reputation, attributing his fame in the
    nineteenth century to a new interest in nature poetry. Now
    finds Herrick "one of the most engaging of our singers" and
    praises Martin's work on his volume (1956.1).

3   ARMSTRONG, RAY L. Review of Poetical Works, by Martin.
    Seventeenth-Century News 14 (Autumn):7-8.
        Praise of Martin's work (1956.1), especially of his ex-
    tensive commentary. Regrets only that he includes Greek
    quotations, for modern readers typically need English
    translations. (See Armstrong's positive review of
    Patrick's text [1963.1], which includes translations
    [1963.3].)

4   BLACKMUR, R.P. "Emily Dickinson's Notation." Kenyon Review
    18 (Spring):224-37.
        As part of a review essay on Thomas H. Johnson's recent
    biography and edition of Emily Dickinson (both by the
    Belknap Press of Harvard University), contrasts Dickinson,
    Herrick, and Rainer Maria Rilke--all three of whom Blackmur
    sees as "nuptial poets." Believes that for Herrick, "di-
    rect experience was accepted only for the sake of something
    else which was to be found in the plentitude of God's
    creation of nature. Thus it is that the clergyman wore the
    sexual garment sweet." Contrasts him with Dickinson, be-
    cause "what was sensuality in Herrick becomes in Emily
    Dickinson the flow of deprived sensation on the quick";
    Dickinson tried to withdraw from the world, but failed
    either to withdraw or to return to real experience. Rilke
    and Dickinson are similar in that both yearned to "create
    mortal images of immortality"; they differ, however: "In
    Dickinson there is the terribilità of our inner escape; in
    Rilke there is the greater terribilità of that impossible
    act, full assent in natural piety."
        Reprinted: Emily Dickinson: A Collection of Critical
    Essays, ed. Richard B. Sewall (Englewood Cliffs, N.J.:
    Prentice Hall, 1963), pp. 78-87.

5   FRANKENBERG, LLOYD. Invitation to Poetry: A Round of Poems
    from John Skelton to Dylan Thomas Arranged with Comments.
    Garden City, N.Y.: Doubleday & Co., pp. 48-50.
        Explication of "To live merrily, and to trust to Good
    Verses" notes that although the poem's structure is that of
    a sermon, it is a merry poem, capped by a "bleary pro-
    nouncement" of the elation that accompanies good poetry.

6   HIBBARD, G.R.   "The Country House Poem of the Seventeenth
    Century."   <u>Journal of the Warburg and Courtauld Institutes</u>
    19:159-74.
        Discusses seven poems (Jonson's "To Penshurst" and "Sir
    Robert Wroth," Carew's "To Saxham" and "To my Friend G.N.
    from Wrest," Herrick's "A Country life: to his Brother,
    Master Thomas Herrick" and "A Panegerick to Sir Lewis
    Pemberton," and Marvell's "Upon Appleton House") which
    celebrate English country houses and the way of life they
    embodied in the early seventeenth century. Notes these
    poems' debts to Horace and Martial, but sees Jonson's addi-
    tions to his Latin models (his emphasis on architecture,
    his insistence on the social function of the house within
    a wider community, and his presentation of the reciprocal
    relationship between human and natural life as necessary
    for social stability) as basic to the English genre.
    Traces significant changes in country-house architecture
    from the end of the sixteenth century to the early eigh-
    teenth century and shows how Jonson presents the Eliza-
    bethan Penshurst as an emblem of a morality based on the
    proper "use" of nature, a morality whose perversion he
    castigates in stage comedies like <u>Volpone</u> and in "Sir
    Robert Wroth." Sees Jonson and his successors as present-
    ing baroque architecture as an embodiment of a vulgar
    threat to civilization. Treats "To Saxham" and "A Country
    life" as poor imitations of "Sir Robert Wroth," but praises
    Carew's and Herrick's other country-house poems as serious,
    excellent works; "A Panegerick" is an effective rebuttal of
    Leavis's judgment of Herrick's poetry as "trivially charm-
    ing" (1935.3). Explains that the opening stanzas of "Upon
    Appleton House" present the last true example of the genre;
    by the time Pope wrote his "Epistle to Burlington," even he
    had to recognize that the traditional life he admired and
    the value system it implied no longer existed.
        Reprinted: <u>Essential Articles for the Study of</u>
    <u>Alexander Pope</u>, ed. Maynard Mack (Hamden, Conn.:   Archon
    Books, 1964), pp. 401-37.

7   HOWARTH, R.G. "Herrick's Epitaph on his Niece Elizabeth."
    <u>Notes and Queries</u>, n.s. 3 (February):89.
        Now realizes that the memorial tablet in St. Margaret's
    Church, Westminster, is a new rather than a restored
    seventeenth-century tablet. (See 1955.3.)

8   _____. "Two Poems by Herrick?" Notes and Queries, n.s. 3
      (February):89.
         Rejoinder to Maxwell, 1955.5. Believes that the person
      who transformed Sejanus' lines from references to personal
      ambition to references to religious joy might have been
      Herrick.
         Discussion continued: 1962.5; 1978.32.

*9   NICHOLSON, HAROLD. Review of Poetical Works, by Martin.
      Observer (London), 25 March, p. 16.
         Cited by Pebworth et al. (1978.28), p. 242.

10   SWARDSON, H[AROLD] R[OLAND]. "Herrick and the Ceremony of
      Mirth." In "A Study of the Tension between Christian and
      Classical Traditions in Seventeenth-Century Poetry." Ph.D.
      dissertation, University of Minnesota, pp. 16-45.
         Shows lighthearted paganism and Christianity merging in
      both the secular and the religious poems to the point that
      the "claims of Herrick's natural world are often made com-
      pelling as a kind of parallel or counter religion." In
      poems like "Corinna," however, pagan elements are sub-
      ordinated to Christian values; in those verses, ceremony,
      ritual, and art elevate erotic experience so that it
      transcends the merely voluptuous. Thus Herrick's poetry
      presents an alternative to narrowly pious Christian
      attitudes.
         See also summary in DA 17:1559. Reprinted in H.R.
      Swardson, Poetry and the Fountain of Light: Observations
      on the Conflict between Christian and Classical Traditions
      in Seventeenth-Century Poetry (Columbia: University of
      Missouri Press, 1962), pp. 40-63.

11   TILLYARD, E.M.W. The Metaphysicals and Milton. London:
      Chatto & Windus, pp. 52-57, 62, 74.
         Examines "To the Virgins, to make much of Time" to show
      that even while Herrick "owes nothing directly to Donne,
      either in substance or rhythm, [he] may have drawn strength
      from the general sense of urgency, of present actuality,
      that Donne helped to give to the lyrical tradition in
      England." Sees the value of the poem not in its para-
      phrasable content but in the way in which Herrick conveys
      his conviction that "fine living" is a possibility even in
      the face of imminent tragedy.

12   Van DOREN, MARK. "A Visit to the Home of Robert Herrick."
      Reporter 14 (22 March):47-49.
         Recounts a chance conversation in Cambridge which led
      him to think about Herrick and to visit Dean Prior. Specu-
      lates about Herrick's life and his ideas about his poetry
      and expresses his belief that Herrick knew what we all
      should remember: "To trust to good verses. That would
      have been his answer to anyone who asked him how important
      lyric poetry was in those times." Closes with the observa-
      tion that criticism in the 1950s is interested "in the
      solemn or confused author whose mind is easy to enter
      because in despair he has left it open"; "Herrick,
      [Horace's] faultless pupil, is passed over for the same
      reason that in so many poems he was perfect--which is the
      precise place for criticism to begin."
         Reprinted as "Robert Herrick Revisited" in Mark Van
      Doren, The Happy Critic and Other Essays (New York: Hill
      & Wang, 1961), pp. 166-73, and in The Essays of Mark Van
      Doren (1924-1972), ed. William Claire, Contributions in
      American Studies, no. 47 (Westport, Conn. and London:
      Greenwood Press, 1980), pp. 65-71.

13   WALTON, GEOFFREY. "The Cavalier Poets." In From Donne to
      Marvell. Edited by Boris Ford. Pelican Guide to English
      Literature, vol. 3. Harmondsworth, England, and Baltimore,
      Md.: Penguin Books, pp. 160-72.
         Presents Herrick as "a poet of charmingly fanciful but
      simple sensibility" who has been overrated by twentieth-
      century critics; sees Carew and Lovelace as more signifi-
      cant exemplars of a school of poets whose work is generally
      inferior to that of their predecessors, Donne and Jonson.
         Several reprints.

1957

1   ECKHOFF, LORENTZ. "Stoicism in Shakespeare . . . and else-
     where." In Studies in English Language and Literature Pre-
     sented to Professor Dr. Karl Brunner on the Occasion of his
     Seventieth Birthday. Edited by Dr. Siegfried Korninger.
     Wiener Beiträge zur englischen Philologie, vol. 65.
     Vienna: Wilhelm Braumüller, pp. 32-42.
        After treating stoicism in Shakespeare, Austen,
     Goldsmith, and Pope, observes that the stoicism in
     Herrick's "The Christian Militant" is modern and European,
     rather than specifically Roman in character (p. 37).

1957

2   FRYE, NORTHROP. <u>Anatomy of Criticism: Four Essays</u>.
    Princeton: Princeton University Press; London: Oxford
    University Press, pp. 299-301.
        Brief use of Herrick as an example of an Epicurean poet
    whose <u>carpe diem</u> poems "accept the limitations of joy in
    experience" and whose "poems on primroses and daffodills
    . . . are . . . close to the fable and emblem tradition:
    so close that there is no incongruity in 'reading a lec-
    ture' from the primroses."
        Several reprints.

3   LEGOUIS, PIERRE. Review of <u>Poetical Works</u>, by Martin. Études
    <u>anglaises</u> 10 (April-June):152-54.
        Describes Martin's edition (1956.1) and "En toute humi-
    lité" provides corrections and additions to the commentary.

4   PINTO, V. De S. Review of <u>Poetical Works</u>, by Martin. <u>Modern</u>
    <u>Language Review</u> 52 (April):259-60.
        Describes Martin's work (1956.1) as thorough and the
    volume as one likely to remain the standard text for many
    years. Provides a few notes that might be considered in
    the next edition.

5   RICHMOND, H.M. "The Use and Development of Certain Tradi-
    tional Themes in the Love Poetry of the Earlier Seventeenth
    Century." Ph.D. dissertation, Oxford University, 620 pp.
        Documents the thesis that Caroline poets were "steeped
    in tradition" and that they "brought a new power of ratio-
    cination to love poetry." Mentions Herrick in passing
    throughout. Developed into 1964.4.

6   STAUDT, VICTOR P. "Horace and Herrick on <u>Carpe Diem</u>."
    <u>Classical Bulletin</u> 33 (March):55-56.
        Analyzes "To the Virgins, to make much of Time" to show
    that Herrick's so-called <u>carpe diem</u> poems are Christian
    admonishments to use time--a fact reinforced by the obser-
    vation that Herrick alludes to the parable of the wise and
    foolish virgins in which Christians are advised to use time
    to prepare for eternity.

7   WATSON, GEORGE, ed. <u>The Cambridge Bibliography of English</u>
    <u>Literature</u>. Vol. 5, <u>Supplement</u>. Cambridge: Cambridge
    University Press, p. 220.
        Additions to 1941.1: the Tannenbaum bibliography
    (1949.1), Martin's <u>Poetical Works</u> (1956.1), Untermeyer's
    <u>Love Poems</u> (1948.1), and nine items under "Biography and

Criticism." (The article by Arvin is in fact about the novelist Robert Herrick.)
See Watson, 1974.18, for The New Cambridge Bibliography of English Literature.

1958

1   CANDELARIA, FREDERICK. "Ronsard and Herrick." Notes and Queries, n.s. 5 (July):286-87.
Adds Ronsard's sonnet "Marie, levez-vous" to Martin's list of sources and influences for "Corinna's going a Maying" (1956.1), noting that Ronsard's and Herrick's poems are similar in imagery and tone and that both conclude on Catullan notes.

2   DUNLAP, RHODES. Review of Poetical Works, by Martin. Modern Philology 56 (August):65-67.
Praises Martin's work (1956.1), especially his commentary, which provides many classical and Renaissance sources and analogues. Finds the text appropriately conservative (with one exception: the Epitaph on the Giles Tomb, which Martin has emended) and approves of Martin's caution in attributing new poems to Herrick. Agrees that the Rosenbach poems are more likely to be Herrick's than Heath's, but notes that even this edition does not provide data that will settle the problem.

3   HOWARTH, R.G. "Attributions to Herrick." Notes and Queries, n.s. 5 (June):249.
Questions some of Martin's attributions of seventeenth-century manuscript poems to Herrick (1956.1). "Epitaph on a man who had a Scold to his Wife" may be the work of Thomas Jordan (who claims it as his own); "To a disdayne-full fayre" is printed in a collection of works by Thomas Pestell; and "Advice to a Maid" appears in a collection of poems by John Hilton. Believes that the "R.H." poems from the Rosenbach manuscript are by Robert Heath, whose poems they resemble more than Herrick's. (Martin's Oxford Standard Authors text, 1965.1, omits these poems--as does Patrick's edition, 1963.1. See 1970.3 for a more extensive argument that this "R.H." is not Herrick.)

4   KERMODE, FRANK. Review of Poetical Works, by Martin. Review of English Studies 9, no. 33:78-82.
Praises Martin's "masterpiece of editorial art" (1956.1) and offers comments relating to what may be learned about

Herrick from his critical notes and commentary. Suggests more French sources might have been mentioned and that Herrick may have used books like Thomas Godwyne's English Exposition of the Roman Antiquities (1614) as sources for various kinds of learning.

5 LEITER, LOUIS H. "Herrick's 'Upon Julia's Clothes.'" Modern Language Notes 73 (May):331.
    Shows how a "submerged metaphor" which he calls the "angler angled" informs the poem; the final admission that Julia's "glittering taketh me" is an ironic, witty reversal.

6 McCALL, JOSEPH DARRYL, Jr. "Factors Affecting the Literary Canon." Ph.D. dissertation, University of Florida, pp. 180-88.
    Uses Herrick as an example of a poet whose reputation has been determined by anthologists; claims that their praise of Herrick as a poet of graceful charming lyrics has been repeated by scholars like Gosse (1903.5), Baugh (1948.2), even by Moorman (1910.11). Notes, however, that Herrick is more often a poet of death, of melancholy, of despair (even the familiar poems are less cheerful than is commonly thought) and that recent scholars like Musgrove (1950.4) have more accurately characterized Hesperides as a book to be taken seriously. Other parts of the dissertation treat the effects of reviews, of critical essays, and of scholarship on short- and long-term reputations of literary figures.
    See also summary in DA 19:1744.

7 ROSS, RICHARD J. "'A Wild Civility': Robert Herrick's Poetic Solution of the Paradox of Art and Nature." Ph.D. dissertation, University of Michigan, 327 pp.
    Explicates poems from Hesperides to show Herrick's search for a way of reconciling "a perfect artful re-creation of nature" and "a frank, undeviating naturalism." Sees the epigrams as treating "nature, which is grotesquely repugnant yet appealing" and the idyllic lyrics as "distinctly art, or unnatural recreation." Finds that the generally chronological structure of Hesperides "records Herrick's achievement of an aesthetic solution for a perennial problem: the disparity between what is and what should be"; Herrick has arranged the poems so that early poems present "an aesthetic solution for natural realities" and the later poems apply that solution to everyday life.
    See also summary in DA 19:1390-91; see 1965.13 for an article derived from this dissertation.

<u>1959</u>

1   ANON. Review of <u>Two Gentle Men</u>, by Chute. <u>Seventeenth-</u>
    <u>Century News</u> 17 (Fall-Winter):28-29.
       A recommendation of 1959.6 which includes "a vivid,
    tolerant, sympathetic picture of Herrick and his society."

2   BRIGGS, K[ATHERINE] M. "The Fashion for the Miniature." In
    <u>The Anatomy of Puck: An Examination of Fairy Beliefs among</u>
    <u>Shakespeare's Contemporaries and Successors</u>. London:
    Routledge & Kegan Paul, pp. 56-70.
       Describes Drayton's, Browne's, Herrick's (pp. 65-67),
    and Sir Simeon Steward's fairy poems as dainty descendants
    of <u>Midsummer Night's Dream</u> and Mercutio's speech in <u>Romeo</u>
    <u>and Juliet</u>. Quotes "Oberons Diet" ("Oberons Feast") to
    show that Herrick's fairyland is "smaller and grosser than
    Browne's and Drayton's." Notes use of folk superstitions
    in Herrick's verse, but observes that the fairies' public
    worship described in "The Fairie Temple" is original with
    Herrick.

3   CANDELARIA, FREDERICK H. "The <u>Carpe Diem</u> Motif in Early
    Seventeenth-Century Lyric Poetry with Particular Reference
    to Robert Herrick." Ph.D. dissertation, University of
    Missouri, 278 pp.
       Treats the classical origins of the motif (Chapter 1),
    its appearance in the middle ages and the Renaissance
    (Chapter 2), Herrick's use of it (Chapter 3), and its
    appearance in other seventeenth-century poets (Chapter 4).
    Emphasizes the unity of Herrick's work even in spite of its
    being divided into one volume of verse that is generally
    secular and one of specifically religious poems. Stresses
    Herrick's debt to the traditional <u>carpe diem</u> motif, rather
    than specifically to Catullus and concludes that Herrick
    represents "the famous unified sensibility of the seven-
    teenth century." An appendix lists Herrick's uses of the
    <u>carpe diem</u> motif.
       See also summary in <u>DA</u> 20:2796.

4   CHUTE, MARCHETTE. "A Biographer and Two Dear Friends She
    Never Met." <u>New York Herald Tribune Book Review</u>,
    27 December, pp. 1, 11.
       Brief biographies of Herrick and Herbert. Says that
    "after I made their acquaintance I found I loved them as
    people."

1959

5   _____. "How a Book Grows." <u>Library Journal</u> 84 (1 September): 2431-32.

    Describes her work on <u>Two Gentle Men</u> (1959.6): the task grew from a project she had projected for eighteen months to more than four years' work as she traced Herbert's and Herrick's religious and political milieu.

6   _____. <u>Two Gentle Men: The Lives of George Herbert and Robert Herrick</u>. E.P. Dutton & Co., 319 pp. Published in London: Secker & Warburg, 1960.

    Noting a number of similarities between Herbert and Herrick--they were born two years apart, they both attended Cambridge University, they both attained posts as clergymen outside of London in 1630, and they both wrote a single volume of verse--pairs Herbert, "the saintly rector of Bemerton" and Herrick, "the somewhat pagan vicar of Dean Prior." Part 2, pp. 155-275, treats Herrick, whom Chute sees as an Elizabethan poet, "deeply rooted in an older England, through his 'dear ancestry' in the town of Leicester." Extrapolates from information in the life records, contemporary documents, Herrick's poems, and twentieth-century historians' accounts of Renaissance England to create a readable treatment of topics such as Herrick's education and friendships, his delight in Devonshire's folk customs, his poetic kinship to the Roman poets and to Ben Jonson, and his royalism. Closes with the comment that Herbert and Herrick, "gentle men in an age that was not gentle," were not proselytizers, but poets.

7 COHEN, HENNIG. "Herrick's 'To Electra.'" <u>Explicator</u> 17 (March): Item 44.

    Observes that "might go proud" refers both to the possibility of the poet's committing the sin of pride and to the likelihood of his becoming sexually excited. Thus Electra's attractions offer both earthly and heavenly dangers.

8 CUTTS, JOHN P. "'Mris Elizabeth Davenant 1624': Christ Church MS. Mus. 87." <u>Review of English Studies</u> 10:26-37.

    Description of this manuscript includes song number 21, a setting for Herrick's "Musicke thou soule of Heauen, care charming spell," which also appears in Bod. MS. Don. c. 57 96 (101). Both here and in the Bodleian manuscript, it has two more lines than the version ("To Musick. A Song") in the 1648 volume.

1959

9   FLETCHER, G.B.A. "Herrick and Latin Authors." Notes and
    Queries, n.s. 6 (June):231-32.
         Adds five Latin sources (from Martial, Horace [2],
    Statius, and Persius) to Martin's list (1956.1).

10 GAMBERINI, SPARTACO. "Robert Herrick, 1591-1674." In Poeti
    metafisici e cavalieri in Inghilterra. Biblioteca del'
    Archivum Romanicum Fondata da Giulio Bertoni, vol. 60.
    Florence: Leo S. Olschki, pp. 198-206.
         Sees Herrick as the first cavalier poet--but a cavalier
    without the faults of graceful irresponsibility cavalier
    poets generally exhibit. Similarly, Herrick follows
    Jonson's classicism, but not his robust temperament. Pre-
    sents work in Hesperides as "delicato, meticoloso, svagato
    e un poco vagabondo"; the poems in Noble Numbers are gen-
    erally less interesting.

11 MORSE, SAMUEL FRENCH. "Alien to Their Time." New York Times
    Book Review, 13 September, 6.
         Review of Chute's Two Gentle Men (1959.6). Praises her
    skill at bringing "Herrick to life in a way that no one
    else before has done."

12 ROLLIN, ROGER B. "Robert Herrick and the Pastoral Tradition."
    Ph.D. dissertation, Yale University, 349 pp.
         Argues that Eliot's criterion that a collection of short
    poems may be a major work if it exhibits "a unity of under-
    lying pattern" (1944.1) is met by Herrick's 1648 volume in
    which the poet-persona is a pastoral poet concerned with
    "the affirmation of life, the confrontation of death, and
    the transcendence of both through Art." Six chapters--"The
    Uses of Pastoral (I): Herrick and the Foreign Tradition,"
    "The Uses of Pastoral (II): Herrick and the English Tradi-
    tion," "The Shepherd as Priest and Preacher," "The Shepherd
    as Sage," "The Shepherd as Lover," and "The Shepherd as
    Poet"--show that Herrick's artistry and his criticism of
    life may be seen in the context of classical and Renais-
    sance pastoral traditions common to poets like Theocritus,
    Virgil, Mantuan, Spenser, the poets whose work is in
    England's Helicon, Jonson, and Drayton, and that Herrick's
    work "deserves to be ranked with Marvell's pastoral as a
    kind of culmination of the bucolic 'movement' in the English
    Renaissance." Includes detailed analyses of representative
    poems in each of "The Shepherd" chapters. Rollin's Robert
    Herrick (1966.6) offers a similar analysis of Herrick's
    pastoralism, without emphasizing--as does this study--the
    place of his poetry in the history of the genre.

1959

13   ROLO, CHARLES. "Bookshelf: Reader's Choice." <u>Atlantic</u>
        <u>Monthly</u> 204 (October):118-19.
            Includes a notice of <u>Two Gentle Men</u> (1959.6) as the work
        of "a painstaking and accomplished biographer" who has
        written "an interesting and thoroughly readable narrative."

14   Van DOREN, MARK. "A Pair of Poets Whose Lives and Lyrics
        Shine Across the Centuries." <u>New York Herald Tribune Book</u>
        <u>Review</u>, 13 September, p. 3.
            An appreciative account of Chute's <u>Two Gentle Men</u>
        (1959.6), which is a book about two poets in a century
        renowned for "the art of intelligent song."

<u>1960</u>

1   ANON. "Two Quiet Lives." <u>Times Literary Supplement</u> (London),
        4 March, p. 146.
            Review of Chute's <u>Two Gentle Men</u> (1959.6). Argues
        against her thesis that Herbert was a pacifist; but is less
        critical of her comments on Herrick, because "the poetry
        explains itself better than any biography can explain it."

2   CANDELARIA, FREDERICK H. "Ovid and the Indifferent Lovers."
        <u>Renaissance News</u> 13 (Winter):294-97.
            Suggests that Ovid's <u>Amores</u>, II.iv, may have been the
        source of Marlowe's, Donne's, Suckling's, and Herrick's use
        of the stance of the indifferent lover.

3   CRUM, MARGARET. "An Unpublished Fragment of Verse by
        Herrick." <u>Review of English Studies</u> 11, no. 42:186-89.
            Notes a recent acquisition by the Bodleian Library,
        Bodl. MS. Engl. Poet. c. 50, which includes some 250 poems
        copied in the first half of the seventeenth century. Re-
        grets that the manuscript was not available to Martin for
        his edition of Herrick's poems (1956.1), for it contains
        "seven poems, and ten lines of an eighth, which were not
        printed in <u>Hesperides</u>, 1648: of these poems, two were not
        in the Harvard manuscript [MSS. Harvard Eng. 626F], which
        was the richest source of unprinted poems available for the
        edition; and the Harvard copyist failed to read two words
        in the third poem, leaving blanks where [this] manuscript
        gives good readings." Prints "Musicke" ("To Musick. A
        Song" in <u>Hesperides</u>), which has sixteen lines in this manu-
        script, eight lines in Bodl. MS. Don. c. 57 and Christ
        Church MS. Mus. 87, and six lines in the 1648 <u>Hesperides</u>.
        Also provides eight major variants from the other Herrick

poems. (The 1963 reprint of Martin's edition [1956.1] includes the eight "new" lines from "Musicke" in the Addenda, p. 586.)

4   LEFKOWITZ, MURRAY. <u>William Lawes</u>. London: Routledge & Kegan Paul, 360 pp. passim.
    Brief mentions of Herrick include the facts that he was living at the "Little Almonry" at the same time Lawes was there, that Herrick wrote a commendatory poem upon Lawes's death, that Lawes is "chiefly remembered for his delightful setting of Robert Herrick's 'Gather Ye Rosebuds While Ye May'" ("To the Virgins, to make much of Time"), and that John Playford mistakenly ascribes Lawes's setting of Herrick's "On the Lillyes" ("How Lillies came white") to Nicholas Lanier. Prints a part of Lawes's popular musical setting for Herrick's "Charon and Phylomel, a Dialogue sung," which Lefkowitz sees as a particularly fine example of the dialogue form.

5   MADDISON, CAROL. <u>Apollo and the Nine: A History of the Ode</u>. Baltimore, Md.: Johns Hopkins Press; London: Routledge & Kegan Paul, pp. 305-18 and passim.
    After defining the Renaissance ode as "a song in the antique manner as distinguished from one in the medieval tradition. . . . the poem that glorified man, his experience, and his works" (Chapter 1), presents discussions of Pindar, Anacreon, and Horace (Chapter 2), the humanist ode (Chapter 3), and the ode in Italy (Chapter 4), France (Chapter 5), and England (Chapter 6; ends with Cowley). Mentions Herrick briefly in early chapters and includes a thirteen-page discussion of him in Chapter 6, where she describes him as "England's first and only Anacreontic poet." Includes most of Herrick's poems in her definition of the ode (the others are generally epigrams "in the ancient sense") and quotes a number of them to show that Herrick is "the great recorder of the country-life of Merry England." Notes influence of other classical poets, especially Horace.

6   WEDGWOOD, C.V. <u>Poetry and Politics under the Stuarts</u>. Cambridge: Cambridge University Press, pp. 75-76.
    Brief mention of Herrick, "whose lyrical art was not attuned to war"; his welcome "To the King, Upon his comming with his Army into the West" in the summer of 1644 is more enthusiastic than were the feelings of most of his countrymen in the west of England.

1960

7   WHITE, HELEN C. "Double Vocations." <u>Kenyon Review</u> 22
     (Winter):160-62.
          Finds Chute's <u>Two Gentle Men</u> (1959.6) a "delightful
     book for the general reader." Praises her work on the
     seventeenth-century milieu in which Herbert and Herrick
     lived and worked.

8   WRIGHT, GEORGE T. <u>The Poet in the Poem: The Personae of
     Eliot, Yeats, and Pound</u>. Berkeley and Los Angeles:
     University of California Press, pp. 30-31. Reprint. 1962.
          Quotes lines 1 through 6 of "The Argument of his Book"
     as an example of his point that lyric poets from the
     troubadours to the Romantics present themselves as singers,
     rather than as individuals with particular qualities. The
     singer is "man in his role of celebrant of human reality";
     by naming the <u>meanings</u> of objects, the singer bestows im-
     mortality upon them.

<u>1961</u>

1   <u>Robert Herrick: Poems from "Hesperides" and "Noble Numbers."</u>
     Selected and Introduced by John Hayward. The Penguin Poets.
     Baltimore, Md., and Harmondsworth, England: Penguin Books,
     220 pp.
          Introduction presents the <u>Hesperides</u> poems as of four
     kinds--amatory, pastoral, occasional, and epigrammatic--
     arranged in apparently random order. A brief survey of
     Herrick's reputation is followed by an evaluation of his
     work as lacking in originality and imagination but as in-
     formed by a "lively and inventive fancy" complemented by
     "a marvellously delicate ear" and great metrical skill.
     Believes that Herrick "wrote too much"--thus a selection
     of his poems will provide the most pleasure.

2   ANON. "Peeping Tom." <u>Times Literary Supplement</u> (London),
     15 December, p. 898.
          Agrees with Swinburne that Herrick's 1648 volume com-
     bines "sweetmeats" and "emetics" (1891.1); is pleased to
     see that in his <u>Robert Herrick</u> (1961.1) Hayward has omitted
     Herrick's grossest poems, but finds the erotic poems to be
     written by a man who is "at times the Peeping Tom of En-
     glish poetry." Does not believe there are enough excellent
     poems from Herrick's hand to fill a "smallish Penguin."

3   HOLLANDER, JOHN. The Untuning of the Sky: Ideas of Music in
     English Poetry, 1500-1700. Princeton: Princeton Univer-
     sity Press, pp. 335-38, 341, 370. Reprint. New York.
     W.W. Norton, 1970.
        Two brief allusions to Herrick and a three-page comment
     on his "rather bald" use of musical allusions in Hesperides.
     Quotes six of the poems in which "Herrick's use of all the
     musical paraphernalia, the instruments, the Orphean myths,
     and the celestial singing itself, is perhaps more than
     anything else directed toward augmenting the repertory of
     integral objects and events programmatically listed in 'The
     Argument of his Book.'"

4   OSGOOD, CHARLES G. "Epithalamion and Prothalamion: 'and
     theyr eccho ring.'" Modern Language Notes 76 (March):
     205-8.
        Includes "An Epithalamie to Sir Thomas Southwell and his
     Ladie" and "A Nuptiall Song, or Epithalamie, on Sir
     Clipseby Crew and his Lady" in a list of eighteen
     seventeenth-century descendants of Spenser's two wedding
     poems.

5   PACE, GEORGE B. "The Two Domains: Meter and Rhythm."
     Publications of the Modern Language Association of America
     76 (September):413-19.
        Argues that the value of traditional metrics is limited;
     subtle metrical analysis demands a knowledge of linguistics,
     that is, an "acceptable theory of language." Presents
     three scansions of the line "Whenas in silks my Julia goes"
     from "Upon Julia's Clothes" to show how linguistic metrics
     can describe and suggest various readings of a poem and
     illustrates rhythm analysis with "The Amber Bead."

6   PECKHAM, MORSE, and CHATMAN, SEYMOUR. Word, Meaning, Poem.
     New York: Thomas Y. Crowell, pp. 23-36, 403-8.
        "His fare-well to Sack" is the first of twenty-five
     poems for which Peckham and Chatman provide syntactic and
     lexical glosses (the syntactic gloss is a diagram) and then
     an interpretational hypothesis (a line-by-line explica-
     tion). "His fare-well" is presented as "a dramatization of
     how a disagreeable necessity is made acceptable by humor
     and good nature." In the second half of the book are two
     more Herrick poems for students to examine independently.

1961

7   PRESS, JOHN. <u>Herrick</u>. Writers and Their Work, no. 132.
      London and New York: Longmans, Green, & Co., 40 pp. Rev.
      ed. 1971.
         Surveys Herrick's life and works "to show the variety,
      subtlety and accomplishments of his finest poems and to
      suggest that he deserves more respect than is commonly
      accorded him nowadays." Allows that much of Herrick's
      verse is coarse, licentious, or trivial, but praises its
      "cunning artistry and musical delight." Emphasizes
      Herrick's borrowings and adaptations from the classics,
      from <u>The Anatomy of Melancholy</u>, and from Jonson's works.
      Accounts for the "inferiority" of <u>Noble Numbers</u> by main-
      taining that Herrick's "intellectual and emotional re-
      sources are too meagre" for divine poetry. Includes a
      select bibliography of twenty-one items.

8   SPITZER, LEO. "Herrick's 'Delight in Disorder.'" <u>Modern
      Language Notes</u> 76 (March):209-14.
         Refutes Bateson (1934.2) and Brooks and Warren (1938.1)
      by showing that the poem's subject--pleasure in disorderly
      dress--is related to a recurring topos in seventeenth- and
      eighteenth-century art theory (what Pope called "brave
      disorder"), by arguing that one need not associate dis-
      orderly dress with a disorderly character, and by noting
      the various qualifiers signaling that the poet is praising
      only some disorder. Criticizes readers who fail to notice
      that the poem's rhyme scheme and syntax reflect the theme
      of the opposition between wildness and civility. Finds the
      topos of "sweet neglect" in Herrick's immediate source (the
      "Song" in Jonson's <u>Epicoene</u>), but observes that Herrick
      modifies that topos by praising "the art that hides behind
      apparent neglectfulness." "Delight in Disorder," then,
      neither presents an "ambiguous" picture nor works by
      "indirection."
         Reprinted in Leo Spitzer, <u>Essays on English and American
      Literature</u>, ed. Anna Hatcher (Princeton: Princeton
      University Press, 1962), pp. 132-38; reprinted 1968.

<u>1962</u>

1   BRIGGS, K.M. <u>Pale Hecate's Team: An Examination of the Be-
      liefs on Witchcraft and Magic among Shakespeare's Contempo-
      raries and His Immediate Successors</u>. London: Routledge &
      Kegan Paul, 291 pp.
         Cites Herrick poems treating witches and topics such as
      the Peter Penny, country sports, and spells to allay love
      and to protect sleep.

1962

2   BUSH, DOUGLAS. English Literature in the Earlier Seventeenth
    Century, 1600-1660. Rev. ed. Oxford History of English
    Literature. New York and Oxford: Oxford University Press,
    pp. 115-19 and passim.
        Revision of 1945.1. Still sees Herrick as "the most
    versatile and, in a limited sense, the most classical" of
    Jonson's successors and continues to stress Herrick's
    "Elizabethan" artistry. Now adds the observation that
    Herrick's classicism is more than "neo-pagan hedonism;
    Herrick's attitude is refined and deepened by his instinct
    for ceremonial, in life and art." Develops his earlier,
    tentative "Nor is Herrick always lacking in seriousness"
    into a statement of the nature of that seriousness: "he
    has the unified vision that was the common inheritance of
    his age, the vision that embraces God and the book of
    creatures in a divine whole." Bibliography (pp. 595-96)
    includes studies like Whitaker (1955.10) and Musgrove
    (1950.4), in which these new apprehensions were first
    articulated.

3   HARRIS, WILLIAM O. "Herrick's 'Upon Julia's Clothes.'"
    Explicator 21 (December): Item 29.
        Explicates the poem to show that stanza 1 treats the
    sound of Julia's clothes, stanza 2, the poet's sight of
    Julia "in (and within) silks."

4   HELMBOLD, WILLIAM C., trans. and ed. Plutarch's Moralia.
    Vol. 6. Loeb Classical Library. Cambridge, Mass.:
    Harvard University Press; London: William Heinemann,
    p. 157n.
        Cites Herrick's "To keep a true Lent" as a parallel to
    Plutarch's interpretation of Empedocles' Frag. 144.

5   HOWARTH, R.G. "Two Poems by Herrick?" Notes and Queries 9
    (October):394.
        Revises his own earlier note (1955.4) with the observa-
    tion that four of the six lines illustrating "Blush" in
    Poole's English Parnassus are by Sidney; the remaining two
    lines are yet to be identified.
        Discussion continued: 1978.32.

6   RØSTVIG, MAREN-SOFIE. The Happy Man: Studies in the Meta-
    morphoses of a Classical Ideal. Vol. 1, 1600-1700. Rev.
    ed. Oslo Studies in English, no. 2. Oslo: Norwegian
    University Press, pp. 73, 113f., 117, 132.
        Revision of 1954.3. Presents Herrick as an exception to
    the rule that the "Stoic austerity of the classical
    sources" of the poetry of retirement "has remained

1962

unimpaired" in the Renaissance: in Herrick's poetry one
finds "the Epicurean sensuousness often expressed by Horace
and Tibullus." Eschewing "philosophical arguments about
happiness," Herrick is content "to describe delightful
scenes of rustic merriment" in poems like "The Country
life, to the honoured Master Endimion Porter," "A Country
life: To his Brother, Master Thomas Herrick," and "The
Hock-cart, or Harvest Home."

7   STARKMAN, MIRIAM K. "Noble Numbers and the Poetry of Devo-
     tion." In Reason and the Imagination: Studies in the
     History of Ideas, 1600-1800. Edited by J.A. Mazzeo. New
     York: Columbia University Press; London: Routledge &
     Kegan Paul, pp. 1-27.
        Works toward a definition of "poetry of devotion" by
     categorizing the poems in Noble Numbers, which she finds
     to be "a large, metrical prayer book [containing] creeds
     and graces, confessions and thanksgivings, litanies and
     dirges, nativity and circumcision songs, plus a large body
     of near-catechetical wisdom." Considers most of Herrick's
     poems to be "considerably different in tone from what we
     have taken to be characteristic of the time": they are
     didactic in tone, they present traditional statements as
     "couplet wisdom," even the "affective prayers" use conven-
     tional images, and their distinctive voice is the adult
     Christian in the role of a childlike ingenu. Compares the
     last nine poems in the volume to poems by Herbert on simi-
     lar subjects to show how those two seventeenth-century
     poets "[move] on a common ground of received tradition and
     a common matter" even while they reveal "the broad range
     and history of the devotional kind." Contrasts Herrick
     with Donne, Herbert, Crashaw, and Vaughan, for Herrick's
     special trait is "the way in which worship is domesticated
     and reenacted in personal and humanistic terms, acclimated
     to the local situation and scene." Concludes that terms
     like "religious metaphysical" are too limited to describe
     seventeenth-century devotional poetry, because they exclude
     Herrick--and even some poems by Donne and Herbert. Less
     spectacular than Donne or Herbert, Herrick is a poet worthy
     of attention.

1963

1   The Complete Poetry of Robert Herrick. Edited by J. Max
     Patrick. The Anchor Seventeenth-Century Series. Garden
     City, N.Y.: Doubleday & Co., xvii + 579 pp. Reprinted in
     the Stuart Editions, New York: New York University Press,

1963, and, with a new foreword and the "correction of a few
minor details," New York: W.W. Norton & Co., 1968.
   Introduction (pp. vii-viii) stresses Herrick's "extraor-
dinarily wide" range of poetic kinds and the "multiple
sensibility" the reader must bring to his work. "Note on
Publication and Reputation" (pp. xi-xiii) suggests that
Herrick's poetry was probably well-received in the seventeenth century and traces his increasing fame from 1796 to
the present day when his "place as one of the greatest
English lyric poets is now secure." Provides a brief
selected bibliography (pp. xv-xvi) and a biographical out-
line (p. xvii). Prints the 1648 volume (primarily after
two copies in the New York Public Library Berg Collection,
the copy in the Rosenbach Foundation Library, and the copy
in the Harvard Library) and a supplement of poems not in
the 1648 volume. Prints variants not available to Martin
(1956.1) and directs the reader to Martin for variants not
printed here. Numbers poems from Hesperides and Noble
Numbers separately (MacLeod's Concordance, 1936.8, may
thus be used with this text). Annotations and textual
notes at the end of each poem are directed toward an
audience less well-versed in biblical and classical studies
than Martin's. Index of titles and first lines.

2   ANON. "Critical Apparatus." Times Literary Supplement
    (London), 30 August, p. 658.
       Brief notice of five Stuart Editions of Renaissance
    writers, including Patrick's edition of Herrick (1963.1).
    Observes that Herrick is currently in vogue.

3   ARMSTRONG, RAY L. Review of Patrick's edition of The Complete
    Poetry. Seventeenth-Century News 21 (Spring and Summer):
    13-14.
       Favorable notice of Patrick's work (1963.1), particu-
    larly of his providing notes appropriate to modern readers.

4   SONG, KYUNG-JOON. "Robert Herrick as a Love-Poet." The
    English Language and Literature (Korea) 14:40-55.
       Presents Herrick's love poems as graceful, sophisticated
    songs.

5   WEEKS, LEWIS E., Jr. "Julia Unveiled: A Note on Herrick's
    'Upon Julia's Clothes.'" CEA Critic 25 (June):8.
       Notes lack of agreement about the poem and questions
    whether its puzzling ambiguity is intentional.

1964

1   BROADBENT, J.B. <u>Poetic Love</u>. London: Chatto & Windus,
    pp. 245-48 and passim. Reprint. New York: Barnes &
    Noble, 1965.
       Surveys English love poetry from the twelfth century to
    the eighteenth. Includes Herrick in Chapter 14, "The
    Metaphysical Decadence": whereas "Cowley is the first
    specialist in decadent Metaphysical modes," Herrick is a
    "specialist in decadent Spenserianism." Emphasizes
    Herrick's focus on sexuality, yet prefers him to Suckling
    and Lovelace "because his poems derive from a recognizable,
    if nasty, personality."

2   KENNER, HUGH. Introduction to <u>Seventeenth Century Poetry:</u>
    <u>The Schools of Donne and Jonson</u>. New York: Holt, Rinehart
    & Winston, pp. xi-xxxii.
       Brief reference to Herrick says his "poetry was no more
    than impassioned play" (p. xxxii). Prints forty-three
    pages of his poems.

3   LOUGY, ROBERT. "Herrick's 'The Hock-Cart, or Harvest Home,'
    51-55." <u>Explicator</u> 23 (October): Item 13.
       Contrasts the last five lines with the first fifty lines
    of the poem to show that "Herrick's sensibility is offended
    by the apparent motives behind the harvest feast." The
    poem ends with a criticism of the selfishness of the man to
    whom it is dedicated.

4   RICHMOND, H.M. <u>The School of Love: The Evolution of the</u>
    <u>Stuart Love Lyric</u>. Princeton: Princeton University Press,
    338 pp.
       Developed from 1957.5. In the course of his examination
    of distinctions between Stuart love lyrics and their clas-
    sical, medieval, and Continental sources, treats "To the
    Virgins, to make much of Time" with Ausonius' "De Rosis
    Nascentibus" and Ronsard's "Mignonne, allons voir si la
    rose" to show that when Renaissance "neo-pagan" poets adapt
    classical themes, they include a "moral tension and
    seriousness" not in their "pagan" prototypes (pp. 59-65).
    Prints "Ile dote noe more" ("A Sonnet"), one of the poems
    attributed to Herrick by Martin (1956.1) but not by
    Patrick (1963.1), as an instance of the "callow self-
    confidence" possible early in the seventeenth century, but
    not after the Reformation (p. 92). A brief explication of
    "Upon her weeping" shows the Stuart poets' "heightened
    sense of how to make a work reverberate in climactic isola-
    tion" (p. 124). Other passing references to Herrick.

5   SANDERS, CHARLES. "Herrick's 'The Carkanet.'" Explicator 23
     (November): Item 24.
         Suggests that the double meaning of the title (a
     carkanet is a necklace and a manacle) is developed in the
     implicit comparisons "of the gift-bearing lover as captor
     or jailer, [and] the ornament-gift (necklace, bracelet,
     etc.) as manacle" throughout the poem.

6   SIMMONS, J.L. "Marvell's 'The Picture of Little T.C. in a
     Prospect of Flowers.'" Explicator 22 (April): Item 62.
         Explication of Marvell's poem includes the theory that
     the warning in the final stanza, "Gather the Flow'rs, but
     spare the Buds," is a "conscious reversal of Herrick's
     warning in his famous carpe diem poem, 'Gather ye rosebuds
     while ye may'" ("To the Virgins, to make much of Time").
     If so, Marvell's line expresses the fear that little T.C.
     "might lose the innocence and purity she now manifests
     through following Herrick's worldly advice."

7   WENTERSDORF, KARL P. "Herrick's Floral Imagery." Studia
     Neophilologica 36:69-81.
         Cites poems from Hesperides to show that Herrick uses
     flower images derived from the Spenserian tradition, from
     personal observation, and from classical mythology as sym-
     bols both of the joys of life, love, and beauty and of the
     sorrows of death and illness. Stresses Herrick's use of
     pagan mythology to point to constant renewal within the
     natural world and argues that Herrick "was in fact unable
     to reconcile the Christian views which he represented
     officially with the paganism to which he felt drawn per-
     sonally."

<u>1965</u>

1   The Poems of Robert Herrick. Edited by L.C. Martin. Oxford
     Standard Authors. London, New York, and Toronto: Oxford
     University Press, ix + 478 pp.
         Brief introduction (pp. v-ix). Pp. 1-419 print same
     poems as in 1956.1; pp. 419-47 print poems not included in
     editions prior to 1956--but omit the eighteen "R.H." poems
     from the Rosenbach manuscript, for "though they carry
     Herrick's initials they do not show many of his most dis-
     tinctive habits of thought or phrasing" (p. viii).
     A "Select Glossary of Uncommon Words and Meanings" is
     followed by indices of titles and first lines.

1965

2   [CROFT, P.J.] "Robert Herrick's Poetical Commonplace Book
        (Lot 146)." Bibliotheca Phillippica: Catalogue of the
        Celebrated Collection of Manuscripts Formed by Sir Thomas
        Phillipps, Bt. (1792-1872). London: Sotheby Sale Cata-
        logue, 28-29 June, pp. 66 and 123-35.
            Describes Phillipps MS 12341 (which was subsequently
        purchased by the University of Texas) as "a highly impor-
        tant manuscript commonplace book of verse and prose con-
        taining twelve pages of verse in Herrick's hand and correc-
        tions by him on numerous pages throughout" (p. 66). An
        appendix (pp. 123-35) presents the contents of the manu-
        script and describes the hand which Croft identifies as
        Herrick's as a less formal version of the hand in the
        fifteen extant letters from Herrick to his uncle Sir
        William Herrick: "Herrick's hand however is a very dis-
        tinctive one, and its identification is never in doubt."
        On the basis of the fact that this hand is the only one re-
        curring throughout the volume, "making corrections on many
        pages," concludes that "the book belonged to Herrick, and
        was compiled under his supervision." Sees the volume as
        important because of its being "the only manuscript poeti-
        cal miscellany which can be shown to have belonged to a
        major poet of the period," because it offers superior
        readings of a number of the poems within it, and because
        it allows us to attribute new poems to Herrick. Noting
        that the "conclusion of one of [the letters in the manu-
        script] is in Herrick's hand," speculates that Herrick
        served as secretary to John Williams (bishop of Lincoln
        in 1621 and lord keeper after that date) between his
        Cambridge graduation in 1620 and his ordination in 1623.
            Responses: 1972.6; 1973.1.

3   D'AVANZO, MARIO L. "Herrick's 'The Mad Maid's Song.'"
        American Notes and Queries 4 (December):55.
            Shows that Herrick reveals the maid's madness in
        stanzas 3 and 4 by having her allude to the phrase "to
        have a bee in one's bonnet"; as early as 1513, the phrase
        was used to mean "exaggerated fancy, craze [sic] and
        foolish or uneasy hope or aspiration for something."

4   DEMING, ROBERT HOWARD. "The Classical Ceremonial in the
        Poetry of Robert Herrick." Ph.D. dissertation, University
        of Wisconsin, 246 pp.
            Locates sources of Herrick's ceremonial poetry in
        Renaissance dictionaries of antiquity and in the rituals
        of the Anglican and Roman Catholic churches of his period.
        Argues that attributes of Herrick's verse that have been
        called "pagan" are, from Herrick's Anglican perspective,

classical predecessors of Christian rituals. Notes that
Herrick's ceremonial mode, which insists on principles of
order, is both a vehicle for proposing and evaluating ideas
about proper social and moral orders and an "artistic surface . . . which conceals and at the same time reveals
these underlying ideas and experiences."
    See also summary in DA 26:5430-31. For articles derived
from this dissertation, see 1967.4; 1968.3; 1969.1; for a
book derived from the dissertation, see 1974.3.

5   HAMILTON, G. ROSTREVOR. English Verse Epigram. Writers and
    Their Work, no. 188. London: Longmans, Green & Co. for
    the British Council and the National Book League, 44 pp.
        Includes three pages (10-12) on Herrick in his survey
    of the epigram in England. Finds Herrick's satirical epi-
    grams "in the worst tradition of Martial"; others are
    "slight and, except for a good clear English, quite ordi-
    nary." Yet admires Herrick's "tiptoe lightness. . . . In
    his own idiom he cannot be surpassed."

6   HÖLTGEN, KARL JOSEF. "Herrick, the Wheeler Family, and
    Quarles." Review of English Studies 16, no. 64:399-405.
        Identifies Herrick's "Amarillis" as Elizabeth Wheeler,
    born in 1589, daughter of Edmund Wheeler, a London gold-
    smith. Suggests that her marriage in 1613 and Herrick's
    leaving London for Cambridge in the same year may account
    for the lovers' separation in two of the Amarillis poems
    and may help to date them. Proposes that the Penelope
    Wheeler whom Herrick praises in two of his poems ("To his
    kinswoman, Mistresse Penelope Wheeler" and "Another Upon
    Her") is the wife of Ambrose Wheeler, a relative of the
    Wheelers mentioned above. Notes that Elizabeth Wheeler's
    brother John was eulogized by Francis Quarles and specu-
    lates that Herrick and Quarles may have known one another.
    Continuation: 1966.2.

7   HUTTAR, CHARLES A. "Herrick's 'The Carkanet.'" Explicator 24
    (December): Item 35.
        Applauds Sanders's analysis (1964.5) and goes on to
    note that the lover-captor is himself captive, "wrapt"
    (line 5); he is "hoist, perhaps, by his own necklace."
    Sees the same irony in "The Braclet to Julia."

1965

8   KIMBROUGH, JOE ARTHUR. "A Critical Study of Robert Herrick."
     Ph.D. dissertation, University of Illinois, 228 pp.
         Rejects recent attempts to make Herrick "intellectually
     respectable," and admires Herrick's versatility, simplicity,
     and delicacy. Sees his interest in concrete, pretty things
     as a defining characteristic, and criticizes the bad taste
     evident in his cruder epigrams. Finds Herrick "the most
     Elizabethan of the Cavalier lyrists."
         See also summary in DA 26:1023-24A.

9   MELLERS, WILFRID. Harmonious Meeting: A Study of the Rela-
     tionship between English Music, Poetry and Theatre, c. 1600-
     1900. London: Dennis Dobson, pp. 110-12.
         Explores the correspondences between Henry Lawes's
     musical settings for "The Primrose" and "Amidst the
     mirtles" ("Mistresse Elizabeth Wheeler") and the poems
     themselves. The music for the former poem is an appro-
     priate combination of simplicity and sophistication; the
     rhythmic structure for the latter has a "sophisticated
     lilt" which "gives to the words a quality at once wistful
     and witty."

10   REA, J. "Persephone in 'Corinna's Going A-Maying.'" College
     English 26 (April):544-46.
         Identifies Corinna as Cora, the Greek equivalent of
     Persephone, the virgin daughter of Demeter, goddess of the
     earth's fertility; in awakening Corinna, Herrick awakens
     springtime. Speculates that Herrick took Corinna's name
     from Ovid's Art of Love.

11   REED, MARK L. "Herrick among the Maypoles: Dean Prior and
     the Hesperides." Studies in English Literature, 1500-1900
     5 (Winter):133-50.
         Re-examines the assumption that Herrick's celebrations
     of country life were inspired by his delight in Devonshire
     and concludes that Herrick's lyrics "grow from and sing of
     England." Observes that seldom, if ever, does Herrick re-
     fer to folk customs unique to Devonshire. Even the cele-
     brations of May Day which Herrick commemorates in
     "Corinna's going a Maying" and in "The May-pole" were
     enjoyed by citizens and courtiers in London; harvest fes-
     tivals like the one described in "The Hock-cart, or Harvest
     home" could be found in nearby Windsor. Herrick's two
     epithalamia, both written some time before his removal to
     Dean Prior, include clear evidence of the poet's knowledge
     and appreciation of English folk customs; and many of the
     lyrics that seem to have been written early in Herrick's
     career contain nature images that could have been derived

from an enjoyment of the fields within walking distance of
the city or even in London gardens. Argues that the significant fact about Herrick's artistic use of rural customs
and English natural scenes is that his poetry fully expresses a facet of English Renaissance poetry introduced
by Spenser: "the growing awareness in the English artistic
sensibility of natural scenery and folk and rural life
other than that of Arcadia or classical verse." Herrick,
then, is a predecessor of Wordsworth.

12   ROLLIN, ROGER. "Herrick's Church Threatened--An Appeal."
      Seventeenth-Century News 23 (Spring-Summer):56-57.
          Account of a recent visit to Dean Prior, where Rollin
      learned (1) that there is a need for repairs to preserve
      the church and (2) that it is in danger of becoming "re-
      dundant" because there are too few parishioners. Requests
      help with a "Herrick Memorial Fund."

13   ROSS, RICHARD J. "Herrick's Julia in Silks." Essays in
      Criticism 15 (January):171-80.
          Examines the theme of art versus nature in Herrick's
      lyrics and then explicates "Upon Julia's Clothes" to show
      that stanza 1 treats "what silks do for Julia" and stanza 2,
      "what Julia does for silks." Argues that in Herrick's
      poetry one often finds "the vibrant culmination of natural
      and artful brought into complete harmony."
      Response: 1967.5.

14   TYNER, RAYMOND. "Herrick's 'Crisped Yew.'" Notes and Queries
      12 (October):380-81.
          Refers to John Parkinson's Paradisi in Sole Paradisus
      Terrestris (1629) and his Theatrum Botanicum (1640) to
      verify his suggestion that the word crisped in "Ceremonies
      for Candlemasse Eve" means "lineal in shape; clean cut and
      sharp in appearance."

15   _____. "Herrick's 'To M. Denham, on his Prospective Poem,'
      3." Explicator 23 (May): Item 72.
          Expands Patrick's annotation of "Pean" (1963.1, p. 310)
      as having a heraldic meaning referring to a black ground
      with spots of yellow to suggest that Herrick "used 'Pean-
      Gardens' as a synecdoche for the general practice of such
      heraldic gardening" as Gervase Markham describes in The
      English Husbandman of 1613. The reference cannot be spe-
      cific because the Denham family's fur was ermine, which
      would have been represented as a white ground with spots of
      black.

16   WOODWARD, DANIEL H. "Herrick's Oberon Poems." Journal of
      English and Germanic Philology 64 (April):270-84.
           Reads "The Temple" (with its introductory poem "The
      Fairie Temple"), "Oberons Feast," and "Oberons Palace" as
      a unified group creating an epithalamion with its tradi-
      tional three parts: the church service, the celebratory
      feast, and the good-nights before the bedding of the newly
      married couple. Shows how Herrick's sacred parody con-
      tributes to his presentation of serious themes that appear
      elsewhere in Hesperides and concludes that Herrick's
      "skillfully directed comedy" presents an "all-embracing
      reverence for life and love as found in nature."

                            1966

1   CLARK, PAUL O. "Herrick's 'The Hock-Cart, or Harvest Home,'
      51-55." Explicator 24 (April): Item 70.
           Disagrees with Lougy's analysis (1964.3) and argues that
      the final lines of the poem include "a hardy acceptance of
      the conditions of life and [rescue] the poem from an anach-
      ronistic proletarianism."

2   HÖLTGEN, KARL JOSEF. "Herrick and Mrs. Wheeler." Times
      Literary Supplement (London), 17 March, p. 228.
           Provides additional information to confirm his earlier
      identification (1965.6) of the Penelope Wheeler whom
      Herrick praises in "To his Kinswoman, Mistresse Penelope
      Wheeler" and "Another upon her" as the wife of Ambrose
      Wheeler; she was the daughter of Thomas Hanchett.

3   _____. Review of eight Stuart editions of Renaissance Liter-
      ature. Anglia: Zeitschrift für englische Philologie 84:
      232-33.
           Paragraph on Patrick's edition of The Complete Poetry
      (1963.1) indicates that although scholars will continue to
      rely on Martin's standard edition (1956.1), all readers of
      Herrick should be grateful for Patrick's explicit annota-
      tions.

4   HUGHES, RICHARD E. "Herrick's 'Hock Cart': Companion Piece
      to 'Corinna's Going A-Maying.'" College English 27
      (February):420-22.
           Agrees with Brooks (1947.1) that "'Corinna's going a
      Maying' is a ritual poem, rooted in the spring festivals
      of antiquity," and with Rea (1965.10) that Corinna "is
      Persephone, Demeter's daughter, hand-maiden to those fer-
      tility rites celebrated in a variety of mystery religions."

Maintains that "The Hock-cart" is a companion poem to
"Corinna," for as it re-enacts the harvest ritual of
autumn, it completes the fertility cycle begun with the
springtime ritual of the other poem.

5   ROLLIN, ROGER B. "Missing 'The Hock Cart': An Explication
      Re-explicated." Seventeenth-Century News 24 (Autumn):39-40.
         Disputes Lougy's explication of "The Hock-cart" (1964.3)
      with the reminder that pastoral is a "singularly apt
      vehicle" for social criticism and the argument that from
      the beginning of the poem Herrick is aware of social and
      economic distinctions between Lord Mildmay and the laborers.
      Maintains that the laborers' "paine" (line 54) is presented
      as a part of the natural order: "Robert Herrick is not,
      alas, a democrat, not a traitor to his class, but merely an
      ordinary (if outspoken) Royalist and Anglican--and an
      extraordinary pastoral poet."

6   _____. Robert Herrick. Twayne's English Authors Series. New
      York: Twayne Publishers; London: Bailey Bros., 231 pp.
         Argues, as in 1959.12, that Herrick is a major poet
      whose 1648 volume fulfills Eliot's requirement that a book
      of short poems may be a major work if it exhibits "a unity
      of underlying pattern" (1944.1). Sees the persona of
      Herrick's volume as a pastoral artist-critic whose
      Hesperides is a "Sacred Grove" "which possesses order and
      richness through its sanctification by art" even while it
      is "alive with real men and gods, and still flourishing."
      Chapters on the themes of transiency, the good life, love,
      faith, and immortality include analyses of representative
      poems to show how the pastoral persona presents and criti-
      cizes life. Stresses the particularly Protestant cast of
      thought in Noble Numbers and the "carefully cultivated
      intellectual and emotional poise" which informs the whole
      volume. Final chapter treats Herrick's reputation, assert-
      ing that he deserves Musgrove's praise: "He was a poet of
      stature less only than the greatest . . . of his age"
      (1950.4).

7   SHUCHTER, J.D. "Herrick's 'Upon Julia's Clothes.'"
      Explicator 25 (November): Item 27.
         Observes the submerged metaphor of "wooing as fishing"
      within the poem and asks whether readers know of other
      examples "of the figure which we might call 'the angler
      taken.'"
         Response: 1967.4.

1966

8   TOBACK, PHYLLIS BROOKS. "Herrick's 'Corinna's Going a Maying'
    and the Epithalamic Tradition." Seventeenth-Century News
    24 (Spring):13.
        Notes Herrick's use of conventions associated with the
    epithalamium in "Corinna" and suggests that the poem's
    being structured as though it were an epithalamium may
    affect its meaning.

1967

1   ALLEN, D[ON] C[AMERON]. "Herrick's 'Rex Tragicus.'" In
    Studies in Honor of DeWitt T. Starnes. Edited by Thomas P.
    Harrison, Archibald A. Hill, Ernest C. Mossner, and James
    Sledd. Austin: University of Texas Press, pp. 215-25.
        Explicates "Good Friday: Rex Tragicus" as a complex
    contemplation (as opposed to a meditation, which "if it
    follows a pious event, squeezes out its moral juices").
    Refers to writers such as Piero Valeriano, Scaliger, Hugo
    St. Victor, and Plotinus as backgrounds for his suggestion
    that Herrick presents the Crucifixion in terms of a great
    tragedy of the fall of a king. Regards Herrick as a minor
    poet, however, and concludes, "But that he intended what I
    have expressed will never be known."
        Reprinted in D.C. Allen, Image and Meaning: Metaphoric
    Traditions in Renaissance Poetry, enlarged ed. (Baltimore,
    Md.: Johns Hopkins Press, 1968), pp. 138-51.

2   BRONSON, BERTRAND H. "Literature and Music." In Relations of
    Literary Study: Essays on Interdisciplinary Contributions.
    Edited by James Thorpe. New York: Modern Language Asso-
    ciation, pp. 127-50.
        Includes comments on Herrick, whom Bronson regards as a
    conscious and competent metrist. Contrasts his work with
    that of his immediate predecessors, "for he demanded more
    subservience [from the musician who set his verses] than
    [earlier lutists] chose to give." Notes his experiments
    with ballad meter and observes how often Herrick's subject
    matter is "seasonally festive and folklike in spirit."
    Believes that "for all his fastidious classicism," Herrick
    is more closely tied to "the popular singing tradition."

3   COWAN, S.A. "A Note on 'The Hock-Cart' by Robert Herrick."
    Seventeenth-Century News 25 (Winter):68-70.
        Notes that the first fifty lines of the poem are "mock-
    serious. . . . The poet [is] superior, sympathetic, and
    amused." Provides two Biblical references (Gen. 3: 17, 19
    and Gen. 8: 20-22) as background to lines 51-55 and suggests

feed (line 44) as a word for the various "fees" involved
between the rustics, the cattle, and Lord Mildmay and
paine (line 54) as a pun on pain, the French word for
"bread." Concludes that Herrick's "position in 'The Hock-
cart' is solidly Christian; his final tone is witty,
ironic, hopeful, and sober all at once."

4 DEMING, ROBERT H. "Robert Herrick's Classical Ceremony."
English Literary History 34 (September):327-48.
 Suggests that Herrick is a representative Anglican for
whom classical ceremony is a precursor of Christian ritual.
Argues that the fusion of classical and Christian details
(the former from poems and handbooks; the latter from
seventeenth-century Anglican and Roman Catholic practices)
in Herrick's ceremonial poetry illustrates Herrick's "devotion to an . . . order of values, values he felt compelled
to assert in the face of Puritan opposition." Notes that
poems like "The Fairie Temple" show Herrick's concern for
order in religious ceremony, while love poems like "To
Julia, the Flaminica Dialis, or Queen-Priest" exploit classical and Christian ceremonies in the service of a religion
of love.
 Revised and expanded in 1974.3.

5 GODSHALK, WILLIAM LEIGH. "Art and Nature: Herrick and History." Essays in Criticism 17 (January):121-24.
 Responds to Ross's assertions (1965.13) that early
Renaissance writers saw art as a perversion of nature, that
"after Donne and Bacon" nature came to be seen as "raw ex-
ternal reality," and that Herrick "reversed the terms" of
earlier Renaissance writers to present nature as a corrup-
tion of art and then attempted to harmonize art and nature.
Cites a number of sixteenth- and seventeenth-century authors
to verify Edward William Taylor's conclusion (Nature and
Art in Renaissance Literature [New York and London:
Columbia University Press, 1961]) that Renaissance writers,
whatever their preference between art and nature, tended to
search for a balance between them. Concludes that while
Ross is a sensitive reader of Herrick's poems, he has mis-
judged Herrick's place in intellectual history.

6 LEITER, LOUIS H. "Herrick's 'Upon Julia's Clothes.'"
Explicator 25 (January): Item 41.
 Observes that Shuchter's note (1966.7) agrees with
Leiter's earlier identification (1958.5) of the metaphor of
"wooing as fishing" and adds that "glittering" in the final
line completes the metaphor. Compares Herrick's poem with
Cowley's "Bathing in the River" and concludes, "More

1967

profound than Cowley, Herrick expresses a psychological
truth--the female catches the male by avoiding him."

7   ROLLIN, ROGER B. "A Thief in Herrick's Hesperides." Notes
and Queries 14 (September):343-45.
    Lists five passages Robert Chamberlain "plagiarized"
from Herrick's "A Country life: To his Brother, Master
Thomas Herrick," observes various temperamental similarities between the two poets, and concludes that the similarities reveal "how wide a gap genius can make" between
two otherwise similar minds.
    Response: 1973.6.

8   SHORT, BRIAN C. Review of Robert Herrick, by Rollin.
Seventeenth-Century News 25 (Spring):12-13.
    Finds Rollin's thesis "provocative and relevant" to in-
vestigations of the real significance of Herrick's volume
(1966.6) and praises his "sophisticated yet reasonable"
readings of individual poems. Suggests that more attention
should now be paid to Herrick's so-called trivial poems,
for his goal in the 1648 volume could have been "producing
tours de force in the handling of 'familiar poetic genres,'"
rather than fulfilling Eliot's goal of a "unity of underlying [thematic] pattern" (1944.1).

9   WINTERS, YVOR. Forms of Discovery: Critical and Historical
Essays on the Forms of the Short Poem in English. [Denver]:
Alan Swallow, pp. 114-16.
    Includes Herrick in Chapter 1, "Aspects of the Short
Poem in the English Renaissance." Contrasts his poems with
lyrics by Gautier and Herbert to show "There is no real intellectual activity anywhere in Herrick"; his "best poems--
and there are many of them--are written with extraordinary
finish, but their content is very small."

1968

1   ANON. Review of Essays, by Ishii. Seventeenth-Century News
26 (Winter):76.
    Summarizes 1968.5 as a "charming and appreciative treat-
ment" of Herrick's work.

2   BERCOVITCH, SACVAN. "Empedocles in the English Renaissance."
Studies in Philology 65 (January):67-80.
    Cites Herrick as one of a number of Renaissance authors
who used "distinctive and identifiable Empedoclean ideas."
Refers to 1962.4 for an instance of Herrick echoing
Empedocles.

3   DEMING, ROBERT H.   "The Use of the Past: Herrick and
      Hawthorne."   Journal of Popular Culture 2 (Fall):278-91.
         Contrasts Herrick's and Nathaniel Hawthorne's "recrea-
      tions of the past" in "Corinna's going a Maying" and "The
      May-Pole of Merry Mount," respectively, showing that
      whereas Hawthorne's resolution of the conflict between
      paganism and Christianity (the forces of "jollity" and
      "gloom") requires the triumph of the sober Puritan idea of
      duty over pagan irresponsibility, Herrick's imaginative
      world achieves a successful fusion of "Christian serious-
      ness" and "delight in physical nature."   Maintains that
      Herrick believes one cannot deny the passing of time or
      escape from death, yet "he can use his art--the ceremony
      of May-day as he would have Corinna experience it--to
      sanctify the old ways of living which will continue to
      remain unchanged."   Notes that seventeenth-century Puritans,
      "like Cleanth Brooks," saw May Day festivals as pagan rit-
      uals: "The urgency and expectation in the tone of the poem
      are the feelings Herrick must have had as he saw the
      Puritans encroaching on the rural festivals and ceremonies."
      Reprinted in the postscript of 1974.3.

4   GUFFEY, GEORGE ROBERT, comp.   "Robert Herrick, 1949-1965."   In
      Elizabethan Bibliographies Supplements, no. 3.   Edited by
      Charles A. Pennel.   London: Nether Press, pp. 13-18.
         Chronological list of sixty-one Herrick items to update
      Tannenbaum (1949.1).   (Numbers 029 and 058 are in fact
      about the novelist Robert Herrick.)

*5   ISHII, SHONOSUKE.   Robert Herrick Kenkyu (Essays on Robert
      Herrick with a Selection from his Poems Done into Japanese).
      Tokyo: Kenkyusha.
         Eleven essays and ten notes in Japanese; summarized in
      English.   Poems from Hesperides translated into Japanese.
      Translated into English and revised: 1974.8.

6   McGOVERN, ROBERT JOHN.   "'A Trust to Good Verses':   Robert
      Herrick's Poetics of Self."   Ph.D. dissertation, Case
      Western Reserve University, 238 pp.
         Places Herrick in the context of his seventeenth-century
      poetic milieu by arguing that Herrick aimed to outdo Jonson
      (Chapter 1); that his poetry constantly employs metaphysi-
      cal images "within a style that suggests simplicity"
      (Chapter 2); that although he is Elizabethan in his sen-
      suousness and his use of Petrarchan themes, especially the
      theme of poetic immortality, he is unlike the typical
      Elizabethan in that his images yield naturalistic effects
      (Chapter 3).   Differentiates Herrick from his contemporaries

on the basis of his pre-Wordsworthian concept of the poet
as a man whose personality is essential to his poetry.
Provides a twenty-page bibliography of editions of
Herrick's poems and of Herrick criticism.
See also summary in DAI 30:3911A.

7   MOLESWORTH, CHARLES. "'In More Decent Order Tame': Marvell,
     History, and the Country-House Poem." Ph.D. dissertation,
     State University of New York at Buffalo, 196 pp.
          Studies seventeenth-century country-house poems, espe-
     cially Marvell's "Upon Appleton House," in light of the
     theory that poems in this genre are informed by their
     poets' concept of the house as an embodiment of certain
     historical values. For an article derived from Chapter 1,
     see 1968.8. Chapter 3, "Carew and Herrick as Jonson's
     Successors," proposes that "A Panegerick to Sir Lewis
     Pemberton" combines "the hedonism of Carew and the stoicism
     of Jonson" and that Herrick "stands below Jonson but above
     Carew, both in the quality of the country-house poem and in
     his sense of history."
          See also summary in DA 29:572-73A.

8   _____. "Property and Virtue: The Genre of the Country-House
     Poem in the Seventeenth Century." Genre 1 (April):141-57.
          Claims that Hibbard's view of country-house poetry
     (1956.6) is limited by his failure to realize that the most
     significant concern of country-house poets is "the uses and
     value of history." Quotes George Puttenham's comments on
     "Historicall Poesie" and Spenser's on the "poet historical"
     to show how closely allied were Renaissance poets' inter-
     ests in history and in epideictic theory. Maintains that
     country-house poems integrate praise of the owners' virtue
     and praise of his estate as a locus amoenus in a way pos-
     sible only in a culture in which land has a social, rather
     than a monetary, value. Relates country-house poetry to
     work on social history by R.H. Tawney and Christopher Hill
     to suggest that Jonson, Carew, Herrick, and Marvell were
     reacting against the social and political upheaval that
     changed Renaissance England into a more crass society.
     These poets present images that delight and instruct: they
     delight by praising excellent estates and instruct by advo-
     cating "the lessons of the multiple and complex relation-
     ships that [they believed] existed between property and
     virtue." Principally a theoretical article, but quotes
     Jonson and Marvell at some length.

1968

9   SMITH, BARBARA HERRNSTEIN. <u>Poetic Closure: A Study of How
     Poems End</u>. Chicago and London: University of Chicago
     Press, pp. 19-20, 39, 44, 69, 108-9, 132n.
         Uses examples from Herrick in several contexts. "Upon a
     child that dyed" is one instance of a poem whose context
     determines our sense of "the probable development and con-
     clusion and thereby our sense of the appropriateness of the
     conclusion that does appear"; since this poem "imitates an
     inscription imitating an utterance," its final lines--"Give
     her strewings; but not stir / The earth, that lightly
     covers her"--seem apt. In "To Electra" (H-663), the final
     line "returns to a strict iambic pattern after the most
     deviant line in the poem"; thus the poem's meter is used
     "to strengthen closure." The final two lines of "The
     Argument of his Book" close a poem whose "paratactic
     structure" (the catalogue of subjects) would otherwise
     seek to continue, for the phrase "I write of Hell" "both
     [breaks] the rhythmic continuity of the poem and [gives]
     particular emphasis and integrity to the remainder of the
     couplet. Closure is also strengthened by the introduction
     of a new verb, <u>hope</u> . . ., by the antithesis <u>Hell</u> . . .
     <u>Heaven</u> and the alliteration that reinforces it . . ., and
     by a number of thematic elements," including the "refer-
     ences to finality" in <u>after all</u>. Briefly mentions the con-
     clusion of "To Daffadills" as a contrast to Herbert's
     "Vertue" and "To the Virgins, to make much of Time" as one
     example of a popular kind "of lyrical argument, the 'per-
     suasion to love.'"

10   WEINBERG, GAIL S. "Herrick's 'Upon Julia's Clothes."
     <u>Explicator</u> 27 (October): Item 12.
         Points out that Julia's loose-fitting clothes are the
     new style recently come to the English court from the
     Continent; the poet's response to their effect is "at
     least partly a response to a specific new phenomenon . . .
     [which] has helped to heighten his awareness and intensify
     his response."

11   WHITEHEAD, J.G.O. "The Tudor Rose." <u>Coat of Arms</u> (London)
     10 (July):110-15.
         Believes that Herrick's reference to his mistress's
     breasts as "strawberries and cream" in several of his
     poems is an allusion to the Tudor rose, which combined the
     red and white roses of the Yorkists and the Lancastrians
     and heralded a time of peace: whether Herrick's mistress
     is real or imagined, her breasts "were the Tudor rose with
     its ideals personified; and that rose stood for . . . a
     return of the Golden Age" lost by the Stuarts.

1968

12   WILLIAMS, RAYMOND. "Pastoral and Counter-Pastoral."
       Critical Quarterly 10 (Autumn):277-90.
          Closes with a criticism of the way of thinking that
       approves the world view of Jonson's Penshurst, Carew's
       Saxham, and Herrick's "The Hock-cart"; finds Herrick's
       picture of workers honoring Lord Mildmay to be "crude in
       feeling, this early and jollying kind of man-management,
       which uses the metaphors of rain and spring to ratify the
       drink as a way of getting more labour (and more pain)."
       Reprinted as Chapter 3 of 1973.14.

1969

1   DEMING, ROBERT H. "Herrick's Funereal Poems." Studies in
      English Literature, 1500-1900 9 (Winter):153-67.
          Uses some twelve funeral poems, including "The Funerall
      Rites of the Rose" which Leavis criticizes in 1935.3, to
      demonstrate that Herrick's ceremonial poems are funeral
      rites intended to sanctify the dead. Argues that Herrick
      uses complementary Roman, Roman Catholic, and Anglican
      ceremonial details to construct poems that are "due and
      proper performance of sacred ceremonies." These ceremonial
      poems serve as mnemonic devices in that each time the poem
      is reread, the person or thing it memorializes is remem-
      bered and the ceremony itself is re-enacted. Thus the
      poetic "rites of sanctification" unite "the ceremonial of
      the past and the ceremonial of the present" and "link the
      mortal world of the poems to the immortal world of remem-
      brance and art."
          Reprinted as part of Chapter 3 of 1974.3.

2   DeNEEF, ARTHUR L. "The Ceremonial Mode of Poetic Expression
      in Robert Herrick's Hesperides." Ph.D. dissertation,
      Pennsylvania State University, 338 pp.
          Presents death and mutability as the major theme of
      Hesperides and argues that "most of Herrick's verse is, to
      lesser and greater degrees, an attempt to go beyond what is
      transient, mutable, and dying." Sees Herrick's use of the
      "ceremonial mode" as a successful method of uniting poet
      and reader in artistic events which clarify the signifi-
      cance of moments in human experience.
          See also summary in DAI 30:4981-82A. For articles de-
      rived from this dissertation, see 1970.1-2; 1971.3-4. For
      a book derived from the dissertation, see 1974.4.

3 HEATH-STUBBS, JOHN. The Ode. London: Oxford University
   Press, pp. 33-35.
      Quotes the odes to Sir Clipsebie Crew and to Ben Jonson
   (H-544 and H-911) as examples of Herrick's use of the
   Horatian ode as remolded by Jonson to create "a miniature
   in which the necessary genuflexion to the Horatian altar
   does not destroy the lightness of tone."

*4 ISHII, MASANOSUKE. "Herrick no 'Good Friday'" [Herrick's
   "Good Friday"]. Eigo Seinen [The rising generation]
   (Tokyo) 115:411-13.
      Cited in 1970 MLA International Bibliography. Vol. 1.
   New York: Modern Language Association, 1972, item 2965.

5 ROLLIN, ROGER B. "The Decorum of Criticism and Two Poems by
   Herrick." CEA Critic 31 (January):4-7.
      Begins by arguing that the literary critic is responsi-
   ble for treating poems with respect: "decorum in criticism" includes care that one's critical hypotheses take
   intrinsic and extrinsic "facts" into account, that one
   distinguish between facts and opinions, that facts dictate
   opinions--not vice versa, and that one "be completely aware
   of the limitations of his own critical approach." Maintains that Lougy (1964.3), Clark (1966.1), Rea (1965.10),
   and Hughes (1966.4) have each violated one or more of those
   dicta in his or her essay on "The Hock-cart" and/or
   "Corinna's going a Maying." In fact, the poems are not
   companion pieces; "Corinna" is a love poem, and "The Hock-
   cart" is about rural life--neither is about an anthropo-
   logical phenomenon.

6 WILLETTS, PAMELA J. The Henry Lawes Manuscript. Aberdeen:
   University Press for the Trustees of the British Museum,
   92 pp.; 22 plates.
      Describes B.M. Add. MS 53723, which contains 325 songs
   by Lawes in his own hand. Praises his settings of song-
   texts by Carew, which she believes to have been much more
   difficult than settings for Herrick, whose "form is still
   that of the Elizabethan lyric" (p. 16). Focuses on Herrick
   on pp. 23-25. Speculates that Lawes and Herrick knew one
   another. Calls attention to the fourteen Herrick songs in
   the manuscript, calling them "early versions of the
   poems. . . . [which] cannot be dismissed as casual
   variants." Prints two completely different versions of
   "Sweet Amarillis" ("Upon Mistresse Elizabeth Wheeler, under
   the name of Amarillis") from the manuscript and Herrick's
   1648 volume and quotes four lines from the two versions of

"The admonition" to show that "the Lawes version is a transitional stage" between a version in a manuscript now at Harvard University (MS Eng. 626 F) and the poem in Hesperides. Notes that Lawes's "Begone thou perjur'd man" is evidently an imitation of Herrick's "Goe, perjur'd man" ("The Curse. A Song"). Sees the manuscript as a valuable source for early versions of poems by Herrick, Carew, and Milton. Plate XXII prints "My mistress blushed," which appears only in the Lawes manuscript (see 1941.2 for Willa Evans's proposal that the song is by Herrick).

1970

1 DeNEEF, A. LEIGH. "Herrick and John Heywood." Notes and Queries 17 (November):408.
Sees Herrick's "The Tythe. To the Bride" as a creative reworking of Heywood's "An account of a mans children" from The fifth hundred of Epygrams (1562).

2 _____. "Herrick and the Ceremony of Death." In Renaissance Papers, 1970. Southeastern Renaissance Conference, pp. 29-39.
Explicates "The Funerall Rites of the Rose," "To Perilla," "Upon a child that dyed," and "Upon a Child. An Epitaph" to show that Herrick's "poetic ceremonials" transcend death, for they are ritualistic poems in which poet and readers re-enact the rituals that sanctify the dead. Treats poems of burial instruction and then the epitaphs which "seek to evoke in the reader the same responses of recognition, pity, and commemoration . . . while at the same time making a plea for those responses even more public and more universal." Claims that Herrick's reader becomes aware of "the significance of this death to him personally, and [Herrick] always takes the reader beyond mourning to a ritual of celebration . . . in which death itself often becomes simply irrelevant."
Derived from 1969.2; expanded in Part 1 of Chapter 5 of 1974.4.

3 DITSKY, JOHN M. "A Case of Insufficient Evidence: L.C. Martin's 'R.H.' Poems and Herrick." Ball State University Forum 11 (Autumn):54-59.
Questions Martin's attributions to Herrick of eighteen poems from a seventeenth-century commonplace book in the Rosenbach Foundation Library (1956.1) by noting, first, that the signature "R.H." could refer to another poet with

1970

the same initials (perhaps Robert Heath). Second, shows
that the eight parallels Martin finds between those poems
and Herrick's lyrics are unconvincing. Attempts, then, to
prove that the eighteen poems are not Herrick's by contrasting "Upon a Carved Cherrystone Sent to Wear in the Tip
of the Lady Jemmonia Walgraves Ear" with "R.H.'s" "A ringe
sent a Gentlew[oman]: with this posy Still beginninge,
neuer endinge" to show that they are markedly different in
technique. Finally, a comparison between Herrick's "To
Marygolds" and "R.H.'s" "The Heliotrope" indicates that the
two men have "clearly discernible personalities." Applauds
Patrick's decision to omit these eighteen poems and seven
others from his Herrick edition (1963.1).

4   HINMAN, ROBERT B. "The Apotheosis of Faust: Poetry and New
     Philosophy in the Seventeenth Century." In Metaphysical
     Poetry. Edited by Malcolm Bradbury and David Palmer.
     Stratford-Upon-Avon Studies, 11. New York: St. Martin's
     Press; London: Edward Arnold, pp. 149-79. Reprint.
     Bloomington and London: Indiana University Press, 1971.
          Includes Herrick (pp. 153-54) as one example in his
     argument that in the seventeenth century, "artists and
     'new philosophers' (i.e., both empirical scientists and
     what we would now call philosophers) were spiritual allies,
     even if they were not always aware of the alliance." Notes
     that one of Herrick's favorite writers was Robert Burton
     and that Herrick examined the "book of creatures" as care-
     fully as did Sir Thomas Browne. Cites "To the little
     Spinners" as an instance of a poem informed by "the percep-
     tion (or convincing illusion) of identity between an actual
     physical process realistically observed and a spiritual
     condition." In poets like Herrick, Herbert, and Marvell,
     "imaginative creation, an inductive leap like a leap of
     faith, has fused sacramentalism and empiricism."

5   JENKINS, PAUL RANDALL. "Robert Herrick's Poems." Ph.D. dis-
     sertation, University of Washington, 180 pp.
          Attempts to find a method of reading Herrick in the con-
     text of his classical predecessors and lyric poetry in gen-
     eral. Concludes that "style is, in the widest sense, the
     content of Herrick's poetic" and speculates that Herrick's
     sprezzatura is a defense against "present trouble."
          Pp. 46-70 of Chapter 2, revised, appear as 1972.10. See
     also summary in DAI 31:3505A.

1970

6   KIMMEY, JOHN L.   "Robert Herrick's Persona."   Studies in
     Philology 67 (April):221-36.
         Uses many brief quotations from the poems to show that
     the persona in Hesperides is a fictional character who
     plays the roles of a poet searching for eternal fame, of
     an aging lover hoping for rejuvenation, and of a Londoner
     banished to Devon. Demonstrates that the poems are ar-
     ranged so the volume as a whole will move "from exile to
     homecoming, from the enjoyment of life to the acceptance
     of death, from a place in the flux of nature to a place in
     the 'artifice of eternity.'" Then in Noble Numbers,
     Herrick's role is that of a confused and penitent sinner
     who finds salvation not in art but in religion. The two
     books are a pair as are Donne's two Anniversaries and
     Browne's Urn Burial and The Garden of Cyrus.

7   _____. "Robert Herrick's Satirical Epigrams." English
     Studies 51, no. 4:312-23.
         Maintains that in his epigrams Herrick is a "keen
     satirist" rather than a "playful pornographer." Shows
     that Herrick, like his Renaissance contemporaries, uses
     witty, pointed epigrams to criticize moral and spiritual
     corruption; his intention is instruction, not titillation.
     Assuming the persona of "the preacher, the social critic,
     the shrewd observer of men and manners," Herrick satirizes
     types of characters whose vices and follies may be found
     in Devon or in London. Most typically, Herrick attacks
     men of his own professions: poets and preachers. Scat-
     tered throughout Hesperides, the epigrams provide variety
     and contrast; they describe the "stark and crude" counter-
     parts to the "delightful and delicate" aspects of Herrick's
     microcosm.

8   MILLER, PAUL W.   "The Decline of the English Epithalamion."
     Texas Studies in Literature and Language 12 (Fall):405-16.
         Sees a loss of faith in the "myth of marriage"--the
     belief that the marriage ritual blesses the wedded couple
     and protects them from disaster--leading to a decline in
     the quality of English epithalamia written after Spenser.
     Traces an increasing concern for the poet's own cleverness
     in the nuptial poems of Fletcher, Donne, Jonson, and
     Crashaw. Contrasts Herrick's "A Nuptiall Song, or
     Epithalamie, on Sir Clipseby Crew and his Lady" with
     Spenser's "Epithalamion" to show a change in seventeenth-
     century perspectives on marriage: whereas Spenser delights
     in orderly ceremony, Herrick is impatient with it.
     Herrick's associating Sir Clipseby Crew's lady with
     "thoroughly human" domestic servants and his wishing

(rather than praying) for her happiness are symptomatic of
the loss of faith in the efficacy of the sacramental powers
of the ceremony and an increasing sense of marriage as a
secular agreement.

9 PARKER, D.H. "The Lyrical Epitaph in the Poetry of Herrick."
   In "The Literary Epitaph in the Seventeenth Century," Ph.D.
   dissertation, Oxford University, pp. 99-121.
   　 Chapter 4 analyzes Herrick's continuation of Jonson's
   lyrical epitaphs (Jonson is treated in Chapter 3, pp. 58-
   97), beginning with comments on Herrick's sharing Jonson's
   concern for skillful craftsmanship, for "a lyrical direct-
   ness of thought and emotion, rather than a show of ingenuity." Then contrasts Jonson's urban perspective with
   Herrick's "Country wit"--a perspective that leads to emphasis on correspondences between human and natural life and
   to the presentation of death "both as an end, and . . . as
   a sharing of new life" within the natural world. Stresses
   Herrick's insistence on ceremonial rituals as affirmations
   of continued life in contrast to Jonson's emphasis on fame
   earned by individual excellence in a social setting. Dis-
   tinguishes between the structures of Jonson's epitaphs and
   Herrick's: the earlier poet's epitaphs end decisively with
   "Martialesque point"; Herrick's smoother versification and
   less pointed conclusions give his epitaphs a more artless,
   unemphatic air.

10 RICHMOND, H.M. Review of eight books, including Robert
   Herrick, by Rollin. Comparative Literature 22 (Winter):
   81-85.
   　 Qualifies a number of Rollin's statements (1966.6), yet
   accepts his thesis that Herrick's verse is "a consistent
   attempt to create a ceremonial vision of the world."

11 SUMMERS, JOSEPH H. "Gentlemen of the Court and of Art:
   Suckling, Herrick, and Carew." In The Heirs of Donne and
   Jonson. New York and London: Oxford University Press,
   pp. 41-75.
   　 Defends Herrick's individual achievements, even while
   showing that his chief poetic "creative presence" is
   Jonson and even while admitting that some of his poems are
   facile, silly, and repetitious. Admires poems like
   "Corinna's going a Maying" in which one can see "what a
   Jonsonian concern with 'how well / Each syllab's answered
   and was formed how fair' could mean for a relatively iso-
   lated poet enamoured with dreams of Rome and Merry England." Appreciates the remoteness, idealization, and
   fragility of Herrick's poetic world.

1970

12   TANNER, JAMES T.F.   "Robert Herrick's Flower Poems."
      Dickinson Review 2:25-34.
          Argues that Herrick, "of all poets," is most accessible
      to young students. Admits occasional "coarseness" in his
      poems, but quotes a number of Herrick's poems about flowers
      to show how agreeably he uses flowers to present his view
      of youthful maidenhood. Notes Herrick's attention to
      ritual even in the flower poems and observes his interest
      in the idea that one should enjoy life.

13   TUFTE, VIRGINIA.   The Poetry of Marriage: The Epithalamium in
      Europe and Its Development in England.   University of
      Southern California Studies in Comparative Literature,
      vol. 2. Los Angeles: Tinnon-Brown, pp. 3, 236-43, 250.
          Sees Herrick's five marriage poems ("An Epithalamie to
      Sir Thomas Southwell and His Lady," "A Nuptiall Song, or
      Epithalamie, on Sir Clipseby Crew and his Lady," "Connubii
      Flores, or the well-wishes at Weddings," "The Entertain-
      ment: or, Porch-verse, at the Marriage of Master Henry
      Northly, and the most witty Mistresse Lettice Yard," and
      "A Nuptiall Verse to Mistresse Elizabeth Lee, now Lady
      Tracie") as evidence that "an inventive poet may still give
      life to old motifs." Shows that Herrick combines the carpe
      diem motif, Catullan themes, English customs, "expertly
      controlled metaphysical conceits," and pagan and Christian
      elements to create successful poems.

14   WEIDHORN, MANFRED.   Dreams in Seventeenth-Century Literature.
      The Hague and Paris: Mouton, pp. 95-97, 104-5.
          Observes that Herrick wrote more dream poems than any
      other seventeenth-century poet. Quotes some of them, not-
      ing how often the dreamer is a naïve, charming lover whose
      dreams are fantasies "shaped by the inner censor."

                              1971

1   BERMAN, RONALD.   "Herrick's Secular Poetry."   English Studies
      52, no. 1:20-30.
          Uses stanza 13 of "A Nuptiall Song" to show that
      Herrick's poetry is informed by the theory of correspon-
      dences and that for Herrick, "the business of the poet, no
      less than that of the lovers, is to 'read, and / Put in
      practice, to understand.'" References to Augustine,
      Titian, Burton, and Milton indicate that Herrick's celebra-
      tion of love is consonant with orthodox Christianity, for
      even though he sees human love as a possible image of
      divine love, he distinguishes between sensate and eternal

1971

love. After noting images with "overtones of creation, ending, and resurrection" with which Herrick reveals both connections between secular and sacred experience and distinctions between life in time and "the permanence of that greater life in which it is located," stresses the particularly Protestant cast of mind of poets like Herrick and Owen Feltham who seek "reality behind sensate appearances." Herrick, then, is not a pagan poet.

Reprinted in Ben Jonson and the Cavalier Poets, selected and edited by Hugh Maclean, Norton Critical Edition (New York: W.W. Norton & Co., 1974), pp. 529-40.

2 BOSS, JUDITH E. "Robert Herrick's Epigrams and Noble Numbers." Ph.D. dissertation, Texas Christian University, 178 pp.

Defends Herrick on the basis of the "Christian tone" she finds throughout his poetry. Notes that Hesperides includes more didactic poems responding to seventeenth-century events than lyrics, and postulates that because the occasional verses were too challenging to be popular only the songs have tended to be anthologized (Chapter 1). Studies the epigrams (Chapter 2); examines Herrick's use, in Noble Numbers, of the structure and content of the Book of Common Prayer (Chapter 3); argues that the secular lyrics are "jocund but chaste" and that their pagan carpe diem themes serve Herrick's Christian morality (Chapter 4).

See also summary in DAI 32:4553A.

3 DeNEEF, A. LEIGH. "Herrick's 'Argument' and Thomas Bastard." Seventeenth-Century News 29 (Spring):9-10.

Contrasts Thomas Bastard's de subiecto operis sui with "The Argument of his Book" to show how Herrick creates "new and original effects" from conventional themes and forms. Observes that both poems move from a catalog of specifics ("somber and satiric" on Bastard's part; "light and festive" on Herrick's) in lines 1-8 to a "more comprehensive overview" in the last six lines. In his final couplet, Bastard presents himself as a "detached observer who comments objectively and definitively on the world's condition"; Herrick uses the word hope to force his reader "out of the comfortable and secure stance of festive affirmation into one of human desire and possible frustration." This speaker, then, is "an emotional, subjective human being."

Incorporated into DeNeef, 1974.4.

1971

4   _____. "Herrick's 'Corinna' and the Ceremonial Mode." South
       Atlantic Quarterly 70 (Autumn):530-45.
          After defining the "ceremonial mode," analyzes
       "Corinna's going a Maying" as a poem in which Herrick
       elevates the May Day festival "into a cosmic ritual of
       unification." Argues that the reminder of death in the
       final stanza forces the reader to see the necessity of
       participating in the ritual celebrated by the poem. The
       poem itself "is the ultimate ceremonial act. . . . [for it]
       heightens and sanctifies, celebrates and demands celebra-
       tion in return." Sees the seduction of Corinna as one
       aspect of the poem's larger goal, for here "the union of
       lovers is a microcosmic representation of a universal
       event." Downplays conflicts between paganism and Chris-
       tianity in the poem, for Herrick uses various religious
       references to intensify his celebratory, ceremonial tone,
       rather than to propose any single religious attitude.

5   FARMER, NORMAN K., Jr. "Robert Herrick and 'King Oberon's
       Clothing': New Evidence for Attribution." Yearbook of
       English Studies 1:68-77.
          Questions the view that Sir Simeon Steward wrote "King
       Oberon's Clothing" by noting that in Folger Library MS.
       V.a. 322 there is a copy of the poem ascribed to "Ro:
       Herricke." Confirms the attribution to Herrick by noting
       that the poem is associated with one or more of the other
       Oberon poems in nine other seventeenth-century manuscripts
       and in two of the three printed books in which the Oberon
       poems are published (A Description of the King and Queen of
       Fayries [1634, 1635] and in Poole's The English Parnassus
       [1657]) and by comparing the poem to other lyrics by
       Herrick. Notes that only Drayton, William Browne, and
       Herrick are known to have been writing descriptions of
       fairy clothing in the mid-seventeenth century, and suggests
       that "King Oberon's Clothing" may have been written in
       imitation of Drayton, whose work it resembles. Records
       variants in other extant manuscripts, with the assertion
       that "the superior--and unique--readings of Folger V.a.
       322, along with the attribution to Robert Herrick, suggests
       that it is in fact closer to the source, and that [the two
       lines missing from the Folger text] were accidentally or
       carelessly omitted." Adds that the evidence that Sir
       Simeon Steward wrote any poetry at all is inconclusive.
       Admits that the attribution to Herrick is also uncertain,
       but suggests the poem be included in future editions of his
       work.

6   HEINEMANN, ALISON. "Balme in Herrick's 'A Meditation for his
    Mistresse.'" English Language Notes 8 (March):176-80.
        Expands pp. 117-19 of 1971.7. Clarifies stanza 5 of "A
    Meditation" by observing that "balme" is a flowering herb;
    the stanza presents the lady's beauty as like "the flower-
    ing herb and its aroma, whose pungency released in the
    steeping or 'transfusing' process gives way almost simul-
    taneously to its evanescence." Stanza 5, then, is appro-
    priate in a poem in which each stanza includes a floral
    metaphor.

7   _____. "The Style of Robert Herrick's Lyrics." Ph.D. disser-
    tation, University of Delaware, 210 pp.
        Provides a stylistic analysis of the poetry by examining
    the poet's five voices--chronicler, sage, singer, peti-
    tioner, and soliloquist (Chapter 2); the structures of the
    poems (Chapter 3); Herrick's poetic language--diction,
    imagery, and metaphor (Chapter 4); and his versification--
    rhythm, metrical patterns, and rime (Chapter 5). Indexes
    the poems that use the five poetic voices (Appendix A);
    charts the numbers of poems using various stanza forms
    (Appendix B); and includes a word count of nouns, verbs,
    and adjectives (Appendix C).
        Pp. 117-19, expanded and revised: 1971.6. See also
    summary in DAI 32:6377A.

8   KIMMEY, JOHN L. "Order and Form in Herrick's Hesperides."
    Journal of English and Germanic Philology 70 (Spring):
    255-68.
        Disagrees with theories (Delattre, 1911.2, and Martin,
    1956.1) that the poems in Hesperides are ordered princi-
    pally by their dates of composition and demonstrates that
    not Herrick but the poet-persona whom Kimmey describes in
    1970.6 is the man whose life is chronicled in Hesperides.
    The early poems are generally lighter in tone; later,
    Herrick treats themes "relevant to the situation of a dying
    and troubled persona living in a world threatened by civil
    war." In the middle of the volume, he moves "from the
    lyrical to the homiletic, from the song to the epigram."
    Even Herrick's shaped poems and metrical patterns reflect
    the shift toward the disciplined, serious poetry of devo-
    tion in Noble Numbers. Thus the order and form of the 1648
    volume show Herrick to be a conscious craftsman who aims to
    represent "the secular and religious world of his time and
    his experience."

1971

9   MINER, EARL. The Cavalier Mode from Jonson to Cotton.
    Princeton: Princeton University Press, 349 pp. passim.
        Chapter 1 defines the "social mode" of the Cavaliers as
    a mean between the private concerns of the Metaphysical
    poets and the public stance of Milton, Dryden, and Pope;
    successive chapters treat key Cavalier themes: "The Good
    Life," "The Ruines and Remedies of Time," "Order and Dis-
    order," "Love," and "Friendship." Includes examples from
    Herrick's poems to show the Cavaliers' treatment of their
    major concern, the good life that includes worldly bless-
    ings and responsible virtue.
        Chapter 2, "The Good Life," excerpted in Ben Jonson and
    the Cavalier Poets, selected and edited by Hugh Maclean,
    Norton Critical Edition (New York: W.W. Norton & Co.,
    1974), pp. 465-79.

10 MORANVILLE, SHARELLE. "The Self and Soul in Robert Herrick's
    Poetry." Ph.D. dissertation, Kent State University,
    160 pp.
        Begins with the premise that Herrick believes that dur-
    ing a human being's "temporal life the soul exists in a
    unique, individual personality. The soul survives immor-
    tality; but the unique self--the 'I'--does not." Examines
    the poems of both Hesperides and Noble Numbers in terms of
    Herrick's dual interest in developing the soul and in en-
    joying life on earth. Includes analyses of poems treating
    "the destructive woman and her effect on the creative eye."
    See also summary in DAI 32:5192A.

11 RAMSEY, JOHN STEVENS. "Magic, Festival and the Order of
    Society: Ben Jonson and Robert Herrick." In "Magic and
    Festivity in English Renaissance Poetry." Ph.D. disserta-
    tion, University of Maryland, pp. 192-286.
        After examining works by Jonson, who uses magic and
    festivals as the bases for masques in which "the court
    discovered and practiced holiday renewal," argues that
    Herrick writes two kinds of poems of celebration and magic.
    In the first half of Hesperides, Herrick includes poems in
    which he suggests that art is "a human magic by which the
    world is transformed to meet the personal requirements of
    the speaker"; in the second half of the book, he goes on
    to present poems that show that "art and life meet in the
    ritual of festivity and magic, each supplying the basis for
    the other." Sees the poet-persona of Hesperides as a suc-
    cessful model "of joyful, festive life."
        See also abstract in DAI 32:3265-66A.

1972

12 SHADOIAN, JACK. "Herrick's 'Delight in Disorder.'" <u>Studies</u>
    <u>in the Humanities</u>, 2. Edited by William F. Grayburn.
    Indiana: Indiana University of Pennsylvania, pp. 23-25.
        Examines "Delight in Disorder," explaining how its
    structure imitates its content and suggesting that its
    praise of "Sweet disorder" is Herrick's "announcement of
    a poetic."

13 SINANOGLOU, LEAH POWELL. "The Poet as Child." In "For of
    Such Is the Kingdom of Heaven: Childhood in Seventeenth-
    Century English Literature." Ph.D. dissertation, Columbia
    University, pp. 71-118.
        Treats Herbert's, Herrick's, and Crashaw's use of the
    persona of a child before God as a result of their desires
    to retreat from "the growing disorders in church and state"
    of seventeenth-century England. Sees Herrick (pp. 95-105)
    delighting in littleness in the <u>Hesperides</u> poems. Believes
    that "the <u>persona</u> of the child gives <u>Noble Numbers</u> an air
    of bedrock sincerity and unquestioning acceptance" and
    argues that the "child's version of Anglicanism" in <u>Noble</u>
    <u>Numbers</u> gives the volume a stability not in <u>Hesperides</u>,
    where time is presented as having the power to destroy
    innocence.
        Revised and expanded: 1977.7; 1978.17; 1979.7. See
    also summary in <u>DAI</u> 35:4558A.

1972

1 ABRAHAMS, ROGER D. "Folklore and Literature as Performance."
   <u>Journal of Folklore Studies</u> 9 (August-December):75-94.
       Uses "Corinna's going a Maying" to show how literature
   uses folklore motifs for its own purposes: in this poem
   Herrick presents tensions arising out of the fact that
   people are <u>not</u> participating in the May Day festivities.
   Argues that this poem transcends conventional <u>carpe</u> <u>diem</u>
   statements as it presents the conflict between the communal activities of the day and the speaker's individual
   goals: "he is using a day of <u>impersonal</u> license to pursue
   what seem to be very <u>personal</u> ends" (the seduction of
   Corinna). Notes that the poem employs pastoral motifs in
   very sophisticated ways.

2 BEER, DAVID F. "'The Countries Sweet Simplicity': Devonshire
   Life in the Poetry of Robert Herrick." Ph.D. dissertation,
   University of New Mexico, 235 pp.
       Explores the influence of Devonshire (where Herrick
   lived for eighteen years before publishing <u>Hesperides</u>) on

1972

Herrick's poems about country life. Notes that their style
is more homely than his other poems, and observes that the
country-life poems are generally those thought to have been
written while Herrick lived at Dean Prior. Parallels poems
with historical writings of the seventeenth century.
Treats nature and Devon itself (Chapters 1 and 2);
Devonshire people (Chapter 3); folk customs (Chapter 4);
and local superstitions and beliefs (Chapter 5).
See also summary in DAI 33:2884A.

3   CAIN, T.G.S. "The Bell/White MS: Some Unpublished Poems."
English Literary Renaissance 2 (Spring):260-70.
Describes the contents of item 25 in the Bell/White
Collection in the library of the University of Newcastle
upon Tyne. Of the two hundred poems in this manuscript
from the mid-seventeenth century, seventy are evidently
unique to this collection. Prints "Herracke on a Kisse to
his Mrs." (fols. 56v-57), which is similar enough to
Herrick's known work to be an early example of his verse,
and "For his Mistris" (fol. 25v), which Cain believes to be
an imitation of Herrick. Lists significant variants in "To
his yonger Mrs" (fols. 26v-27), which Martin prints as
"Advice to a Maid" in 1956.1, observing that they "are
poetically superior to any of those recorded by Martin . . .
[and therefore] may be said to support his attribution."
Versions of "Ones Farewell to Sack" (fols. 30v-31v) and "His
Return and Welcome to Sack" (fols. 31v-33) in this manuscript are close to those in B.M. MS. Sloane 1446. Adds a
selection of eight of the other sixty-eight unique poems,
commenting that although they vary in quality, they "provide
an interesting addition to the available corpus of mid-
seventeenth-century poetry." Plate 1 (following p. 264) is
a facsimile of fol. 56v, which gives the first thirty-four
lines of "Herracke on a Kisse to his Mrs."
Appears as Appendix 1 in 1973.1.

4   CAPWELL, RICHARD L. "Herrick and the Aesthetic Principle of
Variety and Contrast." South Atlantic Quarterly 71
(Autumn):488-95.
Examines the arrangement of poems within Hesperides
against the aesthetic principle of variety and contrast to
show that the volume is carefully structured. Quotes a
number of lyrics from Hesperides and also some not published there to show that the principle of variety and contrast also informs the structures and contents of individual
poems. Suggests that in Herrick's verse "juxtaposition of
contrasting elements" often creates a "balance that is
order and harmony," a moderate golden mean between extremes.

Cites "Upon Man," "Christs Action," "Mistresse Elizabeth
Wheeler," and "The Description" to show Herrick's belief
that the combination of diverse parts "may constitute a
unity of a subtler and higher type than can be achieved by
combining like elements only"; thus Hesperides is like the
seemingly disordered "natural" garden Bacon advocates in
his essay "Of Gardens."

5   CROFT, P.J. Letter to the Editor. Papers of the Bibliograph-
    ical Society of Americ: 66 (Fourth Quarter):421-26.
        Response to 1972.6. Argues that Farmer's comments about
    the Herrick Commonplace Book are often misleading. Believes
    that although Herrick was not necessarily the owner of the
    book, he "was in some way supervising the compilation" of
    it. Again suggests that there may have been a connection
    between Herrick and John Williams during the years the book
    was compiled; adds observation that Herrick addressed two
    Hesperides poems to Williams.

6   FARMER, NORMAN K., r. "Robert Herrick's Commonplace Book?
    Some Observations and Questions." Papers of the Biblio-
    graphical Society of America 66 (First Quarter):21-34.
        Describes the "Herrick Commonplace Book" purchased by
    the University of Texas in 1965, and suggests a need to
    further our understanding of the transmissions of early
    manuscripts. Concludes that the hand attributed to Herrick
    by Croft (1965.2) is "probably" his; suggests that the book
    could have belonged to a friend who asked Herrick to make
    additions or corrections. Notes problems in the pagination
    which may be clarified when the book is disbound. Until
    its provenance is known, believes its primary interest to
    scholars will be in its position as "something of a barom-
    eter indicating the pressures of popular resentment di-
    rected toward prominent persons and institutions" in the
    early seventeenth century.
        For a somewhat different analysis of Croft's conclu-
    sions, see 1973.1. Response to Farmer: 1972.5.

7   GERTZMAN, JAY [A.] "Robert Herrick's Hesperides: A Study of
    the Materials and Intentions of a Seventeenth Century
    Lyric Poet." Ph.D. dissertation, University of Pennsyl-
    vania, 331 pp.
        Distinguishes between Herrick's "playful, recreative
    pastoral" and more didactic pastoral by poets like Virgil,
    Spenser, and Milton. Analyzes rhetorical strategies of
    individual poems from Hesperides to show Herrick's emphasis
    on "describing sensuous pleasure, setting up conditions
    under which it was benevolent and sinless, and conveying a

1972

playful, fanciful vision of this kind of innocence." Uses
the phrase "cleanly-Wantonnesse" to define the genial,
playful mood of Hesperides.
For an article summarizing the argument of this dissertation, see 1974.6. See also summary in DAI 33:1682A.

8   HALLI, ROBERT WILLIAM, Jr. "A Study of Herrick's Hesperides."
Ph.D. dissertation, University of Virginia, 214 pp.
Uses four approaches (reader response, variety, con-
trast, and resonance) and two major themes (beauty and
ugliness, life and death) to investigate Hesperides.
See also summary in DAI 33:3584-85A.

9   HUSON, DOROTHY MATTHIS. "Robert Herrick's Hesperides Considered as an Organized Work." Ph.D. dissertation,
Michigan State University, 205 pp.
Sees the various type sizes used in titles within the
1648 Hesperides as signals to the reader that the volume
is divided into seven sections which parallel the first
seven books of Augustine's Confessions. Suggests that
Herrick arranged his poems to record his early wanton life
and then his increasing awareness of God. The more ex-
plicitly divine poems of Noble Numbers complete the volume,
as do Books VIII through X of the Confessions, by presenting the poet's conversion to Christianity and his commit-
ment to God.
See also summary in DAI 34:275-76A.

10 JENKINS, PAUL R. "Rethinking What Moderation Means to Robert
Herrick." English Literary History 39 (March):49-65.
Discusses Herrick's use of the idea of moderation as an
index of his relationship to Renaissance classicism. Demon-
strates that in "A Country life," "Delight in Disorder,"
"The Lilly in a Christal," and other poems from Hesperides,
Herrick treats moderation as an aesthetic more than a moral
ideal; for Herrick, control and restraint "enforce atten-
tiveness and hone the imagination for a more sustained and
excited release." Argues, then, that the unusual combination of stoicism and epicurism in Herrick's verse results
from his exploitation of "classical wisdom and lore . . .
for the most unclassical of reasons": quite unlike his
predecessor Ben Jonson, Herrick uses classical topoi in
his search for new ways of outwitting old restrictions.

11   LERNER, LAWRENCE. The Uses of Nostalgia: Studies in Pastoral
     Poetry. London: Chatto & Windus, pp. 171-72.
          Includes Herrick in Chapter 8, "Farewell, Rewards and
     Faeries," which focuses on Milton's conflict between Puri-
     tanism and Humanism: "In the last resort, Herrick renounces
     his pagan attitudes and sets his hopes on heaven, but most
     of his poetry was written without this choice being forced
     into attention." Suggests that in Herrick's poetry, as in
     Jonson's, it is difficult to tell "how far [his] paganism
     is literary and nostalgic, and how far he is describing
     what is actually going on."

12   McCLUNG, WILLIAM ALEXANDER. "The English Country House in
     Literature of the Renaissance." Ph.D. dissertation,
     Harvard University, 234 pp.
          Traces the Roman origins of English country-house
     poetry. Describes a number of Elizabethan and Jacobean
     country houses and argues that the "envious show" Jonson
     criticizes in "To Penshurst" is that of houses like
     Theobalds (or Spenser's House of Pride), rather than of
     later, neoclassical buildings by Inigo Jones and his fol-
     lowers. Analyzes seventeenth-century country-house poems
     by Jonson, Herrick, and others.
          For a book derived from this dissertation, see 1977.6.

13   MATTSON, BARBARA DIANE. "A Study of Robert Herrick's
     Hesperides." Ph.D. dissertation, University of Minnesota,
     145 pp.
          Four chapters--"The Art of Herrick's Poetry," "The Auto-
     biographical Impulse of Herrick's Poetry," "Herrick's
     Masculine Sensibility," and "Herrick's Forgotten Verse:
     A Study of the 'Objectionable' Epigrams in Hesperides"--
     argue against those who still see Herrick as a minor poet.
     Comments on Herrick's artistry focus on devices like
     anaphora and alliteration; a chapter on autobiography
     assumes that the poems reveal Herrick's "life, his traits,
     tastes, and varying emotions"; analysis of the epigrams
     places them in the context of classical and Renaissance
     epigrams which are typically "obscene": Herrick is, in
     this respect, no different from his poetic fellows.
     Chapter 3, "Herrick's Masculine Sensibility," contrasts
     Herrick's amatory verse with Donne's, noting that whereas
     Donne treats the range of emotions he experiences, Herrick
     describes the ladies he admires: "He portrays what is be-
     fore him in dream or reality in essentially non-dramatic
     or non-narrative terms." Examines Herrick's dependence
     upon women, his helplessness in the face of their powers,

and his similarities to the Petrarchan poets whose example seventeenth-century poets are often said to eschew.
See also summary in <u>DAI</u> 33:6319A.

14   MINICH, PAUL ANTHONY.   "An Analysis of a Perfect Poetic King-
     dom: Robert Herrick's <u>Hesperides</u>." Ph.D. dissertation,
     SUNY-Buffalo, 238 pp.
        Examines "the interior dynamics and principal modes of
     organization" of a book that "not only thematically ex-
     presses but also embodies Herrick's grasp of himself as a
     creator who psychically inhibits his imaginative linguistic
     creation." Informed throughout by recent aesthetic and
     psychological theories.
        See also summary in <u>DAI</u> 33:5133A.

15   PIEPHO, EDWARD LEE.   "'Faire, and Unfamiliar Excellence':   The
     Art of Herrick's Secular Poetry." Ph.D. dissertation,
     University of Virginia, 206 pp.
        Examines Herrick's original use of figurative language
     from the Petrarchan and classical traditions (Chapter 2),
     his syntax (Chapter 3), his diction (Chapter 4), and his
     versification (Chapter 5) before discussing the implica-
     tions of John Harmar's praise of Herrick's "intellectual
     pleasantry" (Chapter 6). Argues that Herrick's poetry is
     written for a small, educated audience that would appre-
     ciate his playful artistry. Concludes that Herrick's art-
     ful playfulness aims to "invoke extraordinary worlds or
     render the present world more intense."
        See also summary in <u>DAI</u> 33:3664-65A.

16   PRESTON, MICHAEL J.   "Herrick's 'Upon Julia's Clothes.'"
     <u>Explicator</u> 30 (May): Item 82.
        Shows that Ovid's <u>Amores</u>, I.5, is a source for the poem
     and observes that the poet's double vision of his lady is,
     as Schneider notes (1955.7), a vision of her, first, "in
     the trappings of society" (dressed) and, second, "in the
     trappings of nature" (undressed).

17   WITT, ROBERT W.   "Building a Pillar of Fame." <u>University of
     Mississippi Studies in English</u> 13:65-83.
        Surveys Herrick's use of English folklore traditions
     having to do with birds, insects and reptiles, animals and
     fishes, plants, supernatural beings (fairies, witches,
     devils, and ghosts), and holidays: suggests that Herrick's
     attempt to preserve folk customs may be part of a desire to
     make his own poetry "eternally famous."

<u>1973</u>

1   CAIN, T[HOMAS] G[RANT] S[TEVENS]. "The Poetry of Robert
    Herrick." Ph.D. dissertation, Cambridge University,
    289 pp.
        Argues that what some readers have taken for triviality
    in Herrick is in fact "a skilled, graceful and ultimately
    serious form of <u>simplicitas</u>" and that <u>Hesperides</u> is an
    "intellectually unified work" in which Herrick "attempt[s]
    to come to terms . . . with the brutal facts of time and
    death."
        Chapter 1, "Introduction: The Demand for Seriousness,"
    finds the source of Herrick's aesthetic in Sidney's <u>Defense
    of Poetry</u>, which examines "the phenomena of delight, seeing
    it as residing in a discovery of harmony, a congruence be-
    tween the work involved and the moral and physical universe
    around it." Proposes that Herrick's preoccupation in
    <u>Hesperides</u> is the relationship between man and time.
        Chapter 2, "The Structure of <u>Hesperides</u>," notes
    Herrick's many references to his book as a unified work,
    points to the eight introductory and eight concluding poems
    framing <u>Hesperides</u>, defines the volume's title as the name
    for an enclosed garden, and examines a number of the poems
    against a background of Renaissance views of time to argue
    that the poems "make up a collection which form a paradigm
    of the temporal flux, a thread of instants strung out in
    the enclosed and timeless garden of <u>Hesperides</u> to form a
    solid bulwark against '<u>Times</u> trans-shifting' and to bear
    out Herrick's insistence that his collection is a single
    work."
        Chapter 3, "Ben Jonson and the Classical Pantheon," re-
    examines the nature of Herrick's debt to Jonson and to
    classical writers in terms of the Renaissance concept of
    <u>imitatio</u>. Argues that Herrick sees Jonson as a poet who
    "offers his followers the possibility of achieving in the
    vernacular a genuinely classical literature" which will
    endure; Herrick's imitation of Jonson and of classical
    writers is "as a classical poet writing in what he con-
    ceives to be a classical tradition."
        Chapter 4, "The Role of Ceremony in <u>Hesperides</u>," builds
    on Deming's view (1967.4 and 1969.1) that Herrick is inter-
    ested in pagan rituals as significant ways of organizing
    time and of challenging "in some measure the formless move-
    ment of time toward death." Studies poems that examine
    "the continuity of classical and Christian ceremony" and
    lyrics that treat calendrical festivals, and concludes that
    ceremonial poems re-enact occasions in which significant

days are "reborn and [take] their place in the repetitive
cycle of natural law and human ceremony which spaces out,
stabilizes, and finally defeats the flux of time."

Chapter 5, "The Flame of Mankind: Nature and the Regeneration of Man," examines the marriage poetry in terms
of Renaissance celebrations of the regenerative implica-
tions of married love; and Chapter 6, "'Corinna's going a
Maying': Nature and Regeneration of Man (II)," treats
"Corinna" as a "courtly, sophisticated poem" based on May
Day rituals and biblical and classical traditions that re-
mind us that even though individual life is "no more than
a process of decay," one can "preserve . . . the race of
mankind."

Appendix 2 responds to Croft (1972.5) that Herrick
probably "had a very close connection with the Commonplace
Book without necessarily being its sole owner or even its
part owner." Discounts the possibility that it offers new
poems by Herrick as Croft claims (1965.2), and questions
Croft's attribution of "Catch mee a star" to Herrick
(1965.2 and 1973.4), because its "theme is too commonplace,
and its resemblance [to Herrick's known verses] too
casual." Suggests that the attitude toward political
themes expressed throughout the manuscript implies "that
Herrick was less closely aligned with the political estab-
lishment than one might have supposed," yet "they in no way
indicate an unusual or in any way remarkable political
stance." Concludes that the only real significance of the
book to Herrick scholars is the knowledge that "The Welcome
to Sack" and "His fare-well to Sack" are from the early
years of his writing career.

For an essay derived from Chapter 7, "Herrick in Meditation: The Defeat of Time," see 1978.3. For Appendix 1,
see 1972.3.

2   COFFIN, LAWRENCE. "'Liquifaction' [sic] in Herrick's 'Upon
     Julia's Clothes.'" Concerning Poetry 6 (Fall):56-59.
        Argues that the poem imitates the psychological expe-
     rience of the "transfer of identity from lover to beloved."
     Sees the basic analogy of the poem in liquefaction (line 3),
     a word Renaissance preachers used to mean a melting of the
     individual's soul into God. When the poet says Julia's
     "glittering taketh me" (line 6), he acknowledges that his
     "soul is literally carried away by Julia."

3   COLIE, ROSALIE L. "Genre-Systems and the Function of Litera-
     ture." In The Resources of Kind: Genre-Theory in the
     Renaissance. Edited by Barbara K. Lewalski. Berkeley,
     Los Angeles, and London: University of California Press,
     pp. 1-31.
          As she examines "some of the ways in which the idea of
     genre governed . . . and contributed to . . . writers and
     writings in the Renaissance," Colie demonstrates that
     Herrick's "The Argument of his Book" teaches the reader
     that in his "little" poems he has used "large" genres as
     "metaphors, even while he exploits their official topics."
     If we recognize how Herrick plays his work against a lit-
     erary system known to his contemporaries, we see him as "a
     considerable craftsman at the very least" or "a consider-
     able innovator at the very best."

4   CROFT, P.J. Autograph Poetry in the English Language:
     Facsimiles of Original Manuscripts from the Fourteenth to
     the Twentieth Century. Vol. 1. London: Cassell, Items 32
     and 33.
          Item 32: Facsimile and transcription of B.M. Harley
     MS. 367, fol. 154, an elegy entitled "Chorus," which Croft
     attributes to Herrick, who was at Trinity Hall, Cambridge,
     when John Browne, Fellow of Caius and subject of this
     elegy, died in 1619.
          Item 33: Facsimile and transcription of p. 253 of the
     miscellany or Commonplace Book formerly Phillipps MS. 12341,
     now owned by the University of Texas. Croft identifies the
     hand as Herrick's and suggests that the poem "Catch mee a
     star," an imitation of Donne's "Go and catch a falling
     Star," was composed by Herrick.

5   FARMER, NORMAN K., Jr., ed. "Poems from a Seventeenth-Century
     Manuscript with the Hand of Robert Herrick." Texas
     Quarterly 16 (Winter):185 pp. (Paged separately from the
     rest of the volume.)
          Provides facsimiles of the pages from the "Herrick
     Commonplace Book" (formerly Phillipps MS. 12341, purchased
     by the University of Texas in 1965) which contain poems and
     printed transcriptions on facing pages. Introduction
     focuses on the contents of the manuscript, which Farmer
     discusses in terms of its "keen sense of topicality."
     Pp. 8-16 treat seventeenth-century events to which the poems
     refer; then two pages note the few poems with no obvious
     topical references and quote Croft's identification of the
     book as belonging to Herrick and being written, in part, in
     his hand (1965.2). Expresses caution on the latter point,
     inviting the reader to compare the poems in that hand with

a facsimile of one of Herrick's holograph letters printed on p. 4 of this monograph. Concludes, "Whether or not this manuscript is finally determined to have belonged to Robert Herrick," it is a significant document for seventeenth-century studies. Provides a brief list of supplementary readings.

For errata, see 1976.6-8.

6 GERTZMAN, JAY A. "Robert Chamberlain and Robert Herrick." Notes and Queries 20 (May):182-84.

Responds to 1967.7 with the suggestion that Chamberlain's interest in Herrick derives from his reputation in Devon and/or in London in the 1630s as a "recreative, fanciful" poet.

7 HAGEMAN, ELIZABETH H. "Recent Studies in Herrick." English Literary Renaissance 3 (Autumn):462-71.

A topical review of criticism of Herrick from 1945 through 1971. Observes that recent critics have disputed the older view of Herrick as a trivial, slightly immoral poet and that they have continued to admire Herrick's vitality and wit as they have pointed to his Christian, sacramental view of life. Praises Martin's and Patrick's editions (1956.1 and 1963.1) and calls for studies of Herrick and the Book of Common Prayer and of the seventeenth-century music written for Herrick's lyrics.

8 ORAM, WILLIAM ALLAN. "Herrick: The Fictions of Hesperides." In "The Disappearance of Pan: Some Uses of Myth in Three Seventeenth-Century Poets." Ph.D. dissertation, Yale University, pp. 260-305.

Sees Herrick as a conventional Christian poet only in Noble Numbers, whose poems are simple and relatively un-interesting, and argues that in Hesperides, Herrick uses myth "to secularize rather than to sanctify his forms." Believes Herrick's myth focuses on the natural world and excludes the supernatural; for Herrick, poetry has a purely secular function. In his poems, the mind "builds, experiments, plays with a number of hypothetical truths." Other chapters treat Drayton, Milton, and (briefly) Jonson and Waller.

See also summary in DAI, 34, 3423A. Pp. 261-71, with revisions, appear as 1978.26.

9 OZARK, JOAN MARY. "Faery Court Poetry of the Early Seventeenth Century." Ph.D. dissertation, Princeton University, pp. 83-257, 438-79, and passim.

Explicates "The Fairie Temple: or, Oberons Chappell" against the backgrounds of seventeenth-century fairy lore

and of Anglican and Puritan disputes over church ritual to
show that the poem is "an ingenious parody of the Puritan
view of Anglicanism" (Chapter 2). Detailed readings of
"Oberons Feast" (Chapter 3) and "Oberons Palace" (Chapter
4) show that they praise "the good life of feasting and
revelry which the Caroline court represented in Herrick's
eyes" even while they include some parody of that court.
Sees the three poems as a trio "about the fairy king's
worshipping, feasting, and loving." In Appendix 1, argues
that they were written between 1623 and 1626. Other chapters focus on William Browne, Sir Simeon Steward, and
Michael Drayton.
    For an article derived from Chapter 2, see 1981.2.
    See also summary in DAI 34:5115-16A.

10   ROTH, FREDERIC HULL, Jr. "The Poetry of Retreat and the
      Manorial Catalogue of Delights." In "'Heaven's Center,
      Nature's Lap': A Study of the English Country-Estate Poems
      of the Seventeenth Century." Ph.D. dissertation, Univer-
      sity of Virginia, pp. 94-139.
          After chapters on the history of the country-estate poem
      and on Jonson's "To Penshurst" and "To Sir Robert Wroth,"
      treats Herrick (pp. 94-110), Carew, and other seventeenth-
      century followers of Jonson. Sees "A Country life: To his
      Brother, Master Thomas Herrick" as modeled after "To Sir
      Robert Wroth"; but shows that "The Country life, to the
      honoured Master Endimion Porter" is a more mature and
      original example of the genre, for it eschews simple flat-
      tery in favor of a catalogue of the ample joys of the
      countryside. Presents Herrick's only house poem, "A
      Panegerick to Sir Lewis Pemberton," as a celebration of
      the values associated with the golden age and notes that
      Pemberton's house is an emblem of its owner's virtues.
      Declares that "what Breughel is to country-landscape paint-
      ing, Herrick is to country-landscape poetry." Closes with
      a chapter on Marvell.
          See also summary in DAI 34:5120-21A.

11   ROWLEY, VICTOR CURTIS, Jr. "Artifact, Author, and Audience in
      Robert Herrick's Hesperides." Ph.D. dissertation, Ohio
      State University, 178 pp.
          Provides a rhetorical analysis of Hesperides by treating
      it as an only seemingly haphazard group of poems in a
      "poetic Elysium" analogous to Jonson's sylva (Chapter 1,
      "Artifact"); by showing the omnipresence of a single poet-
      persona (Chapter 2, "Author"); and by a consideration of
      "how Herrick uses in poetry readers whom he calls by their

1973

real names" (Chapter 3, "Audience"). Concludes that each
poem must be seen in the context of the entire volume.
See also summary in DAI 34:5121-22A.

12   SABOL, ANDREW J.   Introduction to poems by Robert Herrick.   In
Major Poets of the Earlier Seventeenth Century: Donne,
Herbert, Vaughan, Crashaw, Jonson, Herrick, Marvell.
Edited by Barbara K. Lewalsi and Andrew J. Sabol.   New
York: Odyssey Press, pp. 917-27.
Presents the 1648 volume as "a life's work, epitomizing
and integrating all that he thought and cherished."
Stresses the variety of Herrick's sources and presents a
view of Herrick as a singer of "simple eloquence and un-
fettered joy."   A selected bibliography lists eleven edi-
tions of Herrick and fifteen critical studies.   On pp.
1252-58, prints musical settings for poems by Herrick by
Nicholas Lanier, Robert Ramsey, Henry Lawes, William Lawes,
and William Webbe.

13   TROGDON, WILLIAM LEWIS.   "Classical Mythology in the Poetry
of Robert Herrick."   Ph.D. dissertation, University of
Missouri-Columbia, 310 pp.
Believes that Herrick uses classical mythology because
it offers him "a framework of equivalents that he knows
will endure as long as Western civilization."   Chapters on
"Myth in Herrick's Major Modes," on "Myth and Poetic Technique," and "Mythic Theme and Pattern" demonstrate how
classical myths "help transport the poet to another land,
and once there, they furnish him a part of the material
that will delineate his visions."   Sees this use of classical myth as a unifying element in Hesperides.   Four
appendices catalogue mythical allusions in the poems.
See also summary in DAI 35:1065-66A.

14   WILLIAMS, RAYMOND.   The Country and the City.   New York:
Oxford University Press; London: Chatto & Windus,
pp. 33-34, 72-73.
See 1968.12 for Williams's criticism of "The Hock-cart."
On pp. 72-73, recalls his own childhood anger when he first
read Herrick's "A Thanksgiving," in which the poet offers a
"whine" of thanks for his humble condition.

1974

1   ANON.   Review of Robert Herrick, by Scott.   Economist 252
(3 August):84.
Sees Scott's book (1974.14) as a repetition of others'
work.

2   BACHE, WILLIAM B. "Experiment with a Poem." College Litera-
    ture 1 (Winter):64-66.
         Contrasts seven graduate and sixteen undergraduate stu-
    dents asked to explicate "To the Virgins, to make much of
    Time": most of the undergraduates, but only one graduate
    student, examined the poem's language with care.

3   DEMING, ROBERT H. Ceremony and Art: Robert Herrick's Poetry.
    The Hague and Paris: Mouton, 176 pp.
         Revision of 1965.4; incorporates 1967.4, 1968.3, and
    1969.1. Chapter 1, "Ceremony and Art," relates Herrick's
    use of the ceremonial mode to analyses of play by recent
    writers like Johan Huizinga and argues that Herrick uses
    ceremony as a "mediating device between classical and
    Christian, between play and seriousness, between Nature
    and Art." Presents a number of poems, especially
    "Corinna's going a Maying," to suggest that Herrick's
    attitude toward ceremony is that of a "catholic Chris-
    tianity which is able to accommodate and make poetically
    significant any human or natural activity which is for
    God's greater glory." Subsequent chapters, "Ceremony and
    Cosmos," "Ceremony and Death," and "Ceremony as Cultural
    and Historical Vision," investigate Herrick's use of cere-
    monies "in praise of the old way of life, of fear for its
    passing, of agony over its persecution" and suggest that
    Herrick's poetry can be seen as "conceptualized poetic of
    anti-Puritanism." Closes with a postscript contrasting
    Herrick's historical vision with Nathaniel Hawthorne's and
    (briefly) Marvell's: whereas a natural, pagan ethic is
    "an ideal, an abstraction" presented symbolically by
    Hawthorne and a "metaphoric reality" for Marvell, it is
    "actual reality" for Herrick.

4   DeNEEF, A. LEIGH. "This Poetick Liturgie": Robert Herrick's
    Ceremonial Mode. Durham, N.C.: Duke University Press,
    200 pp.
         Publication, with minor revisions, of 1969.2. Incorpo-
    rates 1970.1, 1970.2, 1971.3, and 1971.4. After defining
    the "ceremonial mode" (Chapter 1), treats four kinds of
    ceremonial poems: pastoral ceremonial (Chapter 2),
    courtly ceremonial (Chapter 3), realistic ceremonial
    (Chapter 4), and artistic ceremonial (Chapter 5). Argues
    the unity of Hesperides, for DeNeef sees Herrick's various
    personae as several aspects of a single singer-persona.
    Throughout Hesperides, Herrick addresses the theme of
    death and mutability in a series of ceremonial poems which
    unite the poet and reader in artistic events clarifying
    the significance of moments in human experience.

1974

5   DOYLE, CHARLES CLAY. "An Unhonored English Anacreon: John
    Birkenhead." Studies in Philology 71 (January):192-205.
        Demonstrates Birkenhead's skill by comparing and con-
    trasting three of his translations of Anacreon with trans-
    lations of the same poems by Herrick, Stanley, and Cowley.
    Whereas Herrick "undermines" the effect of the original in
    his version of Anacreontea, VII ("Age unfit for Love"),
    Birkenhead "undertakes to liven the poem with a vivid
    assortment of new images" in his version (called "Of
    Himself"). In translating the story of Cupid and the bee,
    Birkenhead is superior to both Herrick and Stanley in that
    he, "with more sensitivity than his famous contemporaries,
    has sensed and developed the humor inherent in the situa-
    tion which the Greek poem depicts" (Herrick's version is
    "The wounded Cupid. Song"). Similarly, Birkenhead's work
    matches Stanley's and Cowley's in "The Lute."

6   GERTZMAN, JAY A. "Robert Herrick's Recreative Pastoral."
    Genre 7 (June):183-95.
        Summarizes 1972.7. Presents Hesperides as "a kind of
    locus amoenus: a repository of golden age, soft primitive
    sentiments . . . a congenial place for delineation of the
    recreative, not didactic pastoral behaviour." Analyzes
    "Corinna's going a Maying," "The Argument of his Book," and
    "A Nuptiall Song" as examples of poems informed by "cleanly-
    Wantonnesse," which he sees as a mood of genial, unsophis-
    ticated immediacy.

7   HALLI, ROBERT W., Jr. "Affective Stylistics and Gathering
    Rosebuds." Notes on Teaching English 1 (May):1-2.
        Uses the first stanza of "Gather ye Rose-buds" ("To the
    Virgins, to make much of Time") as an example to show how
    presenting a text to students word by word or phrase by
    phrase will help them see "just what sort of mental exer-
    cise it demands of them."

8   ISHII, SHONOSUKE. The Poetry of Robert Herrick. Renaissance
    Monographs, no. 1. Tokyo: Renaissance Institute, Sophia
    University, 193 pp.
        A revision of 1968.5. Eleven essays and five notes
    treating topics like "Simplicity versus Complexity," "The
    Jocund Muse," and "Death the Black Destroyer." The
    eleventh essay, "Practitioner of Short Verse," appears in
    somewhat different form as 1978.11. "Herrick in Japan--An
    Attempt at a Bibliography" (pp. 176-81) provides a list of
    Herrick items (two in English; the rest in Japanese) pub-
    lished in Japan. Also provides "A Select Bibliography"
    (pp. 186-88) of items published elsewhere.

1974

*9   _____. "Robert Herrick to Nihon--Herrick Shokai no ato wo
         Tadotte" [Robert Herrick and Japan: Searching for the
         introduction of Herrick]. Eigo Seinen [The rising genera-
         tion] (Tokyo) 120:178-80.
            Cited in 1974 MLA International Bibliography. Vol. 1.
         New York: Modern Language Association, 1976, item 4386.

10 KENNEDY, ROY BAYLEY. "Colour Symbolism in the Poetry of
         Robert Herrick." In "The Sources and Nature of Colour
         Symbolism in English Poetry of the Mid-Seventeenth Cen-
         tury." Ph.D. dissertation, Oxford University, pp. 138-50.
            Catalogues Herrick's uses of color epithets, commenting
         on the varied significances of colors like white, red, and
         gold in Herrick's poetry. Other chapters trace sources of
         color symbolism in classical literature, the Bible, and so
         on, and treat five other seventeenth-century poets:
         Milton, Crashaw, Marvell, Vaughan, and Traherne.

11 McFARLAND, RONALD E. "Thanksgiving in Seventeenth-Century
         Poetry." Albion 6 (Winter):294-306.
            After outlining elements central to seventeenth-century
         English devotions of thanksgiving, examines Marvell's
         "Bermudas," Herrick's "A Thanksgiving to God, for his
         House" (pp. 303-4) and Herbert's "The Thanksgiving."
         Stresses the private, humble nature of Herrick's poem,
         which McFarland sees as a literary equivalent of Lancelot
         Andrewes's definition of thanksgiving as "Contentation,
         when we rest in the gifts of God, and are satisfied with
         that which we have."

12 MERCHANT, PAUL. "A Jonson Source for Herrick's 'Upon Julia's
         Clothes.'" Notes and Queries 21 (March):93.
            Parallels the second stanza of the Song from Epicoene
         (I.i.97-102) with Herrick's poem.

13 MOLLENKOTT, VIRGINIA R. "'Gather Ye Rosebuds': An Expanded
         Interpretation." Christianity and Literature 23 (Spring):
         47-48.
            Places "To the Virgins, to make much of Time" in the
         context of other Herrick poems using rose images to show
         that "the advice to 'gather rosebuds' is not to be con-
         strued as exclusively secular advice." Refers to the
         virgin who symbolizes the church (II Cor. 11:12) and to
         the wise and foolish virgins (Matt. 25:1-13) to suggest
         that Herrick urges his virgins to "gather experience which
         is both pleasurable and holy." Notes that those who in
         1926 included the phrase "gather ye rosebuds while ye may"

1974

in the memorial window in the church at Dean Prior and
those who carved the same phrase on a stone at the front
of the churchyard understood that it need not be considered
an invitation to licentiousness.

14   SCOTT, GEORGE WALTON. Robert Herrick, 1591-1674. New York:
St. Martin's Press; London: Sidgwick & Jackson, 200 pp.
    Presents Herrick's life in London, Cambridge, and
Devonshire and discusses his poems to show that "Herrick's
genius [is] one of delicacy matched by subtle feeling."
Thirty-four illustrations picture Herrick, his contemporaries, and places where Herrick lived and worked. Closing
chapter discusses his reputation and lists his songs set to
music in the seventeenth through twentieth centuries. A
chronology parallels events in Herrick's biography with
political, literary, scientific, and artistic events between 1554 and 1680. Includes a selected annotated bibliography of some Herrick editions and studies.

15   SEGEL, HAROLD B. The Baroque Poem: A Comparative Survey.
New York: E.P. Dutton & Co.; Toronto and Vancouver:
Clarke, Irwin & Co., 335 pp.
    In "General Remarks on Baroque Literature," notes that
labels like "metaphysical" or "cavalier" suggest a non-
existent distinction between kinds of poetry: in fact,
poets like Herrick participate in "a single (Baroque)
aesthetic widely cultivated throughout Europe primarily in
the seventeenth century." Prints two Herrick poems in a
section entitled "The World of the Spirit," five in "The
World of the Senses."

16   SPINK, IAN. English Song: Dowland to Purcell. London:
B.T. Batsford, 312 pp.
    Includes a number of brief references to Herrick in
sections on "The new men and the new music," "Henry Lawes's
'tunefull and well measur'd song,'" and "Lanier, Wilson and
the songs of some lesser composers." Prints portions of
Herrick songs set to music by various composers, including
the first bars of "Thou may'st be proud" ("To a disdaynefull
fayre") by both Robert Ramsey and John Hilton.

17   SWAN, JAMES MORRILL. Introduction to "History, Pastoral and
Desire: A Psychoanalytic Study of English Renaissance Literature and Society." Ph.D. dissertation, Stanford University, pp. 1-51.
    Explicates (pp. 11-25) "A Country life: To his Brother,
Master Thomas Herrick" to show the dialectic between pastoral otium and anxiety often found in Renaissance

literature. Sees the poem's avowed purpose, "To teach Man to confine desires" (line 16), as ironic, for the poem aims at both the restraint of desire and the search for confines in which desire may be fulfilled. Here, as elsewhere in the dissertation, Swan considers the complex interactions between personal, familial, and social experience in pastoral literature.

See also summary in DAI 35:3702-3A.

18 WATSON, GEORGE, ed. The New Cambridge Bibliography of English Literature. Vol. 1. Cambridge: University Press, cols. 1195-98.

The Herrick entry lists bibliographies and so on (six); collections (twenty-four); works by Herrick (Hesperides; Poor Robin's Visions, 1677, sometimes attributed to Herrick; and "A song for two voices," 1700 [?]); and some ninety-five biographical and critical items. (The latter category includes two articles--by Arvin and Taylor--which are in fact about the novelist Robert Herrick.)

Hesperides is listed as a source of epigrams and verse satires in column 1336.

1975

1 BRADEN, GORDON McMURRAY. "Robert Herrick and Classical Lyric Poetry." In "The Classics and English Renaissance Poetry: Three Case Studies." Ph.D. dissertation, Yale University, pp. 190-313.

Studies Herrick's debts to Martial, Horace, and "Anacreon."

Printed, with minor revisions, as 1978.2. See also summary in DAI 36:7396-97A.

2 BROADBENT, J.B. "The Imperious Empiricist." Times Literary Supplement (London), 25 July, p. 836.

Essay occasioned by the publications of Deming's, DeNeef's, and Scott's studies (1974.3; 1974.4; 1974.14). Stresses, contrary to Scott's judgment, frustration, wildness, and rebellion within Herrick's poetry. Notes the "rebellion of word against stanza, the way [Herrick's] rhythm can split a line or arch across its end," and argues that Herrick's poems deal with the power relationships at issue in seventeenth-century politics.

1975

3   CAMPBELL, PATRICIA D. "Seemly and Due Order: The Signifi-
     cance of Ceremony in the Poetry of Robert Herrick." Ph.D.
     dissertation, University of New Mexico, 176 pp.
         Treats Herrick's ceremonial poems in the context of the
     early seventeenth-century controversy between Puritans and
     traditional Anglicans over ceremonial customs. Sees
     Herrick affirming traditional values. Emphasizes Herrick's
     Christianity by examining his use of the Book of Common
     Prayer and by pointing to his "sacramental view of nature."
     Also sees Herrick's appreciation of ceremony as related to
     his desire to beautify and to order both art and life:
     Herrick, then, is neither a frivolous nor a trivial poet,
     for he teaches his audience to celebrate life.
         See also summary in DAI 36:3724-25A.

4   CARLSON, ANN STUART. "Robert Herrick's Poetry of Festival."
     Ph.D. dissertation, University of Southern Illinois,
     127 pp.
         Chapters on the poetry of Christmastide, of Candlemas,
     of May Day, of weddings, and of wake and harvest home argue
     that Herrick focuses on secular rather than explicitly
     Christian customs in his poetry about festivals. Describes
     seventeenth-century folk customs to show how common they
     were in Herrick's England. Sees Herrick's dramatization of
     these customs as indicative that his pastoralism is not
     entirely classical, but is at least half English.
         See also summary in DAI 37:3636-37A.

5   CHAMBERS, A.B. "Herrick and the Trans-shifting of Time."
     Studies in Philology 72 (January):85-114.
         Treats Noble Numbers, which "is a decidedly mixed
     affair, liturgical on the one hand, classical on the
     other. . . . the work of a Christian priest strongly
     attracted to classical authors, concepts, and points of
     view," and Hesperides, which is "at least in part, [the
     work] of a classically oriented poet strongly attracted to
     liturgical vocabulary, concepts, and points of view."
     Demonstrates that Herrick's dual perspective results in
     "ambivalence, sometimes of an extraordinary kind" by ex-
     amining "The Fairie Temple: or, Oberons Chappell," "The
     Transfiguration," and "To Daffadills" in the contexts of
     other Herrick poems. Argues that each of the poems should
     be read in the context of the whole book: "The commentary
     provided by poems immediately contiguous to one another is
     amplified by poems which, however widely scattered in
     Herrick's volume, cry aloud to be brought together"; by
     the same token, the two books within the 1648 volume should
     be "read as companion works within which many other

1975

companions can be sought and found." Concludes that
Herrick's triumph is his success in combining classical
and Christian elements as he creates a book presenting "a
serio-comic affirmation of the importance of a transient
world on its way to eternity."

6   DAUBER, ANTOINETTE BUTLER.   "Robert Herrick's Poetry of Play."
    Ph.D. dissertation, Yale University, 202 pp.
        Examines Hesperides in light of the theory that "games
    are a positive cultural force and that the poet's constant
    purpose in Hesperides is to experience the rare world of
    play." Treats poems of social life (Chapter 2), poems of
    sexuality (Chapter 3), the epigrams (Chapter 4), and epi-
    taphs (Chapter 5). Closes by postulating that Herrick's
    poetry is successful, for "Like all play, it metamorphoses
    reality into something more desirable."
        Chapter 4, with slight revision, published: 1976.7.
    See also summary in DAI 36:2841A.

7   DAVIS, WALTER R.   "Recent Studies in the English Renaissance."
    Studies in English Literature, 1500-1900 15 (Winter):
    169-202.
        Includes notice of Ishii's, Deming's, and DeNeef's
    recent books (1974.8; 1974.3; 1974.4). Finds DeNeef's
    "the most illuminating approach to this allusive poet to
    date."

8   FERRARI, FERRUCCIO.   "Robert Herrick, Poeta Religioso."   In
    La Poesia Religiosa Inglese del Seicento. Biblioteca di
    Cultura Contemporanea, 15. Messina and Florence: Casa
    Editrice G. D'Anna, pp. 129-82.
        Quotes extensively from the poetry as he discusses
    "Sintesi di ideali classici e cristiani nella poesia di
    Robert Herrick," "L'aspetto cerimoniale nella poesia pro-
    fana e religiosa di R. Herrick," "I temi cristiani e
    L'aspetto gnomico in His Noble Numbers," and "Cristo,
    mediatore degli uomini. Il colloquio con Dio." Sees
    spontaneity and freshness as Herrick's characteristic
    qualities--even in the religious verse. Finds his expres-
    sions of emotion more simple, yet more genuine than those
    of contemporaries like Donne.

9   GARDINER, JUDITH K.   "Herrick's 'All Things Decay and Die' and
    Jonson's 'To the Immortall Memorie, and Friendship of that
    Noble Paire, Sir Lucius Cary, and Sir H. Morison,' 65-74."
    Explicator 33 (May): Item 76.
        Calls attention to the figure of the falling oak in both
    poems and shows that whereas Jonson uses the oak to refer

1975

to himself, Herrick elaborates "Jonson's self-criticism"
to use the image "as an example of the transience of
England's great age of poetry."

10   HINMAN, ROBERT B.   Review of "This Poetick Liturgie," by
      DeNeef.   Seventeenth-Century News 33 (Winter):93-94.
         Sees DeNeef's book (1974.4) as the most valuable of
      those published in Herrick's tercentenary year, for DeNeef
      eloquently and persuasively presents Hesperides as a book
      evoking "a feeling of joy and festivity" that helps its
      readers transcend the awareness of death and mutability
      that is the book's basic premise.

11   MARKEL, MICHAEL H.   "Robert Herrick: The Idea and the Image."
      In "Ritual and the Individual Vision: The Aesthetic
      Dilemma of the Caroline Love Poets." Ph.D. dissertation,
      Pennsylvania State University, pp. 89-118.
         Contrasts Herrick's courtly love lyrics (which Markel
      sees as unsuccessful imitations of the "aggressively dia-
      lectical strategy" of Carew, Suckling, and Lovelace) with
      "the excellent poems written in his own voice." Sees
      Herrick as one of the earliest seventeenth-century poets
      to escape from the influence of Donne. Believes that
      Herrick's genial temperament is both the quality that
      prohibited him from succeeding in the cavalier mode (which
      is negative in tone) and the quality that defines his suc-
      cessful love poetry. Herrick's skill is not in argument,
      but in the presentation of images that demonstrate his sub-
      ject. Thus Herrick is the precursor, not of Restoration
      poets, but of Coleridge. Other chapters treat Herbert,
      Carew, Suckling, Lovelace, and Marvell.
         See also summary in DAI 36:7439-40A.

12   MARLBOROUGH, HELEN.   Review of The Poetry of Robert Herrick,
      by Ishii.   Seventeenth-Century News 33 (Winter):94-95.
         Describes Ishii's essays (which were written "to intro-
      duce the work of Japanese scholars . . . to the English
      speaking world outside") as interesting to Anglo-Americans;
      finds the essay comparing Herrick's poems to Japanese waka
      and haiku and the bibliography of "Herrick in Japan" espe-
      cially helpful to Western readers.

13   PEBWORTH, TED-LARRY.   Review of Robert Herrick, 1591-1674, by
      Scott.   Seventeenth-Century News 33 (Winter):95.
         Brief criticism of Scott's work (1974.14) as "inconse-
      quential."

1976

14   SABINE, MAUREEN ALICE. "Herrick's 'Pretty Fondlings.'" In
      "The Social and Literary Significance of Childhood in
      Selected Seventeenth-Century Poetry." Ph.D. dissertation,
      University of Pennsylvania, pp. 1-83.
          Uses a number of Herrick's lyrics as typical instances
      of early seventeenth-century poets' interest in, but in-
      complete analysis of, childhood. Sees Herrick's epitaphs
      for dead children against the background of infant mor-
      tality rates in the seventeenth century and his poems on
      family life in the context of the complicated hierarchy of
      Renaissance families. Treats the poet's conception of him-
      self as a child before God in his religious poems; diminu-
      tive, childlike fairies in poems like "The Night-piece, to
      Julia" and "Oberons Palace"; and the little Cupid of the
      amatory pieces. Analyzes poems dealing with games, and
      ends by observing that a study of Hesperides will lead one
      to question the assumption that childhood is absent from
      English literature before the nineteenth century. Other
      chapters treat Crashaw, Marvell, and Traherne.
          See also summary in DAI 36:8080A.

15   SUMMERS, CLAUDE J. Account of the Herrick Tercentenary Con-
      ference. Seventeenth-Century News 33 (Winter):95-97.
          Summarizes papers given at the conference (1978.29),
      including one (by Lee Piepho) not printed in the proceed-
      ings.

                              1976

1   ASALS, HEATHER. "King Solomon in the Land of the Hesperides."
      Texas Studies in Literature and Language 18 (Fall):362-80.
          Noting that Renaissance writers do not generally dis-
      tinguish between the proverb, the epigram, and the apothegm,
      argues that Herrick merges the topics and styles of
      Solomonic proverbs, folk proverbs, and classical epigrams;
      his conflation of these genres "informs not only many in-
      dividual pithy poems but the whole conception of Herrick's
      volume of secular poetry." Sees the persona of Hesperides
      as a Solomonic teacher whose presence unites major themes
      of the book: wisdom, kingship, wealth, and love. Argues
      that Herrick's enigmatic style is that of a gnomic epi-
      grammist and that "the universe of the Hesperides is manu-
      factured out of metaphors from biblical Wisdom literature."
      Cites numerous Biblical passages to make the latter point
      and to show the didactic implications of Hesperides.

1976

2   BREMER, RUDY. "The Eye of the Beholder: Herrick's 'Upon
    Julia's Clothes.'" Dutch Quarterly Review of Anglo-
    American Letters 6, no. 1:34-43.
        Presents an explication that agrees with Schneider that
    Julia "is dressed in the first stanza, but undressed in the
    second" (1955.8). Documents his reading of the poem as "in
    reality upon her body" by examining the rhyme scheme,
    punctuation, the meanings of liquefaction and Vibration,
    and the effects of words like Then, then (line 2) and Next
    (line 4).

3   BROADBENT, J.B. Review of Ceremony and Art, by Deming. Notes
    and Queries 23 (May-June):271-72.
        Finds Deming (whose name he spells "Denning") obscuring
    the meanings of some poems by focusing only on their Roman
    backgrounds; wishes for a wider awareness of political and
    literary contexts for others (1974.3). Concludes that
    Herrick's particular genius is as yet undefined.

4   CAIN, T.G.S. Review of three tercentenary celebrations of
    Herrick. Essays in Criticism 26 (April):156-68.
        Reviews Scott's biography (1974.14) and Deming's and
    DeNeef's studies (1974.3 and 1974.4) of Herrick, all of
    which Cain finds disappointing. Links the publication of
    these variously unsatisfactory books with a felt need to
    celebrate the tercentenary of Herrick's death.

5   CHAMBERS, A.B. Review of "This Poetick Liturgie," by DeNeef.
    Journal of English and Germanic Philology 75 (July):417-19.
        Objects to the "rigor" with which DeNeef categorizes the
    poems; for he has subdivided them into so many small groups
    that his argument that the Hesperides is united by
    Herrick's use of a single "mode," the ceremonial, fails.
    Notes, however, the many excellent readings of individual
    poems.

6   CROFT, P.J. "Errata in 'Poems from A Seventeenth-Century
    Manuscript with the Hand of Robert Herrick. . . . " Texas
    Quarterly 19 (Spring):160-73.
        List of errata in Farmer's transcriptions of poems from
    the "Herrick Commonplace Book" (1973.5), preceded by a
    comment that the transcriptions are "riddled with error"
    and that Farmer's "editorial procedure is in practice
    entirely haphazard."
        Response: 1976.8.

1976

7   DAUBER, ANTOINETTE B[UTLER]. "Herrick's Foul Epigrams."
     Genre 9 (Summer):87-102.
          Publication, with minor revisions, of Chapter 5 of
     1975.6. Places Herrick's epigrams within the classical
     and Renaissance tradition of "pointed" scatalogical epi-
     grams. Argues that Herrick reforms the genre by using a
     whimsical voice rather than the vindictive voice of his
     "anal" predecessors and by using excremental imagery that
     "desublimates various adult pursuits to exhibit the in-
     fantile anality which underlies them."

8   FARMER, NORMAN K., Jr. "A Reply to Mr. P. Croft." Texas
     Quarterly 19 (Spring):174.
          Responds to 1976.6 that Croft's comments are "a disguised
     polemic" rather than "a genuine corrigenda."

9   GLAZER, JOSEPH A. "Recent Herrick Criticism: Sighting in on
     One of the Most Elusive of Poets." CLA Journal 20
     (December):292-302.
          Reviews the revival of interest in Herrick beginning
     with Brooks's essay (1947.1), observing a wide disparity of
     views of "what Herrick was about" and lamenting the ten-
     dency of critics who "seem to be caught up in the unex-
     amined assumption that it is Herrick's ideas--his themes,
     arguments, or literary allegiances--that matter, and not
     the uses to which they are put." Sees Jenkins's article
     (1972.10) as a healthy corrective to other essays written
     through 1974, because of Jenkins's interest in Herrick's
     aesthetics and their effect on the reader.

10   LOW, ANTHONY. "The Gold in 'Julia's Petticoat': Herrick and
     Donne." Seventeenth-Century News 34 (Winter):88-89.
          Disputes Patrick's note to line 2 of "Julia's Petticoat"
     (1963.1) by arguing that Herrick uses gold as a metaphor,
     for "it can be beaten extremely thin, even to the point of
     transparency." Suggests the sixth stanza of Donne's "A
     Valediction Forbidding Mourning" as a source for the
     "leaves of gold" in Julia's petticoat.
          Response: 1976.13; rejoinder: 1978.13.

11   MUSGROVE, S[YDNEY]. "Herrick's Alchemical Vocabulary."
     AUMLA: Journal of the Australasian Universities Language
     and Literature Association 46 (November):240-65.
          Quotes extensively from Herrick's poems and from various
     seventeenth-century books on alchemy (including alchemical
     poems published in 1652 in Ashmole's Theatrum Chemicum
     Britannicum) to show that Herrick uses an alchemical vocab-
     ulary throughout Hesperides and Noble Numbers. Argues that

1976

Herrick and others interested in alchemy see it as a way of "applying to the natural world the anagogical system of Christian metaphor prevalent in the age" and that Herrick's principal subject matter is the transmutation of time into eternity. Believes that <u>Hesperides</u> is a product of seventeenth-century "wit," which Musgrove defines as "the power of giving names to things, and thereby in some sense creating them, or creating them anew"; and proposes that since Renaissance alchemy is based on a Christian belief in perfection through change, one can conclude that Herrick's poetry is "an assertion of delight in beauty and complexity, in life and death and rebirth." Suggests that <u>Hesperides</u>'s title refers to the art of alchemy itself and that the phrase <u>Noble Numbers</u> refers to "purified substances."

12 PALMER, PAULINA. Review of <u>"This Poetick Liturgie,"</u> by DeNeef. <u>Yearbook of English Studies</u> 6:258-59.
    Objects to DeNeef's "over-schematizing" <u>Hesperides</u> in 1974.4, yet praises his readings of individual poems. Notes a contradiction between DeNeef's argument that cere-monial poetry is "closed" and his comments on the reader's responses to them; Palmer, observing Renaissance theories of the didactic nature of poetry of praise, would prefer to call the poems "open."

13 PATRICK, J. MAX. "The Golden Leaves and Stars in 'Julia's Petticoat': A Reply to Anthony Low." <u>Seventeenth-Century News</u> 34 (Winter):89-91.
    Responds to Low (1976.10) that the "leaves of gold" on Julia's petticoat and the stars with which it is "pounc't" are probably similar to those pictured on costumes in il-lustrations in Stephen Orgel's and Roy Strong's <u>Inigo Jones: The Theater of the Stuart Court</u> (Berkeley: University of California Press, 1973). Cautions, however, that one's response to the poem ought to be imaginative, rather than "nitpicking."
    Rejoinder: 1978.13.

14 SCHLEINER, LOUISE. "Herrick's Songs and the Character of <u>Hesperides</u>." <u>English Literary Renaissance</u> 6 (Winter): 77-91.
    Calls attention to the significance of Herrick's song-texts by observing that at least forty settings of thirty-one of his poems survive in manuscript and printed song books from 1624 to 1683--more than for any other major early seventeenth-century poet except Campion, who wrote his own settings. Suggests that the number of settings composed before 1648 indicates that Herrick's verse was

important in London while he lived in Devonshire, but modi-
fies Patrick's supposition that the reprinting of some one
hundred of Herrick's lyrics in twenty-eight collections
between 1648 and 1674 attests to his reputation in the mid-
century (1963.1) by noting that the reprints are of "earlier texts; they attest [only] to Herrick's popularity with
composers from about 1625 to 1650."
     Examines the song-text features of Herrick's printed
poems as indicators of his "poetic method, including his
manner of revising for Hesperides" and proposes that the
song-texts revised for the 1648 volume "should be considered in the special context of generic differences between
song-texts and lyrics to be read." Compares several texts
used in early settings with versions of the poems that
appear in Hesperides to show that the revisions tend to
cut out aspects of the text that are "potentially useful in
song . . . [but] of no particular value for a reader" and
that this cutting process may be related to "the often-
noted effect of lightness or insubstantiality in
Hesperides." Adds, "Another cause for this effect of
lightness in Hesperides is the fact that good song-texts
as poems characteristically have a certain expressive
bareness or suggestiveness which is calculated to leave a
composer room to work" and prints settings by William and
Henry Lawes to show what those composers could do with
Herrick's verses. Closes with the observation that
Herrick's revised songs "remain essentially songs"--even
when the revisions seem to be aimed at the goal of making
them "wittily reasoned lyrics of the speaking voice" popular in mid-century poetry. An appendix lists manuscript
and printed settings of Herrick's verses by nine known
composers (Henry and William Lawes, John Wilson, John
Gamble, Robert Ramsey, William Webbe, John Hilton, John
Blow, and Walter Porter) and one anonymous musician.

15   STEWART, STANLEY. Review of "This Poetick Liturgie," by
     DeNeef. Renaissance Quarterly 29 (Autumn):464-67.
          An ironic review of a book that Stewart believes pre-
     sents "ceremonials in the flutter of every green gown, in
     the inflection of every 'Functionary' and 'Gnomic' aside."

16   SUMMERS, CLAUDE J. Review of Ceremony and Art, by Deming.
     Seventeenth-Century News 34 (Winter):87-88.
          Contrasts Deming's work (1974.3) with DeNeef's (1974.4),
     finding the latter more illuminating. Points, however, to
     Deming's perceptive comments on Herrick's awareness of his-
     torical continuities linking the classical period and the
     Renaissance, to his understanding of Herrick's Christianity,

and to his analysis of Baroque elements in the poems.
Praises some but by no means all of Deming's readings of
individual poems. Includes comments on other recent essays
on Herrick and a nineteen-item bibliography.

17 WALTON, GEOFFREY. Review of "This Poetick Liturgie," by
DeNeef. Review of English Studies 27 (May):217-18.
Disputes DeNeef's assignment of the label "artistic
ceremonial" (1974.4) to some of the poems and expresses
some reservation about DeNeef's having framed his book
around the idea of the ceremonial mode. Finds, however,
much to praise in individual chapters.

18 WARREN, AUSTIN. "Herrick Revisited." Michigan Quarterly
Review 15 (Summer):245-67.
Part 1 surveys Warren's evolving interest in Herrick,
relating his own experience to various studies published
during the sixty years since he first read Herrick's poems.
Takes issue with Eliot's assertion that the "personality
expressed" in the 1648 volume is one of "honest ordinari-
ness" (1944.1), for there is nothing ordinary about
Herrick's poetry and his language is too "subtle" and
"oblique" to fit the word honest.
Part 2 treats the question of the unity of Herrick's
poems: sees him adopting so many personae and using so
many literary traditions that it is difficult to get a
firm sense of Herrick himself. Describes him as a man "of
city and court, of university and its classical culture,"
a man happy with the status quo and pleased with his own
work as a poet.
Part 3 presents Herrick's religion as similar to Walter
Pater's in its eclecticism. Explains his use of imagery
from the Roman Catholic Church by suggesting that for
Herrick religion is valuable because it "binds us to the
past" and thus "binds us together." Examines Herrick's
conflation of classicism and English folk customs, and
argues that "Herrick is the priest and celebrator of life,"
rather than a man restlessly searching for certainties.
Believes poems from Hesperides and Noble Numbers belong
together.
Part 4 turns to the question of Herrick's rank as a
poet. Surveys his reputation, accounting for his achieving
popularity in the 1890s by noting that the sensibility that
appreciated Omar Khayyam and Pater and that reacted against
Victorianism would admire Herrick. Warren's own estimation
of Herrick is determined by his sense of a lack of "calculated structure" or of selectivity in the 1648 volume.
Sees the current admiration for Herrick (like the

admiration of the nineteenth century) as due to his "syn-
cretic religion," for we are sympathetic with his attempt
to create, as Whitaker suggests in 1955.10, a "central
myth" that would reconcile paganism and Christianity.

19   WILCHER, ROBERT.   Review of Ceremony and Art, by Deming.
     Yearbook of English Studies 6:256-57.
          Praises Deming's analysis of Herrick's concern with
     "bringing the past to bear in a meaningful way on the 17th
     century present" (1974.3).   Finds comments on the devo-
     tional poems and medieval lyrics and folk customs particu-
     larly helpful--as is Deming's conclusion that the cere-
     monial poems can be seen "as one form or another of
     conceptualized anti-Puritanism."

1977

1   CHAMBERS, A.B.   "Herrick, Corinna, Canticles, and Catullus."
     Studies in Philology 74 (April):216-27.
          Countering Brooks's analysis of "Corinna's going a
     Maying" (1947.1), argues that Herrick sees pagan and
     Christian rites as complementary--as does the author of
     Canticles, a work to which Herrick alludes in "Corinna."
     Cites passages from the Bible, from seventeenth-century
     biblical commentary, and from classical sources to indicate
     how Herrick conflates classical and Christian themes.
     Parallels Catullus' "Viuamus, mea Lesbia" with "Corinna"
     and with adaptations by Ralegh, Campion, and Jonson to show
     how close Herrick's view of time is to Catullus'.   Closes
     with the idea that Herrick parallels two viewpoints in
     "Corinna" and that "in the serio-comic world of Hesperides,"
     there is no necessity to choose between paganism and
     Christianity.

2   DUBINSKI, ROMAN R.   Review of "This Poetick Liturgie," by
     DeNeef.   Renaissance and Reformation 12, no. 2:130-31.
          Expresses reservations about DeNeef's claim that the
     epigrams are examples of "realistic ceremonial," but
     praises his presentation of Herrick's preoccupation with
     transiency and his intention of defeating death by creating
     his volume of poems (1974.4).   Sees DeNeef's emphasis on
     ceremonial as an outgrowth of Miner's more general comments
     on ceremony in cavalier poetry (1971.9).

1977

3 HALLI, ROBERT W., Jr. "Herrick's 'Upon Prig.'" Explicator 35
   (Summer):22.
        Refutes Kimbrough's judgment that the poem is inept
   (1965.8) by showing that "chev'rell" is a kid leather known
   for its elasticity; Prig, then, owns a purse that would
   stretch out and hold more money than he will ever own. The
   epigram is a successful piece of humorous satire.

4 HALPER, NATHAN. "A Drop of Dew." A Wake Newslitter [sic]:
   Studies in James Joyce's Finnegan's Wake 14:61.
        Notes that earlier readers have observed that
   "bidimetoloves" at 4.19 of Finnegan's Wake is a distortion
   of Herrick's "Bid me to love" ("To Anthea, who may command
   him any thing") and finds a distortion of the line "the
   clear region where 'twas born" from Marvell's "A Drop of
   Dew" ("neatlight of the liquor wheretwin 'twas born") to
   suggest that Joyce presents Marvell as a Puritan counter-
   part to the Anglican Herrick.

5 KIMMEY, JOHN L. "Studies in Cavalier Poetry." English
   Studies Collections 2 (January):1-25.
        Treats four cavalier poets--Carew, Herrick, Suckling,
   and Lovelace--as serious artists, each with a distinct
   aesthetic. Section on Herrick focuses first on "To the
   Most Illustrious, and Most Hopefull Prince, Charles, Prince
   of Wales" and "The Argument of his Book" in which Herrick
   introduces the major image patterns (especially light and
   garden imagery) that will inform Hesperides. Then discusses "Corinna's going a Maying" and other poems in which
   those images are used to create an optimistic vision of
   life and art. Stresses the success of these four poets
   who are too often dismissed with the label "cavalier" or
   seen as derivative "sons of Ben."

6 McCLUNG, WILLIAM A. The Country House in English Renaissance
   Poetry. Berkeley, Los Angeles, and London: University of
   California Press, 192 pp.
        Revision of 1972.12. Shows how poems by Jonson, Carew,
   Herrick, and Marvell in praise of manorial estates owned by
   public servants like the Sidneys (who owned Penshurst), the
   de Grays (Wrest), and the Crofts (Saxham) recommend the
   continuation of traditional moral values. Chapter 1 traces
   elements of the genre to the sponte sua topos in the myth
   of the golden age. Chapter 2 treats the genre in the context of Renaissance England's idealization of England as a
   demi-paradise and the long-standing tradition of the literature of complaint that asserts the degeneration of contemporary life; identifies Joseph Hall's Satire V, 2 (which

includes criticism of a "garish" house) as one source for
the seventeenth-century country-house poems. Chapter 3
outlines the ethical attributes of architecture praised by
the country-house poets by contrasting Penshurst and
Haddon Hall with Longleat and other Elizabethan and
Jacobean "prodigy" houses and by showing how the latter,
in their "acceptance of the principle of conscious design
and display" reveal a new "attitude towards country houses
and towards the country itself." Disputes Hibbard's suggestion that country-house poets attacked the work of Inigo
Jones and his followers (1956.6) by showing that the neo-
classical houses were built too late to have incited the
criticism of poets in the early and mid-seventeenth century; instead, it is the decorated Caroline country house
that serves as the antithesis of the "natural" medieval
house. Chapter 4 analyzes poems by Jonson, Carew, and
Herrick to show how they praise the utility of the estates
whose owners they celebrate. Chapter 5 treats Marvell and,
briefly, later writers whose works contain elements of the
seventeenth-century country-house genre. Thirty-four
illustrations.

7   MARCUS, LEAH SINANOGLOU. "Herrick's Noble Numbers and the
     Politics of Playfulness." English Literary Renaissance 7
     (Winter):108-26.
         Expands ideas about Herrick's Laudianism mentioned in
     1971.13 and 1978.17. Explicates some of the poems treating
     holiday customs against a background of discussion of the
     seventeenth-century controversies over traditional festi-
     vals. Stresses the "solemn warning" implicit in the final
     poems of Noble Numbers as a sign of Herrick's awareness
     that the encroachment of new ideas threatens Anglicanism
     as he has known it.

8   MARTINDALE, JOANNA [HILARY]. "Robert Herrick." In "The
     Response to Horace in the Seventeenth Century, with Special
     Reference to the 'Odes' and to the Period 1600-1660."
     Ph.D. dissertation, Oxford University, pp. 168-96, 384-85.
         Notes Herrick's debts to the Anacreontea, the Greek
     Anthology, and to "Jonson's Horatian manner"--the latter
     in poems like "A Country life: To his Brother, Master
     Thomas Herrick," "A Panegerick to Sir Lewis Pemberton,"
     and "To his worthy Friend, Master Thomas Falconbridge."
     Discusses Herrick's more characteristic voice, that of
     "the small man," and his use of innocent quiet country
     details--both derived directly from Horace. Analyzes a
     number of Herrick's poems to show he has thoroughly assim-
     ilated aspects of Horace's temperament foreign to Jonson

and concludes that Herrick's voice is an individual one, not exactly like either Jonson's or Horace's.

Appendix 1 (pp. 384-85) lists lines from "A Country life" that echo lines from Octavianus Mirandula's Illustrium poetarum flores. Notes, however, that there seem to be a few Horatian allusions not from Mirandula in the poem.

1978

1   BRADEN, GORDON. "Herrick's Classical Quotations." In "Trust to Good Verses": Herrick Tercentenary Essays. Edited by Roger B. Rollin and J. Max Patrick. Pittsburgh: University of Pittsburgh Press, pp. 127-47.

Shortened version of parts of Chapter 3 of 1975.1 and 1978.2. Shows how Herrick quotes classical poets without much consideration of the contexts of the lines he uses: "while Herrick seems very interested in classical poetry, he is not comparably interested in classical poems." Argues that Herrick's attention tends to be on the "verbal texture" of various Latin poets, not on "individual poems as wholes." Yet sees a similarity between Herrick and Horace in that "The Odes and Hesperides each project a self-contained lyric 'world' . . . they are both attempts at realizing contentment with a set of donnees." Moreover, Horace quotes Greek lyric poets as Herrick quotes Latin sources; perhaps the method of quotation exemplified by the two poets "is not incidental but central to at least a certain kind of lyric poetry."

2   _____. "Robert Herrick and Classical Lyric Poetry." In The Classics and English Renaissance Poetry: Three Case Studies. Yale Studies in English, 187. New Haven and London: Yale University Press, pp. 154-258, 269-75.

Derived from 1975.1. Sees Hesperides as "a book about dainty things lived with more or less on their own terms" and maintains that the particular quality of that book is the result of Herrick's "eccentric and sophisticated" use of the classics. Reiterates his belief that Herrick borrows individual lines, rather than whole poems, from Latin poets (1978.1) and calls many of those borrowings "invisible" to all but the most alert source-hunter--as indeed are many of Jonson's borrowings from classical sources. Rejects Catullus as a major influence on Herrick and examines his debts to Martial, Anacreon, and Horace. Emphasizes Martial's Epigrammata as influencing "the overall shape" of Herrick's work, for both are long books of interchangeable,

similar short poems; finds Herrick's poems, however, generally less successful than Martial's. Presents an ex-
tended discussion of the Anacreontea in Renaissance England
and then claims that although Herrick quotes a great many
classical poets, Anacreon is the one with whom he "identifies"; sees Herrick following Anacreon in attempting to
create a dream world within lyric poetry. Finds Horace
most significant for Herrick in that he provides "a sense
of strategy--for, among other things, not wondering what
you are missing." Expands comments on Horace in 1978.1 and
speculates that lyric poets' task is "to learn carefully
how to mean what [they] say." If that is so, lyric poets
may look to the past for affirmation of the principle that
life can be lived: "Bubbles have no history, but they do
have precedents." Appendix, "Herrick's Edition of
'Anacreon,'" describes Estienne's editions of "Anacreon."

3   CAIN, T.G.S. "'Times trans-shifting': Herrick in Meditation." In "Trust to Good Verses": Herrick Tercentenary
Essays. Edited by Roger B. Rollin and J. Max Patrick.
Pittsburgh: University of Pittsburgh Press, pp. 103-23.
      Calls attention to poems in Hesperides that "meditate on
the facts of transience and death without compromise and
without offer of consolation, not even the slender solace
of carpe diem to which Herrick is ready at other times to
resort." Sees poems like "To a Gentlewoman, objecting to
him his gray haires" and "To Dianeme" (H-160) as serious,
dignified poems modeled, in part, on Horace's Odes 1.25
(Parcius iunctas), 4.10 (o crudelis adhus), and 4.13
(Audivere, Lyce), and adds that the "charnel-house imagery"
sometimes found in Herrick's poems is in the same tradition
as Skelton's "Upon a Deadmans Hed." Argues that as they
acknowledge death, Herrick's meditative poems share a
"quiet firmness" with Counter-Reformation treatises on
Christian meditation and that, like some of Herbert's
poems, Herrick's poetry of meditation may be seen in the
context of meditations on the Book of Nature by figures
like Joseph Hall, François de Sales, and Ralph Austen.
Shows that the association of women with flowers that informs many of the love poems is central to meditative poems
like "To Violets" and "A Meditation for his Mistresse";
these poems on death within the natural world are Herrick's
"most complete victory over 'Times trans-shifting.'"

1978

4   CLAYTON, THOMAS. Introduction to Cavalier Poets: Selected
     Poems. Oxford, London, and New York: Oxford University
     Press, pp. xiii-xxiii.
         Stresses the differences between the four poets repre-
     sented in the volume (Herrick, Carew, Suckling, and
     Lovelace), noting that only Herrick is certainly a Son of
     Ben. Says Herrick's work often "enacts the 'social life'
     of a person who finds much of his companionship in his
     imagination"; his best-known poems, such as "Delight in
     Disorder" and "Upon Julia's Clothes," are brief master-
     pieces, difficult to categorize. Prints 151 pages of
     Herrick poems.

5   ELMORE, A.E. "Herrick and the Poetry of Song." In "Trust to
     Good Verses": Herrick Tercentenary Essays. Edited by
     Roger B. Rollin and J. Max Patrick. Pittsburgh: Univer-
     sity of Pittsburgh Press, pp. 65-75.
         Suggests that the poems that are usually anthologized
     are not truly representative of Herrick's work. Cautions,
     therefore, against generalizations drawn from a sampling of
     Hesperides and Noble Numbers. Notes that Herrick's best
     poems are often his songs; postulates that the song, even
     apart from its performance, is a genre in the same sense
     as are tragedy, masque, ballad, and carol.

6   FARMER, NORMAN K., Jr. "Herrick's Hesperidean Garden: ut
     pictura poesis Applied." In "Trust to Good Verses":
     Herrick Tercentenary Essays. Edited by Roger B. Rollin and
     J. Max Patrick. Pittsburgh: University of Pittsburgh
     Press, pp. 15-51; 11 plates.
         Proposes that the "blend of realism and allegory" in
     Marshall's engraved frontispiece to the 1648 volume "in-
     vites the reader to see the poems that follow as "seek[ing]
     a balance between the modalities of naturalism and alle-
     gory." Suggests that most of the poems in Hesperides
     should "be read as speaking pictures, as landskips . . . or
     simply as iconic poems in which the poet contemplates an
     already-formed graphic representation." Speculates that
     the list of painters in "To his Nephew, to be prosperous in
     his art of Painting" and the "white temple of . . . Heroes"
     in "To his Honoured Kinsman, Sir Richard Stone" indicate
     that Herrick knew of the Earl of Arundel's collection of
     paintings. Observes that "To the Painter, to draw him a
     Picture" and "The Eye" depend on the ut pictura poesis
     topos for their meaning and goes on to say that "one's
     perambulations in the Hesperidean garden depend . . . upon
     a reciprocal interplay of the visual and the verbal, the
     one being perceptual and the other being conceptual."

Closes by examining this interplay in the Oberon poems, the
Julia poems, and a few others; concludes that Patrick is
correct in saying "Herrick's Hesperidean garden is most
certainly one whose golden fruits take the shape of poems
[1963.1]. Moreover, it is a garden . . . in which we may
(in the most vivid sense) 'walk amongst' the verbal equiva-
lent of 'bowers, mounts, and arbours, artificiall wilder-
nesses, green thickets . . . and such like pleasant
places.'"

7   GUIBBORY, ACHSAH. "'No lust theres like to Poetry':
    Herrick's Passion for Poetry." In "Trust to Good Verses":
    Herrick Tercentenary Essays. Edited by Roger B. Rollin and
    J. Max Patrick. Pittsburgh: University of Pittsburgh
    Press, pp. 79-87.
        Explores the idea that in Herrick's verse, "poetry is
    the product of a heat which is almost sexual, and his poems
    themselves become objects of his love, capable of arousing
    a delightful excitement that is similar to sexual passion
    and possibly superior to it." Cites Otto Rank's suggestion
    that the poet's creative urge, like the procreative im-
    pulse, derives from the desire to immortalize oneself (Art
    and Artist, 1932; rpt. 1968); and quotes Herrick's poems
    to show that he presents his verses not only as children,
    but also as "mistresses, the actual objects of his love."
    Examines the Julia poems, in which Herrick indicates that
    it is Julia's artfulness, not her physical beauty, that
    evokes the poet's pleasure, and goes on to show that
    Herrick uses similar images to describe his ladies and his
    poetry. Closes with the observation that poetry, even more
    than ladies, provides Herrick pleasure in old age, in "His
    age, dedicated to his peculiar friend, Master John Wickes,
    under the name of Posthumus," he writes of himself as an
    aged poet, revitalized by the seductive power of poetry,
    when he cries, "No lust theres like to Poetry."

8   HALLI, ROBERT W., Jr. "Herrick's 'To Anthea, Who May Command
    Him Anything,' 1-4." Explicator 36 (Spring):19-20.
        Stresses the seventeenth-century meaning of Protestant
    as distinct "on the one hand from Popery, on the other from
    Presbyterianism and Puritanism." The poet's love for
    Anthea, then, is an "orthodox" love for a divine figure.

9   _____. "Robert Herrick's Epigrams on Commoners." South
    Atlantic Bulletin 43 (January):30-41.
        Defends Herrick's scurrilous epigrams (which were popu-
    lar in his own time) by relating them to the Renaissance
    continuation of the ancient theory that the perception of

physical or moral ugliness is "the basic cause of laughter."
Cites a number of the epigrams on common people to show how
Herrick uses puns to create comic contrasts, often between
commoners' presentations of themselves and the true facts.
Includes observations made in 1977.2 to show the sharp
humor directed against those "who vaunt themselves in terms
of wealth, intellect, honor, and physical purity." Argues
that the epigrams on ugliness provide contrast within
Hesperides, for "almost every source of delight in Herrick's
poems on imaginary mistresses has its antithesis in the
coarse epigrams." Even in the epigrams, then, Herrick "is
a careful and consummate artist."

10   HOLLADAY, HAROLD LAKE. "'Chains of Darknesse': A Study of
     Robert Herrick's Hesperides." Ph.D. dissertation, Univer-
     sity of Michigan, 208 pp.
         Rejects the notion that trivial poetry is worthless and
     accepts T.S. Eliot's judgment that Herrick was an "un-
     selfconscious man" (1944.1). Believes that the excellence
     of Herrick's poetry derives from a unified sensibility in-
     herited from the Middle Ages and postulates that Hesperides
     is a complexly diverse book (Chapter 1). Downplays
     Herrick's classicism, arguing that his sensuality and his
     ecstatic moods preclude his being a moderate, classical
     writer (Chapter 2). Sees death and transience as Herrick's
     central preoccupations; his goal is not to transcend death,
     but to make it comprehensible (Chapter 3). Believes
     Herrick's eroticism sometimes "borders on the perverse,"
     sometimes is joyous and healthful (Chapter 4). Observes
     that Herrick's public poetry "articulates a fairly wide
     range of political ideas" (Chapter 5). Includes close
     readings of many poems and relates the poetry to key events
     of Herrick's lifetime.
         See also summary in DAI 39:897A.

11   ISHII, SHONOSUKE. "Herrick and Japanese Classical Poetry: A
     Comparison." In "Trust to Good Verses": Herrick Tercen-
     tenary Essays. Edited by Roger B. Rollin and J. Max
     Patrick. Pittsburgh: University of Pittsburgh Press,
     pp. 187-96.
         Presents five examples of Japanese poems exemplifying
     the qualities of aware ("sensitivity to beauty") and
     okashi ("a state of mind which is at once sober and sensi-
     ble of stern reality") as evidence for his observations
     about key parallels between Herrick's verse and classical
     Japanese poetry. Finds them similarly restrained and sug-
     gestive (though Herrick is somewhat more "loquacious" than
     Japanese poets) and notes that they both treat "the theme

of the transiency of happiness, beauty, and love in poems
dealing with little or young things such as flowers or
maidens." Yet Herrick uses a wider variety of images and
is "more robust and physical" than his Japanese counter-
parts.

12   KAUFMAN, U. MILO. "Herrick and the Search for Secure Space."
     In Paradise in the Age of Milton. English Literary Stud-
     ies, no. 11. Victoria, Canada: University of Victoria,
     pp. 51-56.
          Quotes a number of poems from Noble Numbers to contrast
     Herrick's presentation of paradise as a "womb-like sanctu-
     ary" with "concessions to the abyss" in Milton's represen-
     tation of his paradisal garden. Links Herrick's "claustro-
     phobia" to "the secularizing of space in his century and
     . . . his accommodation of a strangely troubled conscience."

13   LOW, ANTHONY. "Gold Leaves and Petticoats Once More."
     Seventeenth-Century News 36 (Spring):9.
          Responds to Patrick (1976.13) that Herrick might have
     meant to refer to gold leaf in "Julia's Petticoat," for the
     OED gives a definition of leaf from 1567 as "a very thin
     sheet of metal, esp. gold or silver."

14   _____. "Robert Herrick: The Religion of Pleasure." In
     Love's Architecture: Devotional Modes in Seventeenth-
     Century English Poetry. New York: New York University
     Press, pp. 208-34.
          Presents the poems in Hesperides as evidence of
     Herrick's love of sensuous beauty; even the scatological
     epigrams indicate his "simple revulsion from ugliness."
     Cites Røstvig's work on the blending of the Epicurean and
     Horatian traditions (1962.6), but believes that Herrick
     rejects the moderate tone found in poets like Jonson and
     Milton whose works fit Røstvig's explanation. Sees poems
     like "Julia's Petticoat" as foreshadowing a major theme of
     Noble Numbers: "the pursuit of pleasure, guided by God, to
     its uttermost limits--into Heaven itself and 'Life Eter-
     nal.'" Speculates that unlike Crashaw whose "major influ-
     ences were probably affective devotion and mysticism,"
     Herrick's merging of the spiritual and the physical has a
     philosophic basis in treatises on pleasure by Italian
     humanists like Valla, Ficino, and Pico.
          Contrasts Herrick's epigrams with Crashaw's; whereas
     Crashaw strives to "astonish and amaze," Herrick works for
     "simplicity and clarity." Examines some of the seventy
     devotional poems in Noble Numbers to show their "peculiarly
     public and vocal character." Admires meditative poems like

"To his sweet Saviour" and "Good Friday: Rex Tragicus";
they are remarkable contributions to a "well-worn genre."
Although these meditations express a religion of intense
pleasure, the final poem of Noble Numbers makes clear the
fact that Herrick's "ladder of self-gratification leads
finally to selfless love."

15   MACLEAN, HUGH. "'Wit and new misterie': Herrick's Poetry."
      In Familiar Colloquy: Essays Presented to Arthur Edward
      Barker. Edited by Patricia Brückmann. Ottawa: Oberon
      Press, pp. 37-54.
          Examines Herrick's "wit" by noting his use of the term
      (sometimes he uses the word to refer to graceful conversa-
      tion; other times to name "inventive intelligence") and by
      studying Herrick's applications of his own wit. Believes
      that Herrick's wit searches for realities beneath or within
      appearances and cites a number of poems in which "the play
      of wit" creates the "wild civility" that Herrick prefers
      over either "art that is precisely arranged or unadorned
      nature itself." Notes Herrick's many enthusiastic allu-
      sions to the power of music and the poems in which he suc-
      cessfully "[matches] wits with time"--especially "His
      Winding-sheet" in which he transforms the sheet itself into
      his own "wit / Of all I've writ" and "A Nuptiall Song" in
      which he expects the married couple to use their "wit" to
      "teach / Nature and Art one more / Play than they ever
      knew before." Declines to call Herrick a metaphysical
      poet, but observes a significant similarity between his
      wit and theirs.

16   MANLOVE, C[HARLES] N[ICHOLAS]. "Jonson and Herrick." In
      Literature and Reality, 1600-1800. London: Macmillan &
      Co., pp. 16-29.
          Presents Herrick as a less successful follower of
      Jonson--in large part because of Herrick's "fascination
      with phenomena" and his subsequent use of a "centrifugal"
      structure in his poems. Shows, for example, that in
      "Delight in Disorder" and "A Panegerick to Sir Lewis
      Pemberton," Herrick's focus on particulars means his poems
      are "framed," but not "informed," by moral generalizations.

17   MARCUS, LEAH SINANOGLOU. "The Poet as Child: Herbert,
      Herrick, and Crashaw." In Childhood and Cultural Despair:
      A Theme and Variations in Seventeenth-Century Literature.
      Pittsburgh: University of Pittsburgh Press, pp. 94-152.
          Develops comments in 1971.13 and 1977.7. Now sees that
      in Noble Numbers Herrick "played the child to dramatize the
      humble obedience he and more rebellious countrymen owed to

Laudian ecclesiastical authority." Shows how <u>Noble Numbers</u>
responds to the Puritan's threat to his church by "denying
Calvinist teaching about original sin and predestination";
by stressing "shared communal observance" rather than the
idea of "inner individual struggle"; and by a "deliberate
glorification of those base sports and holiday customs" to
which Puritans objected. Observes that the merry world of
<u>Hesperides</u> is threatened by time and still believes that
the "child's version of Anglicanism" in the shorter,
simpler religious poems gives Herrick's <u>Noble Numbers</u> a
tone of "humble certainty beyond the power of time to alter
or destroy."

18 MARLBOROUGH, HELEN. "Herrick's Epigrams of Praise." In
    "Trust to Good Verses": Herrick Tercentenary Essays.
    Edited by Roger B. Rollin and J. Max Patrick. Pittsburgh:
    University of Pittsburgh Press, pp. 159-69.
       Observes that a number of poems within <u>Hesperides</u> are
    epigrams of praise, but that unlike Jonson, who presents
    his epideictic <u>Epigrammes</u> as a theater containing a drama
    with ethical implications, Herrick seems to conceive of his
    complimentary poems as a series of static portraits or in-
    scriptions. These "images of portrait, sculpture, and in-
    scription . . . create a significant pattern--an imagined
    collection--within the larger book, <u>Hesperides</u>"; "The
    pillar of Fame" at the end "may remind us that the epigrams
    of praise are not only social and occasional verses, but a
    significant part of the design of <u>Hesperides</u>." Concludes
    that Herrick's and Jonson's poetry of praise differs from
    "the grandiloquent and politically complex" epideictic
    poetry of Waller and Dryden, for Herrick and Jonson both
    see virtue as "essentially static and timeless ideals."

19 MARTZ, LOUIS L. "Marvell and Herrick: The Masks of
    Mannerism." In Approaches to Marvell: The York Tercen-
    tenary Lectures. Edited by C.A. Patrides. Boston:
    Routledge & Kegan Paul; London: Routledge, pp. 194-215;
    8 plates.
       Postulates "that Herrick and Marvell, along with Carew
    and Lovelace, form a school of English mannerist poets."
    Uses examples from sixteenth-century Italian painting and
    from Herrick and Marvell to define Mannerism as a style
    whose attributes include instability and disjunction (thus
    the seemingly haphazard order of poems within <u>Hesperides</u>),
    the necessity of a "curious" (attentive) audience who will
    see the order in "sweet [pleasing] neglect," and emphasis
    on "the perfectly made detail." Observes that Inigo Jones
    introduced Mannerism to England early in the seventeenth

1978

century and "In the Caroline court Mannerism became almost a way of life, and also a way of death." Like their Italian predecessors, Herrick and Marvell worked in a time of political and religious upheaval; similarly, both groups of artists worked "under the shadow" of classical masters. Closes by using three of Herrick's poems to King Charles ("To the King, Upon his comming with his Army into the West," "To the King and Queene, upon their unhappy distances," and "To the King, Upon his welcome to Hampton-Court") to show how these Mannerist poets convey "the effect of recording the end of an era."

20 MOISSON, THOMAS EDWARD. "Herrick's 'Moist Alchemy': Liquid Imagery in the Poetry of Robert Herrick." Ph.D. dissertation, Harvard University, 238 pp.
Treats Herrick's images of liquidity as symptomatic of an "elegiac point of view" and examines Herrick's "sublimation of liquidity through the metamorphosis of art."

21 MOLLENKOTT, VIRGINIA RAMEY. "Herrick and the Cleansing of Perception." In "Trust to Good Verses": Herrick Tercentenary Essays. Edited by Roger B. Rollin and J. Max Patrick. Pittsburgh: University of Pittsburgh Press, pp. 197-209.
Argues "that in Donne's sense of seeing God in everything, Herrick is a religious poet, even in some poems which seem quite secular from a more traditional religious viewpoint." Compares "Corinna's going a Maying" with Thomas Bateson's "Sister, awake" and "Meat without mirth" with its source in Plutarch's Symposiacs to show Herrick adding "a religious dimension" to his sources. Maintains that even in the love poetry, "there is a sense of organic union with nature and a collapsing of any distinctions between what is natural, what is pleasurable, and what is worshipful." Concludes that those who define religion by "doctrine, theory, and organization" will deny that Herrick is religious, but that those who define religion as the perception of "the sacredness of everything that lives" will see that Herrick, like Blake, is a religious poet.

22 MONTAGUE, GENE. "Herrick's 'Upon Julia's Clothes.'" Explicator 36 (Spring):21-22.
Observes "the central angling image" in the poem; "the two central persons, Julia and the narrator, are assigned three roles--fisherman, bait, and prey. The question is, Who is angling for whom and with what?"

*23   MORI, AKIRA. "Koten ni asonsa Hito: Herrick-shi Hyoshaku"
       [The man who played in the classics: Commentary in
       Herrick's poetry]. Eigo Seinen [The rising generation]
       (Tokyo) 124:318-19.
            Cited in 1978 MLA International Bibliography. Vol. 1.
       New York: Modern Language Association, 1979, item 4751.

24   MURPHY, AVON JACK. "Robert Herrick: The Self-Conscious
       Critic in Hesperides." In "Trust to Good Verses": Herrick
       Tercentenary Essays. Edited by Roger B. Rollin and J. Max
       Patrick. Pittsburgh: University of Pittsburgh Press,
       pp. 53-63.
            Proposes that the persona-critic of Hesperides "is
       groping toward confidence in his own artistry and control,
       an assurance in the immortalizing power of poetry, and a
       mature realization of what Hesperides can and does become."
       Demonstrates that the persona-critic's growth is presented
       in three stages: the first encompasses the first eight
       poems of Hesperides; the second, poems H-9 through H-1122;
       the third, poems H-1123 through "The pillar of Fame."

25   NORLAND, HOWARD B. "A Reassessment of Herrick." Prairie
       Schooner 52 (Fall):295-96.
            Reviews "Trust to Good Verses" (1978.29) as a "hodge-
       podge of critical perspectives and judgments of varying
       quality"; believes the central issue in Herrick criticism
       ought to be Herrick's character as "one of the most con-
       vivial, concise, and witty poets in the English language."

26   ORAM, WILLIAM. "Herrick's Use of Sacred Materials." In
       "Trust to Good Verses": Herrick Tercentenary Essays.
       Edited by Roger B. Rollin and J. Max Patrick. Pittsburgh:
       University of Pittsburgh Press, pp. 211-18.
            Revision of pp. 261-71 of 1973.8. Shows how Herrick
       uses Christian materials--biblical echoes, references to
       ceremonies like burial rites, for example--for aesthetic
       rather than religious purposes. Uses "Corinna's going
       a Maying," "To his Booke" (H-3), "The Funerall Rites of the
       Rose," and "To Perilla" as examples for his argument that
       Hesperides is about "immediate sensuous experience."

27   PATRICK, J. MAX. "'Poetry perpetuates the Poet': Richard
       James and the Growth of Herrick's Reputation." In "Trust
       to Good Verses": Herrick Tercentenary Essays. Edited by
       Roger B. Rollin and J. Max Patrick. Pittsburgh: Univer-
       sity of Pittsburgh Press, pp. 221-34.

1978

    Expands comments on Herrick's reputation in 1963.1 with
a "realistic survey of Herrick's slow rise toward the fame
he now enjoys." Counters Martin's claim that the line
"Some Johnson, Drayton, or some Herick" [sic] in Richard
James's The Muses Dirge (1625), is evidence of Herrick's
high reputation in the 1620s (1956.1) by arguing that
James's poem is merely "a pretentiously erudite, exhibi-
tionistically witty, eulogistic profession of mourning"
and showing that there is no adequate evidence to verify
the claim that Herrick was a well-known poet in 1625; all
we can say is that James, an Oxford man, made "a signifi-
cantly early mention" of Herrick. Quotes the line in context to show that James is probably contrasting Herrick, a
little-known poet, with Jonson or Drayton. Goes on to
argue that Martin underestimates the significance of the
other seventeenth-century references to Herrick; the fact
that some one hundred of Herrick's poems appear in collections published between 1649 and 1674 indicates that his
poetry was popular--as do the many extant manuscript copies
of his verse. Prefers, then, "to accept Wood's statement
that the volume met with popularity on publication, especially among Royalists [1721.1], and to conclude that it
was no more 'neglected' than other volumes of verse published in the late 1640s and 1650s." Agrees with those who
have noted that the 1648 volume appeared at an inopportune
moment in history and speculates that Herrick's seventeenth-
century reputation would have been higher if he had printed
some of his poems in the 1630s, if he had printed a series
of thinner volumes, and if he had omitted the less excellent poems--or arranged the volume so that his finest verses
were not buried within it. Speculates that Herrick wrote
more poetry after 1648, some of which may one day be dis-
covered.

28   PEBWORTH, TED-LARRY, with DeNEEF, A. LEIGH; LEE, DOROTHY;
    SIEMON, JAMES E.; and SUMMERS, CLAUDE J., comps. "Selected
    and Annotated Bibliography." In "Trust to Good Verses":
    Herrick Tercentenary Essays. Edited by Roger B. Rollin and
    J. Max Patrick. Pittsburgh: University of Pittsburgh
    Press, pp. 237-81.

    Presents brief descriptions of significant editions of
Herrick (Part 1), bibliographies and concordances (Part 2),
scholarship and criticism (Part 3, A: before 1910; B:
after 1910), and separately published notes on individual
poems (Part 4). Items included begin with the 1648 volume
and end with 1976. Pebworth explains that this bibliography focuses on scholarship and criticism since 1910 because "Only in the second decade of the twentieth century

did important scholarship begin to appear in quantity, heralded by the critical studies of Delattre and Moorman and spurred by the latter's scholarly edition; and in the last thirty years Herrick scholarship and criticism have noticeably quickened in pace and deepened in perception."

29   ROLLIN, ROGER B., and PATRICK, J. MAX, eds. "Trust to Good Verses": Herrick Tercentenary Essays. Pittsburgh: University of Pittsburgh Press, 291 pp.
        Thirteen essays from the Robert Herrick Memorial Conference held at the University of Michigan-Dearborn, 11-13 October 1974. Additional essays by Rollin and Patrick and a forty-page annotated bibliography of Herrick editions and studies compiled by Ted-Larry Pebworth and others complete the volume. Individual items are summarized under their authors' names in 1978.1, 3, 5-7, 11, 18, 21, 24, 26-28, 30-31, 33, 35.

30   ROLLIN, ROGER B. "Sweet Numbers and Sour Readers: Trends and Perspectives in Herrick Criticism." In "Trust to Good Verses": Herrick Tercentenary Essays. Edited by Roger B. Rollin and J. Max Patrick. Pittsburgh: University of Pittsburgh Press, pp. 3-11.
        Introduces essays from the Herrick Tercentenary Conference as "consolidat[ing] a 'revisionist' view of Robert Herrick. In essence this view maintains that Herrick is a serious and significant artist rather than a minor if skillful craftsman; that his Hesperides is an encyclopedic and ultimately coherent work rather than a miscellany of charming but trivial poems; and that many of those poems exhibit patterns of intellectual significance and emotional depth beneath their polished and seemingly simple surfaces." Observes that work remains to be done on Herrick's prosody, rhetoric, wit, and humor and suggests that Herrick be studied in terms of semiotics, structuralism, and socio-cultural, archetypal, and psychological approaches to literature. Proposes areas of exploration that could reveal how Herrick's reader is involved in "an extensive and complex psychological transaction."

31   SHAWCROSS, JOHN T. "The Names of Herrick's Mistresses in Hesperides." In "Trust to Good Verses": Herrick Tercentenary Essays. Edited by Roger B. Rollin and J. Max Patrick. Pittsburgh: University of Pittsburgh Press, pp. 89-102.
        Examines the etymologies of the fourteen names Herrick uses for his mistresses and concludes that since names like Irene, Myrrha, Biancha, Corinna, and Lucia are "sometimes

employed for their onomastic value," we cannot suppose that Herrick's poems refer to fourteen distinct ladies.

32 SHIPPS, ANTHONY W. "Two Poems by Herrick?" Notes and Queries 25 (October):446.
Identifies two of the lines Howarth guessed were by Herrick (1955.4) as adaptations of two lines from Sylvester's translation of Du Bartas.
For earlier discussions of lines possibly by Herrick from The English Parnassus, see 1955.5, 1956.8, and 1962.5.

33 SUMMERS, CLAUDE J. "Herrick's Political Poetry: The Strategies of His Art." In "Trust to Good Verses": Herrick Tercentenary Essays. Edited by Roger B. Rollin and J. Max Patrick. Pittsburgh: University of Pittsburgh Press, pp. 171-83.
Argues, "As a political poet, Herrick is very seldom merely topical. His ability to incorporate topical issues into a richly complex vision makes several of his poems examples of political discourse of a very high order." Cites some of the epigrams to show that "Herrick's political vision is an orthodox and conservative one" and notes that the positive portrayals of country people in Hesperides "results from a paternalistic rather than an egalitarian attitude." Quotes a number of poems to show Herrick's belief in the "sacred, creative powers" of kingship--a role that Herrick sees as analogous to that of the poet. Disputes DeNeef's suggestion (1974.4) that Herrick's ceremonial poetry "does not lead beyond itself" and argues that Herrick uses the festive ceremonial mode in poems like "A Dirge upon the Death of the Right Valiant Lord, Bernard Stuart" and "To Sir John Berkley, Governour of Exeter" as part of "a carefully devised poetic strategy which utilizes the literal, mundane world as a telling contrast with the celebrated world." Instead of presenting a "timeless Arcadia" in Hesperides, then, "Herrick complexly integrates a sensitive awareness of the real and an imagined apprehension of the transcendent."

34 _____. Review of "This Poetick Liturgie," by DeNeef. Modern Philology 75 (February):297-300.
Sees DeNeef's work (1974.4) as "both exciting and dismaying"--exciting in that DeNeef's treatments of individual poems are "often insightful and refreshingly original," dismaying in his "relentless devotion to an unconvincing thesis." Believes DeNeef underestimates Herrick's Christianity but that he understands and presents him in other relevant Renaissance contexts.

1979

35   TILLMAN, JAMES S.   "Herrick's Georgic Encomia."   In "Trust to
      Good Verses":   Herrick Tercentenary Essays.   Edited by
      Roger B. Rollin and J. Max Patrick.   Pittsburgh: Univer-
      sity of Pittsburgh Press, pp. 149-57.
          Proposes that Herrick's addresses to Endymion Porter,
      "The Country life," and to Thomas Herrick, "A Country
      life," are "not so much pastoral as georgic encomia, both
      in their exhortative tones and in their idealizations of
      the gentlemen addressed as self-restrained, laborious
      master husbandmen of their country estates."   Distinguishes
      between pastoral and georgic by explaining that georgics
      tend to stress description and instruction, to be more
      "realistic" in their presentations of country life, and to
      insist on "the usefulness of labor and self-restraint";
      pastoral tends to present life as a time of happy song.
      Notes Herrick's insistence on Endymion Porter as an exem-
      plary husbandman and contrasts "An Eclogue, or Pastorall
      between Endimion Porter and Lycidas Herrick, set and sung"
      with "The Country life" to show the varying emphases on
      pastoral and georgic elements in the two poems.   Comments
      on the praise of Thomas Herrick in "A Country life" for
      having chosen a life of "discipline and foresight," for
      georgic poetry tends to recommend virtuous self-restraint
      to sophisticated readers and Thomas's choice of a rewarding,
      simple life serves as an example to readers in the city and
      the court.

36   TURNER, J.G.   "The Matter of Britain: Topographical Poetry in
      English 1600-1660."   Notes and Queries 25 (December):514-24.
          Includes "To Dean-bourn, a rude River in Devon, by which
      sometimes he lived," "His returne to London," and "His
      tears to Thamasis" in a list of seventeenth-century poems
      of "panegyric typography."

1979

1   BUSH, DOUGLAS.   Review of "Trust to Good Verses":   Herrick
      Tercentenary Essays, by Rollin and Patrick.   Seventeenth-
      Century News 37 (Spring-Summer):7.
          Summarizes essays edited by Rollin and Patrick in
      1978.29, expressing some doubt about Murphy's and Summers's
      conclusions and serious questions about Mollenkott's defini-
      tion of Herrick's "sacramental" view of experience.   De-
      scribes the bibliography by Pebworth and others as "long
      and useful."

2   COOK, ELIZABETH. "Figured Poetry." Journal of the Warburg
     and Courtauld Institutes 42:1-15.
          Includes "His Poetrie his Pillar," "The pillar of Fame,"
     and "The Cross" ("This Crosse-Tree here") (pp. 10-12) in
     her survey of medieval and Renaissance figured poetry--
     poetry whose shape imitates its content. Sees figured
     poetry as an attempt to "deny the randomness of all the
     forms of the world" and to make human words "overlay, and
     become synonymous with the word which was in the beginning
     and is outside time." Sees the central theme of the 1648
     volume as the power of poetry to deny death. Presents "His
     Poetrie his Pillar," then, as a happy assertion that words
     cannot be thrown down as can stone pillars, and "The pillar
     of Fame" as a visual emblem of the "finish and polish" of
     the whole book. Explains how the words of "The Cross"
     teach the reader how to meditate upon the cross; in reading
     the poem, we are "[brought], worshipping, to its feet."

3   DUBROW, HEATHER. "The Country-House Poem: A Study in
     Generic Development." Genre 2 (Summer):153-79.
          Treats seventeenth-century country-house poems as
     simultaneously adapting and reacting against three older
     genres: Juvenalian verse satire, epideictic epistles in
     praise of significant people, and (especially) pastoral
     poetry including the beatus-ille motif. Argues that
     country-house poems resolve the philosophic dilemma of "the
     conflict between the active and the contemplative life" and
     offer "a solution to one of the major social problems [of
     the period] . . . the irresponsibility of many seventeenth-
     century landlords." Sees "A Panegerick to Sir Lewis
     Pemberton" as different from the other country-house poems
     in its combination of "earthly physicality" and a "digni-
     fied tone created by his many allusions to classical Rome."
     Explains that neither "A Country life: To his Brother"
     nor Jonson's "To Sir Robert Wroth" should be labeled
     country-house poems.

4   FERRARI, FERRUCCIO. L'Influence classica nell'Inghilterra del
     seicento e la poesia di Robert Herrick. Messina and
     Florence: Casa Editrice G. D'Anna, 182 pp.
          Chapters on Herrick's life; Jonson and "The Tribe of
     Ben," Donne, and Burton; the classical tradition in England;
     Herrick and the classics, Herrick as epigrammist; Death,
     ceremonial poetry, and the "Pillar of Fame"; carpe diem
     poetry; flower and fairy poems; the love poems and the
     Anacreontea build to the conclusion that Herrick is far more
     than a writer of songs: he writes poetry in a wide variety
     of genres and moods. As Delattre notes, Herrick is a

modern poet in his presentation of verses that register his
own impressions, observations, reflections, desires, and
worries (1911.2); yet Herrick is also a poet of his time
and one must see his work in its historical and cultural
context. A final chapter surveys Herrick's reputation.

5   FOGLE, FRENCH. Review of "Trust to Good Verses," by Rollin
     and Patrick. Renaissance Quarterly 32 (Autumn):437-40.
         Believes that the various authors of the essays in
     1978.29 have "qualified, expanded, and sometimes stretched
     to extraordinary lengths" ideas expressed by Bush in
     1962.2. Allows, however, that the volume provides many
     "perceptive insights" into Herrick's poetry and offers
     particular praise of Patrick's essay (1978.27) and of the
     bibliography (1978.28).

6   HALLI, ROBERT W., Jr. "Herrick's 'Upon Julia's Fall,' 1-4."
     Explicator 38 (Fall):15-16.
         In this poem and in "Upon Lucia dabled in the deaw,"
     Herrick describes a girl's leg with the word sincerity.
     In the Renaissance, the word was thought to derive from
     sine cera, "without wax." Julia's and Lucia's legs, then,
     are as perfectly smooth as those of a Roman statue that
     does not need mending with wax.

7   MARCUS, LEAH SINANOGLOU. "Herrick's Hesperides and the
     'Proclamation made for May.'" Studies in Philology 76
     (Late Winter):49-74.
         Noting that pastoral is a traditional form in which to
     express political ideas, outlines the seventeenth-century
     controversy over May Day customs to indicate the political
     significance of Herrick's several poems on May Day, espe-
     cially "Corinna's going a Maying." Asserts that "The
     Proclamation made for May" mentioned in "Corinna" refers
     to James I's Book of Sports, for royalists saw the dispute
     over May Day customs treated in that book as "a struggle to
     preserve a vanishing way of life." Sees Herrick's "medi-
     evalizing tendency" and his classicism as strategies to
     counter Puritan arguments against paganism by asserting "a
     vital historical continuity which cannot be broken without
     disastrous consequences." Argues that Herrick's witty,
     even outrageous tone as he unites the sacred (particularly
     references to the Book of Common Prayer and to Anglican
     homilies for the spring season) and the profane is a con-
     scious assertion of an "idealized vision of what England
     could be in the present and how that present should be
     understood within a larger historical continuum."

1979

8   MILLER, EDMUND. "Sensual Imagery in the Devotional Poetry of
    Robert Herrick." Christianity and Literature 28 (Winter):
    24-33.
        After defining the devotional poems as the small number
    of poems in Noble Numbers that "are personal devotions, or,
    if they are ritual poems, . . . represent a very special,
    personalized sort of ritual devotion," discusses their
    imagery. Much of it, according to Miller, can be called
    "Christian Anacreontism."

9   SCHWENGER, PETER. "Herrick's Fairy State." ELH 46 (Spring):
    35-55.
        A structuralist analysis of "Oberons Feast" and "Oberons
    Palace," which Schwenger sees as companion poems dedicated
    to Thomas Shapcott in the 1648 Hesperides. (Omits "The
    Fairie Temple: or, Oberons Chappell" because its satiric
    tone is significantly different from the other two Oberon
    poems.) Examines the menu of Oberon's feast and presents
    a "map" of Oberon's palace to show that the two poems are
    "a single unit": the first poem's images "move from a
    state of spiritual innocence to an awareness of the enclos-
    ing body as a thing of death and sexuality, to a rich and
    erotic projection past the body. The poem's perceptual
    symbol is the concave--the body viewed from within.
    'Oberons Palace' carries on the erotic projection of the
    first poem in showing Oberon ready 'for Lust and action.'
    It then traces his penetration of the convex, past a series
    of elaborate decors, until he attains a sexual goal within
    the palace's center. The poems, viewed thus, only express
    at a deeper level what is plainly being described on the
    literal surface: a feast of accelerating richness and its
    erotic aftermath." Closes with the observation that in
    creating his myth of Oberon, Herrick has presented "common-
    place experience re-enacted in terms of universal, mythic
    significance" which is close to "the idea of ritual--an
    idea which is central to Herrick's poetry and to his mode
    of thought."

10 THOMAS, P.W. Review of Clayton's edition of Cavalier Poets
    and of Rollin's and Patrick's "Trust to Good Verses."
    Review of English Studies 30 (May):213-15.
        Brief mention of the Herrick volume (1978.29) includes
    a protest that Herrick cannot be expected to fulfill the
    same expectations we place on truly major poets; his virtue
    is in the "charm and fleeting pleasures of his lovely cere-
    monials and incantations."

1981

11 TURNER, JAMES [G.] The Politics of Landscape: Rural Scenery and Society in English Poetry, 1630-1660. Oxford: Basil Blackwell, 250 pp., passim.

Mentions Herrick from time to time as he endeavors "to reconstruct the meaning of rural poetry [from 1630 to 1660] in its complex collision with the economic processes of rural life and theories evoked to explain them in their own time," for "Rural poetry always deals with society in general as well as the landscape and the peasantry, its immediate subjects." Sees "The Hock-cart" as an example of verse in which "the depiction of charity . . . [gives] extreme wealth a sweet aspect or sensation of legitimacy."

1980

1 BOSS, JUDITH E. "Herrick's 'Precepts.'" English Language Notes 17 (June):249-53.

Explicates "Precepts" as an example of the "conciseness, compression, wit, and ingenuity" of Herrick's sententious epigrams.

2 DANIELS, F. EDGAR. "Herbert's 'The Flower,' 44." Explicator 39 (Fall):45-46.

Suggests that glide in line 44 of Herbert's "The Flower" and line 17 of Herrick's "To Blossoms" means "fall": in his poem, Herbert sees the fall into death as "the prelude to life"; Herrick offers "virtually a pagan acknowledgment that life has its ending in the grave."

3 WOODALL, KITTY J. "Herrick's 'Corinna's Going A-Maying." Explicator 39 (Fall):29-30.

Argues that the "religious elements" of "Corinna's going a Maying" contradict the speaker's playful, pagan plea for love: "'Corinna' illustrates that paganism cannot replace Christianity."

1981

1 HALLI, ROBERT W. "Herrick's Various Blazon of Beauty." In Renaissance Papers, 1980. Edited by A. Leigh DeNeef and M. Thomas Hester. Durham, N.C.: Southeastern Renaissance Conference, pp. 53-61.

Cites a number of Renaissance sources to illustrate the concept of artistic creation which aims at "variety . . . designed to produce in its audience wonder and admiration, [which are the same as] the effects of God's various

1981

creation upon the mind of a perceptive man." Examines several poems about Herrick's imaginary mistresses to show
that even while Herrick presents "particularity of visual
detail which evokes our wonder and admiration," he presents
not a bevy of individual women but a single "blazon" of
"ideal feminine charms."

2   HOLMER, JOAN OZARK. "Religious Satire in Herrick's 'The
     Faerie Temple: or, Oberons Chappell.'" Renaissance and
     Reformation-Renaissance et Réforme, n.s. 5, no. 1:40-57.
         Derived from 1973.9. Noting Herrick's originality in
     creating a diminutive fairy religion in "The Fairie Temple"
     (for a similar view, see 1959.2) and the Puritans' argument
     that Catholic priests invented fairy lore "for the purpose
     of cloaking their knavish tricks on the laity and for ex-
     acting obedience from them through fear," argues that in
     "The Faerie Temple" Herrick [uses] diminutive fairies as
     the vehicle for his satire of the Puritan view of contempo-
     rary Anglicanism as a 'mixt Religion,' as Romish (papisti-
     cal) and idolatrous (pagan)." Closes with the speculation
     that Herrick's poem may be one manifestation of "a cult of
     curious fairy poems" written by various seventeenth-century
     poets.

3   PALOMO, DOLORES. "The Halcyon Moment of Stillness in Royalist
     Poetry." Huntington Library Quarterly 44 (Summer):205-21.
         Includes Herrick as she cites various uses of the
     halcyon myth by seventeenth-century royalist poets and
     suggests that the myth may be used to define the tone of
     much of their poetry, for its "melodious sweetness and
     graceful images [capture] a state of tranquility . . . yet
     [resonate] with melancholic overtones that express their
     knowledge of disorder and irrevocable change."

Indexes

Author Index

The following includes authors, compilers, editors, and translators of items in this bibliography.

Abbott, Claude Colleer (ed.), 1935.1-2
Abrahams, Roger D., 1972.1
Abrams, M.H., 1953.1
Adams, Joseph Quincy, 1927.1
Aiken, Pauline, 1932.1
Alcott, A. Bronson, 1872.1
Alden, Raymond Macdonald, 1903.1
Aldrich, Thomas Bailey, 1900.1
Allen, Don Cameron, 1967.1
Allingham, William, 1893.2
Alpha [pseud.], 1888.1
Anthony, Edward, 1934.1
Archibald, R.C., 1953.2
Arms, George (comp.), 1950.1
Armstrong, Ray L., 1956.3; 1963.3
Asals, Heather, 1976.1
Ashe, T., 1883.2
Ault, Norman, 1933.1-2
Axworthy, Richard, 1908.1
Aynard, Joseph, 1912.1

B., C.C., 1892.5
B., H.I., 1902.2
Bache, William B., 1974.2
Baker, E.L., 1936.1
Barry, J. Milner, 1850.1-2
Bateson, F.W., 1934.2; 1950.2
Bateson, F.W. (ed.), 1941.1
Baugh, Albert C. (ed.), 1948.2
Bayfield, M.A., 1919.1
Beeching, Henry C., 1903.2

Beeching, Henry C. (ed.), 1905.1
Beer, David F., 1972.2
Belgion, Montgomery, 1946.1
Bercovitch, Sacvan, 1968.2
Berman, Ronald, 1971.1
Bettany, F.G., 1910.5
Blackmur, R.P., 1956.4
Bliss, Philip, 1817.1
Blunden, Edmund, 1921.4
Boas, F.S., 1912.2; 1913.2;
    1914.1; 1917.1
Boas, Henrietta O'Brien, 1904.2
Borish, Murray Eugene, 1936.2
Boss, Judith E., 1971.2; 1980.1
Botting, Roland B., 1929.1
Bouchier, Jonathan, 1875.1;
    1888.2
Bradbury, Malcolm (ed.), 1970.4
Braden, Gordon McMurray, 1975.1;
    1978.1-2
Bremer, Rudy, 1976.2
Breslan, M.L.R., 1902.12
Briggs, Katherine M., 1959.2;
    1962.1
Briscoe, J. Potter (ed.), 1899.1
Briscoe, John D'Auby, 1936.2
Broadbent, J.B., 1964.1; 1975.2;
    1976.3
Broadus, Edmund Kemper, 1931.2
Bronson, Bertrand H., 1967.2
Brooke, Tucker, 1948.2
Brooks, Cleanth, 1938.1; 1939.1;
    1947.1

Subject Index

The following is a list of subjects mentioned in the annotations of this bibliography. Readers are advised to consult general studies related to specific topics, including notes and commentaries in various editions of Herrick's poems.

Editions
-complete works, 1648.1; 1823.1;
    1844.1; 1846.1; 1856.1;
    1859.1; 1869.1; 1876.1;
    1884.1; 1890.1; 1891.1;
    1893.1; 1898.1; 1915.1;
    1921.1; 1928.1; 1956.1;
    1963.1; 1965.1
-selected works, 1810.1; 1839.1;
    1877.2; 1887.1; 1895.1;
    1899.1; 1900.1; 1904.1;
    1905.1; 1906.1; 1923.1;
    1948.1; 1961.1
Elegies, 1932.1; 1939.3
Elizabethan poets and poetry,
    1874.3; 1896.4; 1897.1, 3;
    1901.3; 1905.5; 1910.6;
    1913.6
Emblem tradition, 1957.2
Empedocles, 1962.4; 1968.2
Empiricism, 1970.4
Endymion (mythical figure),
    1944.4
England's Helicon, 1959.12
English character of Herrick's
    poetry, 1823.1; 1856.2;
    1883.2; 1892.11; 1900.1;
    1903.4; 1905.2; 1908.1;
    1913.5; 1927.1; 1935.2;
    1948.5, 7; 1960.5; 1965.11;
    1975.4
English customs, 1970.13
Epicureanism, 1859.2; 1876.1;
    1905.3; 1911.4, 6; 1935.6;
    1957.2; 1962.6; 1972.10;
    1978.14
Epideictic poetry, 1968.8;
    1978.18; 1979.3
Epigrams, 1853.1; 1875.2; 1876.1;
    1883.2; 1887.4; 1892.3-4;
    1897.3; 1910.11; 1912.5;
    1915.9; 1917.5; 1927.1;
    1933.7; 1940.1; 1947.3;
    1958.7; 1965.5; 1970.7;
    1971.2; 1972.13; 1975.6;
    1976.1, 7; 1978.9, 14, 18,
    33; 1979.4; 1980.1
Epitaphs, 1970.2, 9; 1975.6, 14
Epithalamia, 1875.2; 1936.3;
    1961.4; 1965.11, 16; 1966.8;
    1970.8, 13; 1973.1; 1975.4

Eroticism, 1956.10; 1978.10;
    1979.9
Estienne, Henri, 1941.3; 1978.2
Euphuism, 1903.3
Excremental imagery, 1976.7
Exeter, Earl of, 1721.1
Exeter, siege of, 1910.15

Fairfax, Thomas, 1910.15
Fairy lore, 1930.4; 1933.8;
    1973.9
Fairy poems, 1856.2; 1875.2;
    1877.1; 1880.1; 1883.2;
    1903.3; 1911.2; 1912.4;
    1921.4; 1931.4; 1959.2;
    1971.5; 1975.14; 1979.4, 9;
    1981.2.   See also Oberon
    poems
Fane, Mildmay, Earl of
    Westmorland, 1892.9; 1954.3;
    1967.3; 1968.12
Fellowes, E.H., 1954.1
Feltham, Owen, 1971.1
Fertility rites, 1965.10; 1966.4
Festivals, 1971.11
Ficino, Marsilio, 1978.14
Fictional accounts of Herrick's
    life, 1920.1; 1932.5
Field, Barron, 1854.1
Figured poetry, 1979.2
Firth manuscript, 1915.1
Fletcher, John, 1917.1; 1947.8;
    1970.8
Flower images, 1964.7
Flower poems, 1936.7; 1970.12;
    1971.6; 1979.4
Folk customs, 1851.2; 1853.1;
    1892.7; 1897.9; 1911.2;
    1959.2, 6; 1965.11; 1968.3;
    1972.1-2; 1975.4; 1976.18
Folklore, 1972.17
"For his Mistris," 1972.3
Frost, Robert, 1948.3
Fuller, Thomas, 1875.4
Funeral poems, 1969.1

Gallus, 1932.1
Gamble, John, 1976.14
Garden imagery, 1965.15; 1977.5
Gautier, Théophile, 1902.10;
    1967.9

Medical vocabulary, 1895.3
Medieval attributes of Herrick's
    poetry, 1935.1; 1979.7
Meditative poems, 1978.3, 14
Melancholy, 1859.2; 1893.4;
    1896.1; 1901.2; 1916.1;
    1928.4; 1958.6
Metaphysical style, 1868.1;
    1897.5; 1899.3; 1935.5;
    1939.1; 1953.4; 1968.6;
    1970.13; 1978.15
Mildmay, Lord. See Fane,
    Mildmay, Earl of Westmorland
Milton, John, 1855.1; 1889.1;
    1893.3; 1897.3; 1900.1;
    1906.2; 1910.10; 1912.4;
    1916.1; 1920.2; 1944.3;
    1969.6; 1971.1, 9; 1972.7,
    11; 1973.8; 1974.10; 1978.12,
    14
Mirandula, Octavianus, 1977.8
Mistresses, 1900.1; 1910.6;
    1911.2; 1927.3; 1930.1;
    1948.1; 1968.11; 1978.31;
    1981.1
Moderation, 1972.10
Montaigne, Michel de, 1902.8
Montrose. See Graham, James
Musarum Deliciae, 1796.2
Musical allusions, 1928.3;
    1961.3; 1978.15
Musical settings. See song-texts
Mutability, 1969.2; 1974.4
Myth, 1931.4; 1932.2; 1964.7;
    1973.8, 13; 1979.9; 1981.3

Naps upon Parnassus, 1796.2;
    1889.3; 1906.4
Noble Numbers
-title, 1976.11
-unity of, 1962.7

Oberon poems, 1876.4; 1891.1;
    1896.1; 1903.3; 1910.11;
    1965.16; 1971.5; 1973.9;
    1978.6; 1979.9. See also
    Fairy poems
Occasional poetry, 1971.2
Odes, 1916.2; 1930.3; 1936.11;
    1960.5; 1969.3
Omar Khayyam, 1901.2; 1976.18

Onomastics, 1978.31
Orgel, Stephen, 1976.13
Ovid, 1902.8; 1925.2; 1932.1;
    1956.1; 1960.2; 1965.10;
    1972.16

Paganism, 1859.2; 1875.2; 1880.1;
    1903.6; 1906.2; 1911.1;
    1916.1; 1917.5; 1934.2
Paganism and/or Christianity,
    1859.2; 1868.1; 1887.4;
    1891.2; 1904.5; 1910.4;
    1931.4; 1932.2; 1936.10;
    1942.1; 1947.1; 1948.12;
    1950.4; 1955.10; 1956.10;
    1957.6; 1962.2; 1964.7;
    1965.4; 1968.3; 1970.13;
    1971.1-2, 4; 1972.11; 1974.3;
    1976.18; 1977.1; 1980.2-3
Parkhurst, John, 1947.3
Parkinson, John, 1965.14
Parodies of Herrick, 1887.2
Parody, 1973.9; 1981.2
Parry, Sir George, 1910.15
Parsons, Thomsen, 1936.10
Pastoralism, 1880.1; 1898.3;
    1902.1; 1903.3-4; 1911.2;
    1913.4; 1935.8; 1939.3;
    1948.5; 1959.12; 1966.5-6;
    1968.12; 1972.7, 11; 1974.6,
    17; 1975.4; 1978.35; 1979.3,
    7
Pater, Walter, 1976.18
Peacham, Henry, 1929.1
Pembroke family, 1897.9
Pepys, Samuel, 1900.1; 1906.3;
    1910.6
Persephone, 1965.10; 1966.4
Persius, 1939.3; 1959.10
Personae in Herrick's poems,
    1944.2; 1962.7; 1966.6;
    1970.6-7; 1971.3, 7-8, 11, 13;
    1973.11; 1974.4; 1976.1, 7,
    17; 1978.24
Pestell, Thomas, 1958.3
Petrarch and Petrarchism, 1903.3;
    1910.11; 1945.4; 1968.6;
    1972.13, 15
Phillipps MS 12341. See Herrick
    Commonplace Book
Philostratus, 1895.4

(Reviews)
-of Nott, 1810.2
-of Palgrave, 1877.1
-of Patrick, 1963.2-3; 1966.3
-of Pollard, 1892.1-4, 10-11;
    1902.10; 1905.2
-of Roeckerath, 1931.1; 1932.4;
    1933.9
-of Rollin, 1967.8; 1970.10
-or Rollin and Patrick, 1978.25;
    1979.1, 5, 10
-of Saintsbury, 1894.1; 1896.3
-of Scott, 1974.1; 1975.2, 13;
    1976.4
Revisions of poems, 1915.1, 3,
    9; 1917.1, 5; 1952.2; 1954.1;
    1959.8; 1960.3; 1969.6;
    1976.14
Rilke, Rainer Maria, 1956.4
Ritualistic poems, 1970.2;
    1979.9. See also Ceremonial
    poems
Robinson, Gwilliam, 1860.2
Robinson, Mary, 1947.9
Roman Catholicism, 1903.3;
    1965.4; 1967.4; 1969.1;
    1976.18; 1981.2
Roman Poetry, 1896.4; 1969.1
Ronsard, Pierre de, 1910.1;
    1912.6; 1945.4; 1958.1;
    1964.4
Rose images, 1974.13
Royalism and royalist poetry,
    1856.2; 1901.2; 1911.2;
    1936.9; 1946.3; 1959.6;
    1966.5; 1979.7; 1981.3
Rural poetry, 1876.3; 1911.2;
    1979.11

Sacramental view of nature,
    1946.3; 1950.4; 1970.4;
    1975.3
Sacred parody, 1965.16
Saint Margaret's Church, memorial
    tablet in, 1955.3, 9, 11;
    1956.7
St. Victor, Hugo, 1967.1
Sallust, 1898.4; 1902.8
Sandys, George, 1927.2
Satire, 1939.3; 1940.1; 1970.7;
    1977.3; 1978.9; 1981.2

Scaliger, Julius Caesar, 1940.1;
    1967.1
Scudamore, Lord, 1948.10
Seldon, John, 1892.9; 1897.9
Seneca, 1898.4; 1902.8; 1912.2;
    1940.2
Sententious couplets, 1940.1
Shakespeare, William, 1888.5;
    1897.3, 9; 1900.1; 1901.2;
    1904.5; 1912.4; 1922.4;
    1927.1; 1930.4; 1935.1;
    1936.7; 1940.2; 1950.4;
    1959.2
Shapcott, Thomas, 1910.15; 1979.9
Shelley, Percy Bysshe, 1880.1;
    1897.8; 1910.11; 1935.4;
    1950.3
Shirley, James, 1954.1
Sidney, Sir Phillip, 1903.3;
    1962.5; 1973.1
Sidney family, 1977.6
Silverton, 1910.15
Singer, poet as, 1960.8
1648 volume
-frontispiece, 1769.1; 1824.1;
    1876.1; 1894.2; 1978.6
-order of poems in, 1876.1;
    1884.1; 1890.1; 1891.1;
    1892.8; 1895.1; 1896.4;
    1897.3; 1903.6; 1910.6;
    1911.2; 1912.6; 1913.3;
    1940.1; 1956.1; 1970.6-7;
    1971.8; 1972.9
-unity of, 1933.7; 1944.1;
    1959.3, 12; 1966.6; 1973.12;
    1975.5; 1976.18
-variants in, 1903.7-8; 1905.4;
    1917.1. See also Hesperides.
Skelton, John, 1978.3
Skeltonics, 1843.1; 1948.6
Smith, E., 1824.1
Song-texts, 1910.8; 1911.2, 7;
    1927.1; 1933.1, 5-6; 1941.2;
    1947.9; 1948.11; 1952.2;
    1953.3; 1954.1; 1959.8;
    1960.4; 1965.9; 1967.2;
    1969.6; 1973.12; 1974.14, 16;
    1976.14; 1978.5
Sons of Ben, 1887.1; 1903.5;
    1904.8; 1931.2; 1939.3;
    1945.1; 1947.8; 1977.5;
    1978.4; 1979.4

Poetry Index

The following includes poems by Herrick and poems attributed to Herrick mentioned in the annotations. Titles are spelled and numbered as in J. Max Patrick's edition of The Complete Poetry of Robert Herrick (1963.1). Poems not numbered are those Patrick does not accept as Herrick's.

Copyediting directed by Ara Salibian.
Text formatted and produced by Fred Welden.
Camera-ready copy typed by Geraldine Kline
    on an IBM Selectric.
Printed and bound by Braun-Brumfield, Inc.,
    of Ann Arbor, Michigan.